PRAISE FOR
KARL BARTH'S CHURCH DOGMATICS *FOR EVERYONE*

This exciting new volume makes Karl Barth's *Church Dogmatics* accessible for pastors, students, and laypersons in a whole new way through an interactive reading guide that is both engaging and easy to navigate. Whether you are new to Barth's theology or a seasoned reader, this volume offers valuable resources for everyone.

—**Kait Dugan**, managing director for the Center for Barth Studies, Princeton Theological Seminary

Like a Mozart symphony, Karl Barth's *Church Dogmatics* has motifs and recurring themes that weave through its pages. However, it takes a gifted ear to hear the themes of Barth's thought in his often paragraph-long sentences. Dr. Marty Folsom is one who has that ear for Barth's music, with the added gift of helping the ungifted to hear it too.

—**Richard Keith**, pastor, Corowa Presbyterian Church, NSW, Australia

I would recommend this helpful book as a companion for the church when picking up Barth's *Dogmatics* for the first time. Barth needs to be read; this resource can provide the encouragement to do so!

—**Cherith Fee Nordling**, sessional lecturer, Regent College

Pope Paul VI said that Karl Barth was the greatest theologian since Thomas Aquinas. That is praise enough to support serious study of Barth's theology. Marty Folsom encourages just that in this new introduction. *Karl Barth's* Church Dogmatics *for Everyone* provides an accessible and commendable initiation into the theology of Karl Barth.

—**Paul D. Molnar**, professor of systematic theology, St. John's University, Queens, NY

D0022202

Folsom couldn't be more right! Barth has been admired, and criticized, more than he has been read. In this breakthrough series, Folsom is taking *Church Dogmatics* down from the upper shelf it often fills in the pastor's study, blowing off the dust, and illuminating its pages for the benefit of parched souls and practical living.

Restoring deepest meaning to theology as "queen of the sciences," I hear Torrance and Macmurray applauding as Folsom provides us a lens to introduce us not only to Barth but more importantly to the God who is revealing God uniquely in Jesus Christ, the God apprehended (not comprehended!) in faith, the God who loves us more than He loves himself, the God who is truly *for us*!

One of Folsom's greatest contributions in this series is to provide not only an accessible entre to Barth but also an infrastructure that can be easily utilized for personal or group study. Such a format is only fitting for the discovery of the triune God, who is, in unity, persons in community!

—**Jeff McSwain**, founder, Reality Ministries, Inc.

This series sets out to communicate with clarity and imagination the insights that define the work of the greatest theologian since John Calvin. Written for nonprofessional theologians, its lucidity makes it accessible to a very wide audience. The additional essays by Julie Canlis and others are no less easy to read than Marty's text and are, without exception, outstanding. This series opens a door to the thought of Karl Barth for people who might otherwise miss out on the insights into the faith of this theological giant. This would be an ideal series for church discussion groups who wish to think through the Christian faith in great depth.

—**Alan J. Torrance**, emeritus professor of systematic theology and founding director of the Logos Institute, University of St Andrews, Scotland

KARL BARTH'S *CHURCH DOGMATICS* FOR EVERYONE

—— VOLUME 1 ——

The Doctrine of the Word of God

A Step-by-Step Guide for Beginners & Pros

MARTY FOLSOM

With additional essays by:

Douglas Campbell

Myk Habets

Richard Keith

Julie Canlis

James Chaousis

John Vissers

Andrew Torrance

Steve Guthrie

Illustrations by Abigail Folsom

ZONDERVAN ACADEMIC

ZONDERVAN ACADEMIC

Karl Barth's Church Dogmatics *for Everyone, Volume 1—The Doctrine of the Word of God*
Copyright © 2022 by Marty Folsom

Requests for information should be addressed to:
Zondervan, *3900 Sparks Dr. SE, Grand Rapids, Michigan 49546*

Zondervan titles may be purchased in bulk for educational, business, fundraising, or sales promotional use. For information, please email SpecialMarkets@Zondervan.com.

Library of Congress Cataloging-in-Publication Data

Names: Folsom, Marty, 1958- author.
Title: Karl Barth's Church Dogmatics for everyone : a step-by-step guide for beginners and pros /
    Marty Folsom.
Other titles: Church Dogmatics for everyone
Description: Grand Rapids : Zondervan, 2022. | Series: Karl Barth's church dogmatics for everyone |
    Volume 1 has additioanl essays by: Douglas Campbell, Myk Habets, Richard Keith, Julie Canlis,
    James Chaousis, John Vissers, Andrew Torrance, Steve Guthrie, and illustrations by Abigail
    Folsom. | Includes bibliographical references. | Contents: V.1. Doctrine of the Word of God --
Identifiers: LCCN 2022005656 (print) | LCCN 2022005657 (ebook) | ISBN 9780310125679
    (paperback) | ISBN 9780310125686 (ebook)
Subjects: LCSH: Barth, Karl, 1886-1968. Kirchliche Dogmatik. | Theology, Doctrinal.
Classification: LCC BT75.3.B373 F65 2022 (print) | LCC BT75.3.B373 (ebook) | DDC
    230/.041--dc23/eng/20220302
LC record available at https://lccn.loc.gov/2022005656
LC ebook record available at https://lccn.loc.gov/2022005657

Scripture quotations marked KJV are taken from the King James Version. Public domain.

Scripture quotations marked NLT are taken from the Holy Bible, New Living Translation. © 1996, 2004, 2015 by Tyndale House Foundation. Used by permission of Tyndale House Publishers, Inc., Carol Stream, Illinois 60188. All rights reserved.

Any internet addresses (websites, blogs, etc.) and telephone numbers in this book are offered as a resource. They are not intended in any way to be or imply an endorsement by Zondervan, nor does Zondervan vouch for the content of these sites and numbers for the life of this book.

All rights reserved. No part of this publication may be reproduced, stored in a retrieval system, or transmitted in any form or by any means—electronic, mechanical, photocopy, recording, or any other—except for brief quotations in printed reviews, without the prior permission of the publisher.

Cover design: Brand Navigation
Cover art: Dreamstime
Interior design: Kait Lamphere

Printed in the United States of America

22 23 24 25 26 27 28 29 30 31 32 /TRM/ 15 14 13 12 11 10 9 8 7 6 5 4 3 2 1

Dedicated to Douglas A. Campbell,
Friend, mentor, courageous adventurer,
and faithful servant of the Word of God

CONTENTS

PREFACE

WHY READ THIS BOOK?

- To be introduced to the most significant theologian of the twentieth century, Karl Barth, and his most significant theological work—in a way accessible for everyone.
- To be guided through Karl Barth's monumental *Church Dogmatics* (hereafter *CD*) as its 9,000 pages proclaim Jesus.
- To rediscover Jesus and be renewed through this journey.

WHO SHOULD READ THIS BOOK?

- Everyone! Ordinary people, leaders, theologians, and explorers will benefit from this book.

HOW THIS BOOK COULD BE READ

- Regardless of who you are, start with the introduction so you are prepared for what follows.
- If you are new to the *CD*, spend ample time in the first seven chapters to orient yourself to all that follows.
- If you have been introduced to the *CD* but have been stopped by the intensity and immensity of the whole, read this book as a tour guide that will introduce you to theological thinking that is meant to transform the Church. Do not worry about having a copy of the *CD* at your side.
- If you have been reading the *CD* for years and wish for a deeper understanding, read this book as a companion to the *CD*; start with this book and then enter the original texts with an inquisitive mind to see all the additional insight to be gained.

SHARE THE JOURNEY

This book may be used as a study guide for private training or a chart for learning with a group. Consider reading it with friends, fellow students or ministers, or create a reading group. This book is a humble servant to make clear one of the greatest works of theology ever written. It is immensely valuable to learn its methods and goals in coming to know God.

Barth never intended us to have a mastery of his text; he wanted us to have an encounter with the personal God revealed in the living Word, Jesus. This Jesus is known through the written Word of the Bible. But the Word comes to life when it becomes a spoken and lived word in our lives. Take it one step at a time. Take time to discover what rapt attention can highlight in the landscape you are passing through. You might be astonished by what begins to be revealed. Let the discovery process increase your enthusiasm for more of what might feed your whole being. *Bon voyage*!

Finally, this is a book to find enjoyment with a master. Barth loved Mozart. He learned much from that master. When Mozart first heard another master, J. S. Bach, in 1798, he was amazed. "When the singing was finished he cried out, full of joy: 'Now there is something one can learn from.'"[1] Hopefully you will learn from the majestic work of Barth and come to enjoy its complexity and mystery with a satisfaction that leaves you wanting more and full of joy to share with others as the Word of God brings you into a new kind of freedom. Barth loved Mozart and would begin the day listening to him; he even wrote a book about Mozart. May both of these masters bring music to your soul.

---

1. Christoph Wolff, *Johann Sebastian Bach: The Learned Musician* (New York: Norton, 2001), 463.

HOW TO READ THIS BOOK

GETTING ORIENTED: Who Are You and Where Are You Going?

You are going on an adventure. Exploring the world of Barth studies is one level of that expedition. Entering the world of knowing the God who has come to us in Jesus Christ is the deeper dimension. To that end, take time to reflect on who you are and how to get the most from this book. In assessing your goals, what follows here will help you consider how to proceed in delving into the field of discovering the personal God and why it matters to you and those you serve.

BASICS FOR EVERYONE

1. **Read the Introduction.** This short section serves as the legend to the map for your journey. It introduces you to the structure of the book and each chapter's internal arrangement and offerings. It will focus your mind for what follows.

2. **Read selectively.** This work has many layers. In many ways, it is introductory for your particular understanding. Beyond that, it also explores the outworking of Barth's theology for church and academy. Thus, it embodies a constructive character in furthering the science of knowing the triune God at levels spanning from the simple to the complex. Additionally, it explores life in light of the living God for communities and for personal life together.

3. **Live into the story of discovery.** The book's format invites you to begin a journey with Barth in knowing the God who knows us and speaks to us. You will do well to note that the chapter title, images, and focus statement work together to facilitate your entry into the story that guides the investigation. Each chapter's image moves you into the experience of investigation.

4. **Take it one step at a time.** Expect short sentences and paragraphs. Take each as a thoughtful step instead of a casual jaunt. Be intentional in engaging the complex thoughts of Barth, which are here condensed and presented in accessible language. Read slowly to savor the insights as though you had a week in your favorite city and wanted to enjoy each moment and encounter.

5. **Get the big picture.** The design of this work is to start you very generally and to move into the landscape of the material with greater clarity and complexity. Unless you are familiar with Barth, start at the beginning to bring the successive sections into focus. This will be true for all five volumes of this series.

6. **Make notes on places to dig.** This book is a tour guide to the *Church Dogmatics*. If its thirteen parts were easy to read, I never would have written this book. They are like the Alps or the Amazon Rainforest. They are majestic but best explored with a guide. Some stops along the way are better places to focus your visit than others. As you go, note where you want to read the *CD* in full and not merely the summary. This book is a portal, but you need to leave markers as a reminder to return and dig for deeper treasure.

7. **Think about constructive change in your thinking.** If you are reading this book, you are someone who is up to something big. You are looking for theology to make a difference. Barth had a big vision and might be compared to Einstein, who changed the world of the natural sciences. Both open our understanding to live more fully in the light of reality. Keeping Barth's specific kind of scientific investigation in mind, you will find each chapter provides overt insights and clarifying questions to develop your thinking about what is possible in theological thinking and possible outcomes for a flourishing life in the light of God's grace.

FOR A BEGINNER

1. This is a perfect book for beginners as well as advanced scholars. The language starts simple and introduces new words as you progress.

2. Take extra time in the first seven chapters. They give you the lay of the land for the whole of the *CD* (*Church Dogmatics*), not just this first volume.

3. Think of the book as an adventure course into the wilderness. It will give you tips and tools for finding your way around and enjoying your expedition.

4. Recognize you have come to study a majestic mountain of books, but the real point is to come to know the living God. That is the gold. Barth believed that theology was about learning to listen to the God who speaks, not just talking about God. God speaks; you learn to listen. Then live in the love extended to you.

5. I have kept very short paragraphs. I have whole pages of single sentence paragraphs. This is for you. One footstep at a time is implied by that cadence. Each step makes a rich, distilled point. Give it time to sink in. Don't hurry. Learn to love the distinctions made as an experience, like tasting a tray of cheeses to note the qualities of each or sampling sauces for a great feast.

6. Feel free to skip material that doesn't apply at this point in your learning. If you are not a pastor, student, or professor, you can skip sections designed for them. Or maybe check them out if you feel the nudge.

PRACTITIONERS

1. If you are in ministry, counseling, the arts, science, or any kind of leadership, you are a practitioner. This book is intended to expand your horizon.

2. The material of the book introduces the study of God not as an object to be observed but as a personal God to enlarge your capacity to serve. This God brings perspective and insight into an embodied life expanded by God's creative presence.

3. The essays in the back of the book are written by practitioners to get you started. Listen to them to find new perspective in this quest to discover fresh possibilities for your field.

4. Try to improvise on the material. Barth wanted to serve an active community to break down abstract thinking and avoid boring books when thinking about God. He wanted to see a world aflame with joy and creativity. Try reading this book with another person who shares your interests and improvise together. See what new thing you can create as you companionably listen to the text and then generate new ideas.

5. Check out the insight sections at the end of each chapter. They fill in a missing piece for those who like "so what?" kinds of engagements. They get you out the door and alive to birth new "ah-ha" experiences.

6. Start a journal. Take notes on old thinking to reconsider and new thoughts that come. These may engage your understanding of God, caring for people, revitalizing a relationship, creating a work of art to make a difference, or starting a new venture. Any of those are possible with any chapter. Listen, linger, and let your imagination be moved by the Spirit to come alive.

PROFESSORS AND STUDENTS

1. Professors and students have a symbiotic relationship; both benefit from the other's presence. This book can be like a shared meal. Professors know the recipe but want students to learn to become masters themselves. This book lends itself to this apprenticing; the student gets bite-size beginnings so as not to choke.

2. For a professor who is student-centered, this book gives an entry like few others into the complexity of the life of the triune God. It begins with a focus on the one person, Jesus, who opens all the insightful dynamics for life in concert with God and in communities.

3. Learning theological topics from simplicity to complexity allows for more integrated learning. Each chapter offers fresh meat, alternative ways of cooking it up, and ways to develop the skills needed for mastery. Theory and practice in being human make more sense when explored in the presence of this dynamic God. This God created the world as the context for the arts, sciences, and the many forms of helping people. This book aligns the learner with God to open the world of thought and practice for a shared life of service.

4. This book inspires the learning relationship by engaging small texts latent with big ideas. Barth moved theology from fragmented thinking to unified thought in the light of the Creator. He resists theology that labels and boxes up ideas and arguments. Barth preferred to shake the world by calling readers to come and meet a person. His goal was to invite communities of people to develop together in response to the revelation of God.

5. Reading this book seminar-style is a perfect stepping stone for think-tank engagement. It lends itself to conversations for expanding what is actual and possible with God. Discussing what difference it makes to have a living, dynamic God, instead of definitions and descriptions, can bring theology to life in a living greenhouse of ideas.

6. The insights for pastors and for theologians in this book are focused on students. They provide outcome-based thinking about why each chapter matters for the practices of competent leadership.

7. This book lends itself to developing laboratory experiences. That is, each chapter engages theology as it impacts real life—our ultimate laboratory. For example, the last section of each chapter offers a clarifying question to both reflect on and start conversations. I have students who use these questions to interview family members, neighbors, friends, or strangers on the street. This is transformative

for student and interviewee alike. Then, returning to class to discuss the experience creates a gateway to expanded learning.

INVITATION TO ACADEMICS

1. An academic lives in a community of learners and experts. Their key role is to expand and improve the field of their expertise. Research and publishing are the frontier for progressive development of the field. Barth had a vision for expanding the field of theology by returning to its central subject—Jesus Christ. Not all theology books get you to the living center. This one does.

2. This book deals with a classic text that is more admired than read; it makes *CD*'s contents available with efficiency. While there are a few original quotes, this book mostly provides fresh compressed restatements of vast amounts of material. Though you may not quote it, this book may give you a framework of thinking that would have taken years to glean.

3. Many books on Barth require an extended education in Barth studies to understand. Thus, many people do not read the secondary literature, which is voluminous, in addition to not reading the original text of the *CD*. This book, *Karl Barth's* Church Dogmatics *for Everyone*, is academic enough to provide a deep grasp of complex thoughts in the theology of the master theologian of the twentieth century. It is also accessible enough to invite a novice to join the conversation. Students need a place to get on the train; academics need a train to get them to their destination.

4. This book follows the structure of the *CD*. Therefore, it makes a helpful study companion to discern the gist of Barth's theology. Use it as a guide to each section. Allow the questions to inspire research and writing.

5. Academic study involves equipping the next generation. Barth has been key in the last century in theology, but the best works may be yet to come. Consider inviting students to read this book to search for research topics or to get acquainted with Barth as part of their narrowing of their vision for research.

6. Read the essays in the final section of the book. Consider connecting students from different disciplines to engage Barth to enrich their work. Theology was once the queen of the sciences. This is possible again if we follow Barth's lead. He uniquely helps to reboot the sciences to think out of the life and works of the creator God who invites humanity to live in joyful service in all aspects of life.

INTRODUCTION

This is great! It's the book I would have liked as a companion before picking up the *Dogmatics*.
—Cherith Fee Nordling, *commenting on this book*

WE'RE GOING ON AN ADVENTURE

This book is intended to give a slow and savoring engagement with Karl Barth's great work, the *Church Dogmatics* (we will note as *CD*). The thirteen parts that make up the *CD* can be overwhelming to read. You might feel unprepared, as if you were climbing a mountain in flip-flops. What if we took it one step at a time so we could appreciate and be transformed by the whole work? That is our goal.

Some people are frightened by the words *church* and *dogmatics*. *Church* for Barth is not merely a local congregation or building; it is a people who hear and respond to the love of God and act like it in gathering and loving. *Dogmatics* is often associated with people who are opinionated and unwilling to consider others. For Barth, *dogmatics* is an exercise in clarifying whatever we say about God and whatever we say God has said, to make sure that it is true to God. This means we cannot throw around our opinions about God, but we must be faithful to God's words and actions in our presentations of God. All that follows in these chapters is an exercise in careful listening that calls us to a life of loving response to the God who shows up in Jesus.

Barth began this adventure calling his expansive work *Christian Dogmatics*. But he found that this title focused too narrowly on the individual Christian and not enough on the living God. This God is his focus. God informs, shapes, and invigorates the Church as a community in relationship with God, one another, and the world. A simple name change provided a radical transformation of focus from a set of rational beliefs into a receptive conversation about knowing the living God personally in community.

Each chapter in this book is intended to bring the *CD* into clearer focus with tools for the adventure of knowing the living God through Barth's majestic work that opens the way.

We're going to begin with the big picture. Imagine the *CD* is Earth, and we're viewing it from outer space. As the chapters progress, we'll zoom in and enter Earth's atmosphere. We want to bring the whole work into a manageable picture to then parachute into the landscape of the *CD*, observing all the vivid insights as we explore each part. That's when things start to get bumpy and fun as we interact with the *CD* and it with us.

Therefore, that big picture perspective will start in chapter 1, looking at the whole of the *CD* in one word. That is one step, as a clear snapshot of the whole as if looking from outer space (it would look pretty small). Then we will move closer and closer to bring into focus layers of profound thought presented so that the parts become visible, mapped out as a portion of the whole.

This book you are reading contains 31 chapters, seven of which are introductory. From chapters 8 through 31, we are looking at what are called "paragraphs" in Barth's *CD*, but these paragraphs feel more like chapters. Don't be fooled; they can be quite large. The § symbol means paragraph. So when you see a title that looks like "§ 1. The Task of Dogmatics," that is Barth's title for what feels like a chapter, but we will refer to them as paragraphs. This first book of the series on the *CD* looks at § 1–24. These first twenty-four paragraphs make up *CD* 1.1 and 1.2. This is the normal shorthand for referring to each of the volumes and parts of the *CD*.[1] The two parts referred to in this book explore *CD*, volume 1, "The Doctrine of the Word of God." Later books in this series will explore the three other volumes. Additionally, a fifth volume will survey what Barth gave as the basic structure and content of *CD* 5, based on his own works, as well as adding essays by specialists on that material.

TOOLS FOR THE JOURNEY

Each chapter in this book will offer a set of tools, components to help you on the way. What follows here is a base camp preparation to ready you for the journey.

Chapter Titles: As you put on your Barth boots to explore, begin by looking for the chapter titles. These are each shaped to orient you so you can gain perspective on where you are in the process of narrowing in to the picture set before you as a step to focus on. Each chapter title names where you are on the map.

---

1. Hence *CD* 1.1, 1.2, 2.1, 2.2, 3.1, 3.2, 3.3, 3.4, 4.1, 4.2, 4.3.1, 4.3.2, 4.4. Some books may use *CD* 1/1, 1/2, etc. Others may use the Roman numerals, *CD* I/1, I/2, II.1, II.2, etc.

Focus Statement: Next, in each chapter, you will see a focus statement that reveals the point of that chapter as it opens up the vista. Each focus statement will feature bold text and a larger font size to get your attention. In the section called Text you will find what the focus statement is pointing to.

Each chapter's focus statement will employ the metaphor of imaging the *CD* as a mountain to be hiked and enjoyed with a competent guide. Metaphors are like glasses or binoculars to help us see clearly what is going on around us. We will then see the connection to Barth's point in this chapter.

Introduction: Then an introduction will scope out the purpose of the chapters. Starting at chapter 8, we land in the text of the *CD*, and this will help give us a sense of what Uncle Karl intended us to understand in each section under consideration. These are like route notes to prepare us.

Context: Next will come some helpful details to discern how big of a step we are taking. We will see the context of where we are within the scope of each particular chapter—how far we will be hiking. It will refocus us on which volume of the *CD* we are in, how many pages we are snapshotting, and so on. Also included is a list of subsections that Barth had structured within the paragraph; these subsections show the big topics laid out before us as stepping stones to cross the terrain. In this book, we will cover the text of the first two books shown in the image below.[2]

Karl Barth	Karl Barth	Karl Barth	Karl Barth	Karl Barth	Karl Barth	Karl Barth	Karl Barth	Karl Barth	Karl Barth	Karl Barth	Karl Barth	Karl Barth
Church Dogmatics	*Church Dogmatics*	*Church Dogmatics*	*Church Dogmatics*	*Church Dogmatics*	*Church Dogmatics*	*Church Dogmatics*	*Church Dogmatics*	*Church Dogmatics*	*Church Dogmatics*	*Church Dogmatics*	*Church Dogmatics*	*Church Dogmatics*
I/1	I/2	II/1	II/2	III/1	III/2	III/3	III/4	IV/1	IV/2	IV/3.1	IV/3.2	IV/4
1932 (1936 ET)	1938 (1956 ET)	1940 (1957 ET)	1942 (1957 ET)	1945 (1958 ET)	1948 (1960 ET)	1950 (1961 ET)	1951 (1961 ET)	1953 (1956 ET)	1955 (1958 ET)	1959 (1961 ET)	1959 (1962 ET)	1967 (1969 ET)

---

2. This illustration in all its forms through this and following volumes was created by Wyatt Houtz.

📖 **Text:** We then will engage the text, referred to in the focus statement, at an easy gait. We can walk at our own pace; it is not a race.

Chapters 1–7 make up part 1 of *Karl Barth's* Church Dogmatics *for Everyone,* and the chapters approach the whole of the *CD* to get us ready to see the particular sections of the text. Thus, chapters 1–7 cover more than *CD* 1; they also cover *CD* 2, *CD* 3, and *CD* 4 (see above).

Starting with chapter 8, the rest of this book covers *CD* 1.1 and *CD* 1.2. At this point, the chapters will begin to serve up the introductory summary that Barth provided to begin each section. That brief statement will be our beginning text. Each chapter that follows in this book and future books in the series will cover one paragraph of the *CD.* Remember, when we say paragraph, we do not mean a small section of sentences. Each paragraph in the *CD* can range from fifteen to over one hundred pages. The entirety of the *CD,* including the fragment Barth did not finish, contains seventy-eight paragraphs. In this book we will cover the first twenty-four paragraphs.

✹ **Summary:** What follows is a summary of what is to be enjoyed on our journey.

A set of concise statements is provided that express the heart of the section being considered. Thus, we can stroll with leisurely steps and stop often to appreciate. Like much social media, these are small and separate snapshots for easy viewing. Each statement attempts to provide simple language for the complex beauty we are traversing. Each summary statement is one or two sentences long and yet could be a sermon. Each can be enjoyed separately, but they are developing the flow of Barth's thoughts. By reading slowly and reflectively, we can relish the full text without being overwhelmed or exhausted. These statements are about the size of a text message or a short tweet. Each is intended to have that invigorating punch that makes one want to talk about it or share it to social media.

In a nutshell, these summary statements give the gist of what that segment of the trail in the *CD* is saying. This book is all about nutshells. Once we have surveyed the larger sections, like a mountain meadow spread before us, we will be better able to read these smaller statements as if they were one step at a time—one that will not easily leave our memory. Reading the *CD* is a transformative experience. We may wish to further dive into the wilderness of the actual text to relish and wrestle with the vast detail Barth brings.

🔬 **Commentary:** A few closing comments clarify the key concepts in each chapter. These observations take one last focused glance at what we might take away from this leg of the journey.

Conclusion for the Church: In that Barth's *Dogmatics* is for the *Church*, this section includes a statement on the conclusion for the Church. This implies that what we are learning is not an end in itself but is an invitation to a larger adventure in our own neighborhood.

Insight for Pastors: An insight for pastors note at the end of each chapter invites pastors to see the value of each section of the trail as it applies to serving a church to encounter and know the living God.

Insight for Theologians: Finally, an insight for theologians section is an invitation to higher levels of engagement. These proposals clarify how we use theology to participate in life with God, the Church, and with the humans God so loves. These statements are an invitation to the academy not merely to exist for itself but also to discover how to serve others in hearing and responding to the living God.

Clarifying Questions: The clarifying questions are intended to help us think through our theological interpretations. They allow us to assess whether we align with Barth as we see the "Yes" of God and the "No" that is implied.

A MAP OF WHAT FOLLOWS

As previously stated, part 1 of this book, "Getting the *Church Dogmatics* in Focus," surveys the *CD* as a whole.

Part 2 and part 3 of this book designate where we are in the journey, showing which part of the *CD* we will engage. Part 2 focuses on *CD* 1.1, and part 3 covers *CD* 1.2.

Finally, part 4 of this book contains a collection of short essays by extraordinary thinkers who appreciate the *CD*. As those who excel in their fields of study, each has been asked to articulate in a punchy essay why they value *CD* volume 1 and how *CD* 1 is of great importance for their discipline.

I have maintained the masculine for God (He, His, Him, etc.) because we will encounter this in the *CD*, and it is best to clarify its use here. Barth does not think of God in male terms; only humans have these gendered attributes. This is a personal term that maintains that God is personal and not a force, power, or idea—not an *it*. Jesus was male, but that in no way elevates the masculine in that Jesus came in the most humble and lowly way possible. Thus, these pronouns are to be read merely as referring to the personal being of God in three persons.

WHO WAS KARL BARTH?

Karl Barth was a Swiss Reformed theologian who lived from 1886 to 1968 and changed the world of theology.

Barth is the Einstein of theological thinking, opening a new era of scientific discernment in understanding God and the world. Both Barth and Einstein developed new scientific methodologies. They both opened the way to see the whole of reality as the context for the parts that exist in dynamic relation to each other.

Barth greatly influenced most of the great theologians of the twentieth and twenty-first centuries. Thus, he is key for understanding the theological landscape today.

Barth's name is correctly pronounced *Bart* and rhymes with *cart* and *art*. The *h* is silent.

## PART 1

GETTING THE
CHURCH DOGMATICS
IN FOCUS

Karl Barth	Church Dogmatics	I/1	1932 (1936 ET)
Karl Barth	Church Dogmatics	I/2	1938 (1956 ET)
Karl Barth	Church Dogmatics	II/1	1940 (1957 ET)
Karl Barth	Church Dogmatics	II/2	1942 (1957 ET)
Karl Barth	Church Dogmatics	III/1	1945 (1958 ET)
Karl Barth	Church Dogmatics	III/2	1948 (1960 ET)
Karl Barth	Church Dogmatics	III/3	1950 (1961 ET)
Karl Barth	Church Dogmatics	III/4	1951 (1961 ET)
Karl Barth	Church Dogmatics	IV/1	1953 (1956 ET)
Karl Barth	Church Dogmatics	IV/2	1955 (1958 ET)
Karl Barth	Church Dogmatics	IV/3.1	1959 (1961 ET)
Karl Barth	Church Dogmatics	IV/3.2	1959 (1962 ET)
Karl Barth	Church Dogmatics	IV/4	1967 (1969 ET)

## CHAPTER 1

THE VIEW FROM OUTER SPACE

FOCUS STATEMENT: This chapter introduces the simplicity of the *CD* in *one word*—Jesus. Think of seeing the *CD* from a space station. What is its outstanding feature? This point of view is rare and majestic in its simplicity and reveals what is important.

INTRODUCTION: Yes, we want to begin by hearing an overview of the *CD* in *one word*. It is the big picture in a single, infinitely rich *Word*—Jesus. We are taking a single glance at a vast and deep subject, seeking the clarity that comes when seeing an immense thing, like Earth, from a distance. Except what we see in the *CD* is a person.

CONTEXT: The whole of the *Church Dogmatics* consists of four volumes, divided into thirteen books (fourteen including the posthumously published fragment), outlined into seventeen chapters, expressed in seventy-eight paragraphs (including the unpublished fragment), translated onto 8,353 pages, and detailed in some 6,000,000 words in the English text.[1]

Relationship: This is the purpose for which God chooses to connect with humanity in a restorative relation, and that purpose is embodied in the name and life of this person who comes to restore relationship with His creation.

TEXT: Jesus

SUMMARY: The meaning of the whole of the *CD* in one word, or Word—Jesus—as we shall come to see, is an expansive encounter with this one person.

COMMENTARY: The life of the church consists in hearing and knowing Jesus and living in response.

---

1. David Guretzki, *An Explorer's Guide to Karl Barth* (Downers Grove, IL: InterVarsity Press, 2016), 145.

Even in this one word we see that we are focused on:

- **The personal.** We have the name of a person.
- **The particular.** We are paying attention to one specific person's name.
- **Intent.** The name Jesus means "God saves," and this already reveals what He is up to.
- **The God-human story.** In the name of this person, we are met by the God who initiates and completes reconciliation in this story of saving and restoring.
- **Relationship.** This is a purpose for which God chooses to connect with humanity in a restorative relation and that purpose is embodied in the name and life of this person who comes to restore relationship with His creation.
- **History.** This name is the Greek translation of a Hebrew name, Yeshua, embodying the story of God's saving history with Israel.
- **The end goal of unity between God and humanity.** This one person, Jesus, is both the God who saves and the human in whom saving is completed for all humanity.

CONCLUSION FOR THE CHURCH: The Church has one focus. To be the Church, we focus on Him alone. But Jesus also opens up the world of knowing God and ourselves. Notice what I did not choose as the one-word summary:

- **God.** A generic category that people fill in, to fit their own liking. This is an abstract term that misses the point in letting God be known.
- **Salvation.** A focus on God's benefit to humanity, which starts in the wrong place.

INSIGHT FOR PASTORS: The *CD* is about the person who is the touchstone for God and humanity to meet. All discussion will be grounded in His life and activity. All preaching is intended as an echo of His voice. Preaching that intends to make better Christians or a better community outside of Jesus will be missing the point of theology for the Church.

INSIGHT FOR THEOLOGIANS: Theology must begin by listening to God. Theology proceeds by listening to Jesus' articulation of all He embodies as God and human, providing a proper context and content for theological discussion. Later, we will see that this excludes all forms of trying to know God outside God's self-revelation.

? CLARIFYING QUESTIONS: Does your theology aim at knowing Jesus *or* knowing about Jesus? Is Jesus a person to be engaged *or* an object of study? Further yet, is Jesus dispensable from our theology?

 CHAPTER 2

THE VIEW FROM EARTH'S ORBIT

FOCUS STATEMENT: The point of this chapter is to capture the *CD* in *one phrase*. As we enter Earth's orbit, we become aware of the shape and contours of this orb in front of us. With an enveloping glance, we begin to recognize an outline of land and water—the first glimpse of Earth's character.

INTRODUCTION: Jesus is revealed as God. Jesus uniquely shows us God, not at a distance, but with us and for us. From our simple vantage point, we begin to discern simple outlines and to distinguish discernable parts in relation to each other—to see God in relation to humanity.

TEXT: Jesus Christ, the Lordly Servant, God for and with Humanity

SUMMARY:

All theological thinking arises from what is known in Jesus.

Jesus acts to reveal both true God and true humanity; the content of that revelation is to restore humanity to God.

God really is like what we see in Jesus.

Jesus comes as a servant to bring us home, restoring the broken relationship.

COMMENTARY:

In this one phrase we see:

- Jesus is for us and with us.
- God is an embracing God. The story of God is acted out in history, not in the heavens. In Jesus, God engages humanity within God's good creation.
- Jesus is the fulfillment of the messianic story of the servant who comes to rewrite the brokenness of the past into the fulfillment of God's love in the future.

- The humiliation that is the choice (election) of God is intended to restore all humanity from loss and alienation and to facilitate an eternal encounter and embrace.
- The dual role of Jesus, as fully God and fully human, is to be the paradox of all meaning, the possible impossibility of being both human and divine, thus serving as the raw data for all our theological conversation. He is true God and true human; all true statements about either must begin with Him.
- God has both created and entered the earthly sphere to rule and to serve with glory and humiliation.
- God is involved, God is present, and God sustains human existence.

INSIGHT FOR PASTORS: Theology is not abstract; it is the active engagement by God with humanity to work for the restoration of an estranged relationship. Ministry lives as a participation in this active, restorative service of God.

> God really is like what we see in Jesus.

INSIGHT FOR THEOLOGIANS: Proper theology must focus on the God-human relation as mediated through Jesus. Theology should interpret all His actions and words as revealing all of God and all of true humanity.

CLARIFYING QUESTIONS: Does your theology focus on a person *or* on a system of thought or impersonal religion? Does Jesus come to personally address you, *or* does He come to teach you truths about God and life?

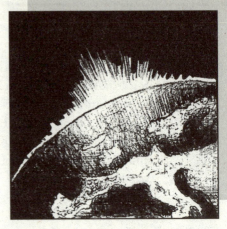

CHAPTER 3

THE VIEW FROM 40,000 FEET

Space Shuttle Reentry View

FOCUS STATEMENT: The point of this chapter is to capture the theme of the whole *CD* in *one long sentence*. As we come closer to Earth, we become selective in where we want to land. We still have a big picture of the globe before us, but we find our focus point on the broad landscape. The grand structures of Earth, once impossible to see, now unfold before us. Oceans and continents, the eye of the hurricane, day and night become visible. We begin to see the continent on which we live, orienting us to discern a simple outline of the content of the *CD*. More and more, we become oriented as we descend toward Earth and home.

INTRODUCTION: This chapter opens the vision that Jesus is the very history of God. Jesus becomes the basis for knowing and being known by the God who calls for an attentive response. In knowing the whole of God's dynamic life, we find the basis of all of our human knowing and acting together. That is the storyline of the *CD*. As we approach Earth, we want to make sure we are landing where we will be met by our intended people in the intended place.

TEXT: The science of God explores the revealed God through an encounter with the actuality of God made known in Jesus Christ—the person spotlighted in Scripture as the One who comes to restore our relation to His Father and the Spirit, concretely knowing the creative work of this triune God; Jesus, as the restoring Word, has transformed and is still transforming all creation through personal connection and fulfillment.

SUMMARY:
The task before us is scientific discovery. This is not science that looks only at the impersonal, natural world. This science includes persons finding a

revelation that speaks, not focusing on a silent object only waiting to be observed. We are to engage and understand what in God is other than ourselves, as God reveals, and then to speak and act appropriately in response.

The focus of our study is provided in the observable being of Jesus Christ, who steps into human history.

Scripture is the scientific report on the reality known through Jesus. But this is even more than a report; it is a portal to enter into dynamic relation with the God who speaks, addressing us and calling for response.

Jesus is not alone as an autonomous individual; to observe and hear Him is also to know and hear His Father and to be given ears to hear by the Holy Spirit.

COMMENTARY:

In this long sentence we see that:

- We are engaged in science, knowing and speaking about the triune God who is ever in relation to God's creation. Science finds language to reflect on what is actual in the reality engaged by humans. Reality is not limited to human experience, but science is limited to that which humans study.
- No speculation or projection allowed; theology must be based on the actual in space and time.
- We are entering reality to be transformed in our thinking, not the other way around.
- Scripture points to the living Word who reveals God's personal life and activity in this world, not merely in the heavens.
- Creation is the context for the text of covenant relationship (I am your God; you are My people). That relationship is initiated and fulfilled by the One freely loving God whose love cannot be conditioned.
- All history, space, and time operate within a dynamic of relations that fulfills God's intention to restore all things.

> All history, space, and time operate within a dynamic of relations that fulfills God's intention to restore all things.

INSIGHT FOR PASTORS:
Science is not a cold calculated study of the objects of the world; rather, for Barth, science is an open investigation of all that God is, does, and creates so that we see the meaningfulness of life in the context of God's life. The Church is the visible people who mirror His life and love. In deeply clarifying God's self-giving, we have the basis

for science as a clear articulation of what it means to relate to what is other than ourselves, a science of knowing this personal God as a community of personal knowing.

INSIGHT FOR THEOLOGIANS: As a discipline, theology must become more holistic in its scientific thinking so that it engages more fully the God who creates, reconciles, and redeems. It must learn to unpack all its theological work within the intentions and actions of God. This means it must make sense in the world to serve God, the Church, and the world, as we see in Jesus. Science, as traditionally used, must follow as a study of the creation after one comes to know the Creator. The ordering of this science is critical to understand the reality of the Creator-creation relationship.

? CLARIFYING QUESTIONS: Does your theology engage with the triune God who comes to you *or* with forms of reasonable thought that enable arguments regarding God's nature and benefits?

## CHAPTER 4

THE VIEW FROM 30,000 FEET

View from an Airplane

🔭 **FOCUS STATEMENT:** The point of this chapter is to capture the structure of the volumes of the *CD* in *one very long sentence*. Now the landscape opens below us. Now we see the mountains, rivers, lakes, and plains. From this height, the vista is still vast, but it is textured with mountain crests and carved valleys as the scene unfolds.

🖋 **INTRODUCTION:** Although thirteen books sit on the shelf as the set of the *CD*, four divided volumes segment the whole (*CD* 1 consists of two parts, *CD* 2 consists of two parts, *CD* 3 consists of four parts, and *CD* 4 consists of five parts). This chapter seeks to summarize this visible layer of engagement. *CD* 5 was never written, but it would have been on the Spirit and God's redemption. We may sense it in the distance. From an airplane, we can see vast stretches of land or water, but we cannot quite grasp the whole in one glance. We can identify main features that help us identify where we are above that land mass, but details are lost in the expanse.

Each of the four volumes of the *CD* has its own structure as well. They each begin with the form and content of God's revelation in Jesus. They each deal with the human side of the relation as made clear by coming to know Jesus. They go on to deal with the impact of the topic for the God-human relation. They envision the future intention of God bringing fulfillment of His purposes to the world. Each culminates with an ethical section, discussing how life might be lived in response to and participation with God in our daily human lives. This repeated rhythm reveals the dynamics of the God-prepared life that leads to a loving, freeing relationship in action.

📖 **TEXT:** The task of dogmatics is the Church's clarification of and eventual encounter with the God revealed in Jesus, who speaks as God and opens knowledge of

His Father and the Holy Spirit for human apprehension in the "Word of God," in order to incorporate the Church into God's mission (*CD* volume 1);

and so the Son reveals God so that the fullness of God may actually be known as the triune God who informs "The Doctrine of God"; the Church avoiding all forms of projecting human experiences onto God (natural theology), but persistently focusing on the one who loves in freedom and graciously elects to be for and with humanity, embracing all humanity in the man Jesus Christ, so that we may live in joyful response to His faithfulness (*CD* volume 2);

and thus, we discover in "The Doctrine of Creation" that the Creator has covenanted with humanity and has created humans for correspondence within God's providential care, and consequently to live as fellow creatures, facilitated in a life of interactive partnership, encountered in space and time by the work of the Spirit; even when humans choose to find life in something other than God, He remains faithful (*CD* volume 3);

The five volumes of the *CD* may be seen as a story of God stepping on the stage that God fashions, telling all of who God is, what *has been* done, what *is being* done, and what *will be* done in the final state when God's intentions of freeing love are achieved toward all God creates, cares for, and brings to fulfillment by God's power and loving choice.

so that we awaken to the fact in "The Doctrine of Reconciliation" that God radically acts to restore God's lost covenant-partners in such a way that God's reconciliation of humanity overcomes all human failing and arouses humans to the definitive reality of God's act on our behalf, by which He gathers us as a community by the Holy Spirit within the vastness of Jesus' transforming work to restore relationship, which is entirely the outworking of God's grace, in order to revitalize humanity within God's faithful, loving, hopeful provision of God's self (*CD* volume 4)

—there is hope for more to be brought about in knowing God's completion, that is, the hope in "The Doctrine of Redemption," but this future is veiled in clouds that envelop what is to come in God's final redemption (*CD* volume 5 —never written).

✠ SUMMARY:

The triune God wants to be known.

We know God in Jesus.

Jesus reveals His Father and the Spirit.

Jesus reveals what it means to be fully human.

Humanity is known as the covenant partner restored in Jesus.

Humanity suffers in choosing what God has not chosen, walking away to nothing rather than living in the lordship of love and freedom offered in Jesus.

Restoration is God's act that completes God's intended renewal of relationship with His creation.

The Bible is a Word that originates in the Word of God in Jesus, who reveals the whole of the God-human relation.

The Church's existence is established and maintained in its inseparable connection to the sustaining life of grace from the Father, made actual through Jesus, and made present by the Spirit.

COMMENTARY:

In this winding comprehensive sentence presented above as the text, we have an overview of the whole *CD* in its present state.

- Notice how the actions of God precede all human knowing from A (God's self-revelation) to Z (God's final redemption by the Spirit). This is called revelation.
- God reveals God. That is the starting point of theology. All our knowledge is grounded in this reality. We are God's creation who receive what God shares.
- The intended five volumes of the *CD* may be seen as a story of Jesus stepping on the stage that God fashions, telling all of who God is, what *has been* done, what *is being* done, and what *will be* done in the final state when God's intentions of freeing love are achieved toward all God creates, cares for, and brings to fulfillment by God's power and loving choice.
- Jesus is the visible face of God. He makes apparent His Father and discloses the activity of the Holy Spirit, who facilitates our knowledge and transformation as we discover ourselves as the children of God.
- God's action does not replace human action and responsibility; rather, it creates the playing field for the possibility of genuine human interaction playing in fulfilling response.
- For a brief glimpse at the volumes, here is my summary of each in less than 250 characters:
  - *CD* 1: God is revealed to humanity in the person of Jesus in an extension of freeing love. The writers of the Bible witnessed the dynamic personal life that created the text of the Bible and the community who gathered around the person, text, and proclamation of the still-speaking God.
  - *CD* 2: God has chosen to be for humanity and enacts this in the person of Jesus. In spite of human attempts to discover, grasp,

or replace God, the faithfulness of God is to be free in loving humanity and expressing that life concretely in Jesus, fulfilled in the life of the Church.

- *CD* 3: God has created the world for a covenant connection with His creatures. The fulfillment of this possibility is in the actuality of Jesus as the one true human who actualizes the God-human relation in which we are made partakers.
- *CD* 4: God restores what is fractured and lost in relation to His beloved creation. In the person of Jesus, the decisive act of God is fulfilled which restores what was lost. The judgment of God is not against humanity but is rather the transformation of the relationship for an outworking of grace.
- *CD* 5: By the Spirit, God is bringing creation to His intended end. Even in our present existence, the Spirit empowers humans to live what God intends, not following our human cravings. The Spirit makes present what is unseen but true in the embodiment of the life of grace offered in Jesus and His promises.

INSIGHT FOR PASTORS: The whole of the *Church Dogmatics* is a reflection on the active life of God at work to bring the Church into being, to sustain the Church, and to restore human existence as God intended. We are called to come home, not clean up our performance. All ministry shares in the mission of God to reconcile, restore, and live in a communing relationship nurtured by God's love that continues to sustain His ministry in our location.

INSIGHT FOR THEOLOGIANS: The Church is a scientific community who lives in response to the actuality of God's being and act, served by theologians who work to help the Church fulfill the mission of God. To serve the Church, theologians call for thoughtful reflection and action so that all humans, and especially the Church, might participate in the triune God's restorative work. The Church exists to bring people into community as a fulfillment of communion with Jesus in a life together. Barth has restored the vision of the academy and the Church like no other theologian by calling leaders to listen to Jesus and not look for means to fulfill human agendas and desires in shaping the Church.

CLARIFYING QUESTIONS: Does your theology begin with God's self-giving and never depart from that source, *or* do you prefer mediating tools, finding God through nature, conscience, or some other human portal into the life of God?

CHAPTER 5

THE VIEW FROM 14,000 FEET

View from a Mountaintop

FOCUS STATEMENT: The point of this chapter is *to capture the published volumes of the CD in a brief overview* as they sit on the shelf and to see them as one continuous landscape. Step back and soak it in as we survey the entire set of the *CD* in one paragraph. It is like a glorious look from a mountain that fills our panoramic vision with grandeur.

INTRODUCTION: Here we have come to the physically structured form of the *Church Dogmatics*. We are trying to grasp the whole while seeing it separated into volumes and parts. Each number below (1.1, 1.2, etc.) names one book in the set. This is like sitting on the edge of a vast vista. We see where we are sitting, on the mountain with glaciers, rivers, and other basic features. But we are also aware of the glorious 360° glance, as we turn in varied directions, and it seems to go on forever.

Looking at the *CD* can feel like a vast landscape one must try to comprehend but never can. But we are ready. Attempt to read the text below in one big breath. Feel the wonder in the rushing torrent of the experience as you sense the movement of God toward humanity (and you). Sense the breathtaking spectacle of God made visible in the open and dynamic revelation of God coming to be known in Jesus. When we are on top of a mountain, we can see for miles. For Barth, to sit with Jesus is to see eternity and all it contains. The vista around us on the mountaintop is unfathomable, but we can begin to absorb it if we survey in segments, in an unhurried rotation. Everything in view on a clear day is either limited or opened up by our capacity to observe, our knowledge of what we are looking at, and the availability of tools (maps, compass, binoculars, etc.) that help us identify what is available before us. With a good guide, the surrounding region is revealed.

The *CD* is a massive work that aims at knowing the unknown with the tools to awaken us to what can be known.

TEXT: The landscape of the *CD* begins with:

1.1 the adventurous task of the Church patiently positioned to hear the God who is the Revealer, Revelation, and Revealedness of Godself. Thus, God personally provides the ability to respond and participate in God's active encounter. This dynamic moment becomes available in God's glorious self-giving in

1.2 the threefold Word of God revealed as: living (Jesus), written (Bible), and preached (Church witness). This harmonic revelation of the Word amazes us, and generates an ongoing human response. God shows us Himself and in doing so provides the means to validate appropriate human hearing and teaching as an authentic invitation to know God, with God alone as the author and measure of its trustworthiness.

2.1 Through this self-display, God is available to be explored by focusing on God's acts of free, loving encounter and speech to humanity. We must say no to constructions of theology that build on natural human capacities. Consequently, we are able to faithfully apprehend God as we are met by the personal threefold fellowship that is God's life as Father, Son, and Holy Spirit. Overwhelmed by this gracious triunity, we humans are awakened with gratitude for God's gift, and as we discover God's gift to humanity, we are invited into shared knowledge of Godself as a free, loving response

The whole of the *CD* explains what God has done to embrace all He has made.

2.2 to the unconditional will of God, seen in the loving action of God's electing to be for humanity. This election occurs in the person of Jesus Christ and not in selecting a few individuals. He bears away our rejection as He gifts humanity with the provision of new life. This life is lived as a community renewed by Jesus' act. By the Spirit, we are personally awakening to the gift

3.1 that is based on God's original intention to create a world for covenant partners to live in the context of His created provision. This goes back to the beginning of God's activity in coming to us, fulfilling the glory of God's purposes by establishing an ultimate "yes" for all persons, a "yes" that is the fulfillment of love and, at the same time, a "no" to all that opposes loving relations. Consequently,

3.2 we are especially focused on the "yes" of the One True Human, Jesus Christ, who fulfills freedom in fellowship on behalf of all humanity as a faithful covenant partner, in whom humans find coexistence with God as a gift that invites a renewing participation in God's fulfillment as the Lord of time, whereby

3.3 God stands against all loss of relation. Thus, humans may choose to follow or not, but God always providentially sustains us so that we might continue on with God despite the destructive options available to us in a world engaged by angels and demons, in order that

3.4 we might learn to live in ongoing practical loving action in response to God's ever-present, freeing love, to learn the life of provisional care that shapes our familial life, grows our neighborliness, and transforms us as hearers who act responsively in what becomes the loving form of Christ-informed ethics.

4.1 This God-intended place of covenant relation has been initiated and completed by the humiliation of Jesus Christ, who takes our human cause to be restored, overcomes the disruption of human lostness, and comes as the judge judged in our place to reconcile us to right relation with God as a fulfillment of the very covenant that initiated creation

4.2 in which Jesus is triumphant in His quest into the far country to set humanity back into being a people gathered to share divine love, built to represent God's loving intention through sharing God's work in the world, with the Church being set apart for this very purpose

4.3.1 as an overcoming of the present struggles we encounter, and instead we look forward to the final state and thus become able to endure the time between the times (resurrection and return) as we share in God's transforming work as those sent to be a missional people of the Mediator who calls humans to life,

4.3.2 entering into the vocation of being a community empowered by the Holy Spirit to bring hope that looks forward as a witness that awakens and acknowledges the gift of God's invitational life

4.4 so that all might experience freeing faith as an answer to the gift of God with a gratitude that is made visible in a baptism that points to God

[*The Christian Life*—lecture fragments] and enables us to see special ethics as a grateful response to the Reconciler, bringing honor to God's name, and resisting rebellious powers, to see the kingdom coming.

✠ SUMMARY:

The thirteen or fourteen parts of the five *CD* volumes move us toward clearly focusing on God through Jesus.

The *CD* tunes us into the address of God to humanity uniquely revealed in Jesus.

The whole of the *CD* explains what God has done to embrace all He has made.

All of the *CD* flows toward clarifying God's act in Jesus to restore the God-human rupture and bring a renewed creation made possible by God's act of restoration.

COMMENTARY:

The extended paragraph above attempts to trace the flow of thought of the *CD* by paying attention to their presentation as a set of volumes.

- *CD*'s chapter and paragraph divisions give additional perspective on the vista we are beginning to clarify.
- The paragraph above follows a logic that bridges the whole yet sees the flow of logic from God's initiating activity all the way to human participation in response.
- When read as a paragraph, this narrative gives a sense of the grand scope of God's creative, reconciling life that invites a freeing life of loving response for humans through Jesus. All human love is an echo of Jesus' love for humanity. We love because He first loved us.

INSIGHT FOR PASTORS: Each of the volumes is part of a dynamic movement from God for humanity, proclaimed in the Church, and intent on creating a freeing faith in response to God's ongoing presence. A volume aiding pastors resides at the end of the set. These aids can help incorporate the *CD* into resources for preaching. But in this section, we are seeing the revealed strategy of God in being made available for human response. The exploration of what God has shown of Himself and His way of being with us awakens a revitalizing of what ministry looks like as an extension of God's ministry.

INSIGHT FOR THEOLOGIANS: The *CD* volumes are an extended discussion of reality when seen in the light of God's revelation in Christ; this is the foundation of theological reflection that calls the Church to action in once again making the science of God reorient humanity back to the creating, sustaining, and restoring God.

CLARIFYING QUESTIONS: Does your theology follow the course of discovery opened by Jesus and the mission He pursued, *or* does it follow the logic of philosophical investigation in its language, methods, and conclusions? Does your understanding of God resonate with the Jesus of the Bible?

CHAPTER 6

THE VIEW FROM 5,000 FEET

View from a Mountain Loop Trail

FOCUS STATEMENT: The point of this chapter is to capture the *seventeen chapters of the CD as a substructure.* The trail and the destination come into focus. We are called to a particular trail that leads to a specific destination. Yes, there is a chapter structure to these volumes, a thoughtful trail, so to speak, that does not follow the structure of the published volumes. These chapters present an inner logic that is often missed. Reset your brain to the logical flow as we look at the chapters of the *CD*, not the volumes or paragraphs.

INTRODUCTION: It is easy to miss, but the *Church Dogmatics* contains an introduction, plus sixteen chapters (and chapter 17 is in the book *The Christian Life*, posthumously published from a draft taken from lecture notes). In this present chapter, we will follow the chapters of the *CD* as the skeleton of the entire *CD*. First, we will simply list the chapters of the *CD*, then follow with an overview of the logic of the chapters. I am thinking of my own Mount Rainier in Washington State at this point. The Wonderland Trail is an expansive adventure that takes many days to complete. But the trail provides access to the whole mountain, to experience with sweat and joy.

TEXT: *Table of Contents of the CD by Chapters* found below:

Overview of the Logic of the Chapters:

The task of theology begins with the acknowledgment that the Christian Church speaks of God, and when done properly, theology is a knowledge that arises from God and encounters the Church with a trustworthy knowledge (introduction).

The Christian Church is a speaking Church and its speech is grounded in God's personal speaking in Jesus Christ, as witnessed to in the Bible, and this informs the content of the Church's proclamation as sharing God's speech and act (chapter 1, "The Word of God as the Criterion of Dogmatics").

But God is the focus, the one God made visible and audible exactly where God has made known God's revelation (in Jesus) coming from the Revealer (the Father) so that we may be drawn into a knowing relation made possible by God (the Holy Spirit) in an encounter with this living God (chapter 2, "The Revelation of God").

The God revealed exists as three "Thous" who meet the human "I" for a relationship. The Father is seen as our Father, who initiates the sending of the Son, who, in turn, shows us and reconciles us to His Father by the Spirit, who in love restores us as children (chapter 2, part 1, "The Triune God").

God became a human for the purpose of freely becoming available in space and time to embrace us in God's time and story and to reveal God's mystery as a reconciling event that displays God's intent to reconcile with humanity (chapter 2, part 2, "The Incarnation of the Word").

But we are not passive or alone in the face of God's act; we are given freedom to respond as we are filled with the Holy Spirit, who opens us for freely receiving love in the place of our attempts to prepare ourselves, as though God needed our self-perfecting to be acceptable rather than freely working out of God's grace (chapter 2, part 3, "The Outpouring of the Holy Spirit").

Humanity is not without a witness to the living Word, Jesus; we have the Bible as witness to God's revelation. God gives authority to this Word and invites a listening obedience whereby the Church finds its freedom in coming to know and love the living God (chapter 3, "Holy Scripture").

Therefore, the Church listens, proclaiming what it has heard, attuning the Church to know and devotedly follow the one it loves and joyfully obeys (chapter 4, "The Proclamation of the Church").

Knowing God is a personal response facilitated by the Spirit, who draws our knowing to be a loving discovery of the truth God gives in His Son and confirms by the Spirit, while at the same time clarifying what is not God so that we will be nourished by God's grace alone as we abide in His life and love (chapter 5, "The Knowledge of God").

> In this brief summary, one can see the activity of God as a triune, personal mission of creating, restoring, and bringing hope to humanity as the ongoing, shared life of freeing love.

What we find in knowing God is that God loves us in freedom. The expansive life of God is unconstrained and unearned, self-generous and expressed in ways that meet real human needs (chapter 6, "The Reality of God").

The particularity of God's love for humanity is in the fact that God chose us to be restored by His own free choice in Jesus to be unconditionally for us and with us, freely determining to deal with humanity's rejection of God as well as restoring participation in relation again, utilizing community and persons to be gathered and graced to bear God's witness to the world (chapter 7, "The Election of God").

The good news is that God's election to love humanity becomes the command of love, which is to be lived as if one has been indeed claimed and empowered to witness to the love bestowed. God is gracious and judges us with grace, dealing with our failures by the death and resurrection of the Son, making us right in relation and free to live under God's care (chapter 8, "The Command of God").

God's good work began at creation. God expressed His free love in the act of providing a world and inhabitants to be the focus of God's concern.

God covenants with creation to benefit all that God makes through His ongoing acts of providential care (chapter 9, "The Work of Creation").

Humanity is the central focus of God's concern and only truly known in Jesus Christ since all others bear the damage of the human rejection of God. But humanity is called home to be restored, renewed as covenant partners with God and one another as whole beings in relation to all God creates, in the place and time God gifts (chapter 10, "The Creature").

God does not abandon humanity but unveils the fatherly care provided by God, especially in Jesus Christ. Humans may choose otherwise than to receive God's care, but this is to choose nothing; since God gives all good things, not choosing God is choosing nothing. But God's intent is that Earth be filled with the presence of God's kingdom to triumph over all opposing chaos (chapter 11, "The Creator and His Creature").

As God has created and sustained the creation, He now in love compels the human to respond in joy and gratitude as the form of worship, resulting in a shared life of loving encounter with God and neighbor in the freedom of service that is the act of love for the other within the time and place where we live (chapter 12, "The Command of the Creator").

The central act in the God-human story is God's grand restoration called reconciliation, so that God will be known and God's purposes made complete—for this Jesus came to Earth. God takes confused and willful humanity and salvages us to be made right in relation, transformed to love, and empowered for service (chapter 13, "The Subject Matter and Problems of the Doctrine of Reconciliation").

This is accomplished through Jesus as He goes from heaven into the far country of humanity and brings us home in Himself. Jesus crucifies the guilt of humanity and gifts us with the promise of forgiveness and life to be gathered and awakened to share in the life of the Servant to whom the Spirit awakens us (chapter 14, "Jesus Christ, The Lord as Servant").

But the story is not over. Jesus is raised to bring us to live under His care and direction, sharing His life of love. Although we are lazy and in misery, He fills us with Himself and builds us up by the Spirit to lovingly build a community that lives from and for love (chapter 15, "Jesus Christ, the Servant as Lord").

Jesus' ministry of reconciliation is not merely a point-in-time occurrence; it is lived in the ongoing activity of Jesus as mediator of the truth. In the face of all the falsity of humanity, Jesus calls us to live faithful and true lives that facilitate the service of God and humanity to one another. The Spirit sends us out into the world to accomplish this task, bringing hope and healing to point toward the fulfillment of God's purposes. Our participation in baptism is a proclamation of the actuality of Christ, the faithfulness He brings to nurture us, and the hope the world needs to encounter (chapter 16, "Jesus Christ, the True Witness").

The joyful response of those who answer the call of reconciliation is to know the Father's love and to live in response, seeing His kingdom coming, connected in prayer and the hope of His peace to rule in the world (chapter 17, "The Command of God the Reconciler").

SUMMARY:

The chapters follow a logic of first focusing us on the God we are discovering.

The personal God is then unveiled in a process of exploring what is known of God.

In the light of whom we are studying, we can then see that God has acted and spoken to humanity in Jesus.

Jesus is the clarifying person who alone can bring us to know God and true humanity.

In faith Jesus came on a mission to bring God's presence to humanity so that we might live in loving, joyful response.

The Bible and the *CD* recount a grand story of God's restoration in reestablishing God's relational intention to create a life of shared love.

COMMENTARY:

- In this brief summary, one can see the activity of God as a triune, personal mission of creating, restoring, and bringing hope to humanity as the ongoing, shared life of freeing love.
- We will look more closely at these sections as we survey the paragraphs that are subsets of the chapters.

INSIGHT FOR PASTORS: Although many miss these chapters within the structure of the *CD*, these strata reveal that the *CD* is about God initiating and facilitating the ongoing dialog between God and His people to compel us freely in love to participate in God's life in the world. These chapters offer a picture of the story of God, like looking at a family album and seeing the chapters of life that have shaped the family. If a church sees these topics not as theoretical topics but as movements in the story of the family of God, then the possibility of being drawn into that family increases exponentially. Rather than getting people in the pews, think of getting people to live within the story of God's life as their story.

INSIGHT FOR THEOLOGIANS: These chapters remind us that the science of God is about God and not about what God can do to improve the lives of individual Christians. But this God will not be without humanity, so we know God as a personal being who embraces humanity.

? CLARIFYING QUESTIONS: Does your theology focus on the task of the Church to listen to the Lord and continually renew its participation, *or* does it focus on the individual being saved, the Church being powerful, or Christianity becoming the dominant religion to save the world?

CHAPTER 7

THE VIEW FROM 1,200 FEET

View from the Trailhead

FOCUS STATEMENT: The point of this chapter is to introduce a list of the *seventy-eight paragraphs of the* CD *with brief summaries*. This chapter is a detailed account of the parts of the trail, the sights along the way, and insights to navigate the trail right from the start.

INTRODUCTION: The *Church Dogmatics* (*CD*) are divided into seventy-eight "paragraphs" that are as long as a book in some cases, but we are wise to see them as another level of surveying the *CD*. Each paragraph is indicated with the § symbol, beginning with § 1, "The Task of Dogmatics." At the trailhead, a map often shows us in miniature what appears in grandeur before us. There is an obvious connection between the map and the trail, but one can orient us and the other overwhelm us at the thought of traversing its expanse. Breathe deep, check the map, and let it fill you with delight at what is to come.

In the *CD*, each paragraph includes a short, bolded summary written by Barth. You will find this at the beginning of each section; it will help us summarize the contents. Beginning with chapter 8 in this book, each paragraph opening summary will be indicated by the following: 📖 **TEXT**.

In the index volume of the *CD*, the paragraphs are listed along with their descriptive summaries in a section called "Contents of the *Church Dogmatics.*" Preacher's aids are also included in the index volume, which hints at Barth's intended readership. That supplemental volume is a valuable map of the territory, much like the information board at a trailhead.

At the end of this chapter, I have included an image of the contents of the thirty-one-volume study edition that further breaks down the content into smaller sections (and it adds a helpful tool for study).

We will set off taking big strides by simply listing the titles of the seventy-eight paragraphs (§) in the left column so they are easy to see. This provides a map at the trailhead of a long trail with seventy-eight sections that provide a particular view of the land as we circle the mountain. In the right column is a one-line summary of each paragraph to help you begin to flesh out the contents.

For now, we will exclude the volume and chapter titles of the *CD* so we can observe the increasingly detailed landscape visible in the paragraph titles. See if you can discern a flow of thought with just the paragraph titles.

📖 **TEXT: Simple List of Paragraph Titles and Summary:**

#	Name	Summary
§ 1	The Task of Dogmatics	The Church must speak faithfully.
§ 2	The Task of Prolegomena to Dogmatics	Theology must begin with Jesus, not human insight or Church tradition.
§ 3	Church Proclamation as the Material of Dogmatics	The Church talks about God talking to humanity.
§ 4	The Word of God in Its Threefold Form	The Word of God is preached, written, and revealed.
§ 5	The Nature of the Word of God	The Word is God addressing humanity.
§ 6	The Knowability of the Word of God	Humanity hears the Word of God in order to know God.
§ 7	The Word of God, Dogma and Dogmatics	Dogmatics is a careful testing of the truthfulness of our hearing and speaking.
§ 8	God in His Revelation	God alone reveals God in His revelation.
§ 9	The Triunity of God	God is revealed as Father, Son, and Spirit, who meet humanity.
§ 10	God the Father	God is Father and the Creator of all and the One who reveals.
§ 11	God the Son	God is revealed in person as Son of the Father.
§ 12	God the Holy Spirit	God makes us children who share the love of God by the Spirit who embraces us.
§ 13	God's Freedom for Man	God loves as a freedom for humanity.
§ 14	The Time of Revelation	God creates and gives meaning to the time of His meeting with humanity.

#	Name	Summary
§ 15	The Mystery of Revelation	God takes on human form in order to include humanity into God's life.
§ 16	The Freedom of Man for God	God speaks so that humans may freely respond as beloved children.
§ 17	The Revelation of God as the Abolition of Religion	God's gracious self-giving exposes all false relations pretending to be God's Word.
§ 18	The Life of the Children of God	God enlivens His own children to express themselves as found and loved by God.
§ 19	The Word of God for the Church	God is the Word speaking personally, beheld in the Bible, and attended to in the Church.
§ 20	Authority in the Church	God is the Lord over Scripture as the Church studies and submits to its intentions.
§ 21	Freedom in the Church	God gives the Bible to create free, joyful obedience toward God in each person.
§ 22	The Mission of the Church	God gives the Church a share in God's address that reveals God's life to the world.
§ 23	Dogmatics as a Function of the Hearing Church	God calls the Church to be attentive to God's address and to prepare to share.
§ 24	Dogmatics as a Function of the Teaching Church	God summons the Church to teach the God revealed in Jesus.
§ 25	The Fulfillment of the Knowledge of God	God is known when revelation becomes embraced and loved in personal connection.
§ 26	The Knowability of God	God faithfully gives God's self to be known in Jesus and by the Spirit so we may participate.
§ 27	The Limits of the Knowledge of God	Only God knows God; claims made outside God's revelation are inadmissible.
§ 28	The Being of God as the One Who Loves in Freedom	God's very being is in love; this is freely extended to humanity.
§ 29	The Perfections of God	God is complete in a life of abundance that gives in grace.
§ 30	The Perfections of the Divine Loving	God is consistent in all God's ways of loving.
§ 31	The Perfections of the Divine Freedom	God is consistent in all God's ways of being in time, space, and activity.

#	Name	Summary
§ 32	The Problem of a Correct Doctrine of the Election of Grace	God chooses to be for humanity and to engulf all humanity in being loved in Jesus.
§ 33	The Election of Grace	God, in Jesus, embraces alienated humanity and restores them home to God's self.
§ 34	The Election of the Community	God uses Israel and the Church as representatives of God's mercy and promises.
§ 35	The Election of the Individual	God rejects the godless void that humans choose and elects to personally gift life.
§ 36	Ethics as a Task of the Doctrine of God	God is committed to human well-being and so engages to elicit human response.
§ 37	The Command as the Claim of God	God's claim on our life compels us to seek this life intended for us.
§ 38	The Command as the Decision of God	God decides to be for us and with us, and we stand and move because of His choice.
§ 39	The Command as the Judgment of God	God judges humans as wrongdoers and also restores them for eternal life with God.
§ 40	Faith in God the Creator	Jesus is the faithful God and true human whose being opens our humanity to God.
§ 41	Creation and Covenant	God creates all that is not God, covenanting with humanity as the goal of creation.
§ 42	The Yes of the Creator	God affirms goodness through all God creates.
§ 43	Man as a Problem of Dogmatics	God makes known the true nature of humanity in Jesus Christ.
§ 44	Man as the Creature of God	God has made humans capable of personal response.
§ 45	Man in His Determination as the Covenant-Partner of God	God made humans for encounter with God and each other as fulfillment.
§ 46	Man as Soul and Body	God made humans inseparably embodied and simultaneously interrelated (soul).
§ 47	Man in His Time	God appoints a time for humans to live within as covenant-partners.
§ 48	The Doctrine of Providence, Its Basis and Form	God oversees the care of humanity most succinctly in the provision of Jesus.

#	Name	Summary
§ 49	God the Father as the Lord of His Creature	Jesus is the Image of the fatherly care of God toward creation.
§ 50	God and Nothingness	The sphere of life God has not chosen has no being; it exists as what is refuted by God.
§ 51	The Kingdom of Heaven, the Ambassadors of God, and Their Opponents	God provides messengers to ward off opposing forces of chaos.
§ 52	Ethics as a Task of the Doctrine of Creation	God's command is already the beneficial means for creaturely life.
§ 53	Freedom before God	God wills for human freedom to come through dynamic connection with their Creator.
§ 54	Freedom in Fellowship	God calls humans to love one another as an enjoyment of God and humanity.
§ 55	Freedom for Life	God compels humans to honor their own life and consequently to serve others.
§ 56	Freedom in Limitation	God gives humans time to fulfill a vocation as fellow-humans.
§ 57	The Work of God the Reconciler	God takes the lost cause of alienated humanity and makes it His own.
§ 58	The Doctrine of Reconciliation (Survey)	Jesus, as very God and very human, makes at one the restoration of God and humanity.
§ 59	The Obedience of the Son of God	Jesus goes into the far country to bring us back from death to life.
§ 60	The Pride and Fall of Man	Jesus' death and resurrection disclose the serious guilt of humanity.
§ 61	The Justification of Man	Jesus has attained what humanity cannot, a renewal that we may acknowledge.
§ 62	The Holy Spirit and the Gathering of the Christian Community	Having renewed them, the Spirit gathers humans to be ready for life.
§ 63	The Holy Spirit and the Christian Faith	The Spirit awakens humans to acknowledge and participate in Jesus' death and life.
§ 64	The Exaltation of the Son of Man	Jesus reveals a life of exalted servanthood, that by the Spirit we might share in it.
§ 65	The Sloth and Misery of Man	Jesus' resurrection reveals the self-centered inhumanity and anxiety He transforms.

#	Name	Summary
§ 66	The Sanctification of Man	By God's loving act, humans are given a new form of existence to live freeing love.
§ 67	The Holy Spirit and the Upbuilding of the Christian Community	The Spirit empowers the Church of Jesus Christ to benefit humanity with Jesus' life.
§ 68	The Holy Spirit and Christian Love	The Spirit draws human life to correspond to the life of God.
§ 69	The Glory of the Mediator	Jesus has made the one way for knowing God.
§ 70	The Falsehood and Condemnation of Man	Jesus overcomes the falsity of human thinking and acting and claims humanity for Himself.
§ 71	The Vocation of Man	In fellowship with Jesus, humans are empowered to speak and act with Jesus.
§ 72	The Holy Spirit and the Sending of the Christian Community	The Spirit empowers humans to be a community who calls all humanity to hope in Jesus.
§ 73	The Holy Spirit and Christian Hope	The Spirit enlightens the Church to live with cheerful expectation of God's fulfillment.
[§ 74]	Ethics as a Task of the Doctrine of Reconciliation	God's reconciliation creates the context for human covenant participation in Jesus.
[§ 75]	The Foundation of the Christian Life (Thesis)	In baptism, humans confirm the faithfulness of Jesus, marking a new life of participation.
[§ 76]	The Children and Their Father	As God is Father and humans are God's children, they are liberated by the Spirit to live as such.
[§ 77]	Zeal for the Honor of God	Christians live in the already and not yet as those attuned to the primacy of God's Word.
[§ 78]	The Struggle for Human Righteousness	Christians live as those responsible to agree with divinely ordained safeguards for peace.

 **COMMENTARY:**

- Allow yourself to skim the sentences to get the overarching flow of the *CD*.
- This brief hike through the woodlands and meadows of the *CD* shows the lay of the land so we can see the big picture with increasing clarity.
- These seventy-eight paragraphs focus on God's action in Jesus to open the understanding of the Church and persons to live with gratitude in response to God's actions.

- We will continue our journey by traversing each paragraph (§), so prepare to shift your thinking from looking at the *whole* of the *CD* to examining *one paragraph* at a time. The next chapter engages the first paragraph of the *CD*, called "The Task of Dogmatics" (§ 1). Put on your hiking boots!

INSIGHT FOR PASTORS: The list of paragraphs orients the reader to see that much more exploration lies ahead to clarify the meaning and application of God's way of being in the world. As we move toward contact with reality, the text calls us to reframe our thinking in light of Christ. This reorientation is the first task of pastoral ministry. An outline is like a melody line, the main thrust of a song that reveals its themes and provides context for its rich variations. In learning the tune of Barth's masterpiece, we are invited to improvise in our context while listening to Barth's melody line. This listening and improvising informs the dynamics of ministry that is living and active, not controlling and theoretical.

Be sure to check out the "Aids for the Preacher" at the end of the index volume, stretching from pages 263 to 552 (almost 300 pages!). One could use the index to look up what Barth says about the verse you are preaching on that week. In the study edition of the *CD*, you can reference any of the Greek words you might encounter. One could also do a whole sermon series based on these pastoral aides. These tools facilitate difficult tasks and equip us for the wilderness.

INSIGHT FOR THEOLOGIANS: Like a wonder-struck scientist who has figured out how to study while keeping the object of study alive, the paragraphs of the *CD* are an adventure in exploring the dynamic life of God and humanity, both in healthy forms and in correcting errors.

Theologians may survey the paragraphs and summaries to discover topics that intrigue them. Barth's *Dogmatics* is not orderly in the same manner as many American systematic theologies. Thus, this guide helps navigate the countryside for people who wander off the trail, who are charting new trails, or who feel lost and need orientation.

CLARIFYING QUESTIONS: Does your theology follow the life and activity of God down to every detail, *or* does it build frameworks that attempt to make God reasonable, appeal to how God will make life better, or try to provide winning arguments for a secular society? Are you aware of the breadth of the topics of theology, *or* have you focused only on a subset of the things that interest you? This chapter may open your eyes to new things you hadn't studied before.

THE BIG PICTURE

The original volumes of the *Church Dogmatics* have been reprinted by T&T Clark in an expanded thirty-one volume edition. Their organization, listed below, gives a helpful glance at the overall flow of the material.

14 Vol. Edition	31 Vol. Edition	

VOLUME 1: The Doctrine of the Word of God

1.1	1 § 1–7	The Word of God as the Criterion for Dogmatics
	2 § 8–12	The Revelation of God: The Triune God
1.2	3 § 13–15	The Revelation of God: The Incarnation of the Word
	4 § 16–18	The Revelation of God: The Outpouring of the Holy Spirit
	5 § 19–21	Holy Scripture
	6 § 22–24	The Proclamation of the Church

VOLUME 2: The Doctrine of God

2.1	7 § 25–27	The Knowledge of God
	8 § 28–30	The Reality of God I
	9 § 31	The Reality of God II
2.2	10 § 32–33	The Election of God I
	11 § 34–35	The Election of God II
	12 § 36–39	The Command of God

VOLUME 3: The Doctrine of Creation

3.1	13 § 40–42	The Work of Creation
3.2	14 § 43–44	The Creature I
	15 § 45–46	The Creature II
	16 § 47	The Creature III
3.3	17 § 48–49	The Creator and His Creature I
	18 § 50–51	The Creator and His Creature II
3.4	19 § 52–54	The Command of God the Creator I
	20 § 55–56	The Command of God the Creator II

VOLUME 4: The Doctrine of Reconciliation

4.1	21 § 57–59	The Subject-Matter and Problems of the Doctrine of Reconciliation Jesus Christ, the Lord as Servant I
	22 § 60	Jesus Christ, the Lord as Servant II
	23 § 61–63	Jesus Christ, the Lord as Servant III
4.2	24 § 64	Jesus Christ, the Servant as Lord I
	25 § 65–66	Jesus Christ, the Servant as Lord II
	26 § 67–68	Jesus Christ, the Servant as Lord III
4.3.1	27 § 69	Jesus Christ, the True Witness I
4.3.2	28 § 70–71	Jesus Christ, the True Witness II
	29 § 72–73	Jesus Christ, the True Witness III
4.4	30	The Christian Life (Fragment), The Doctrine of Baptism
INDEX	31	Index with Aids for the Preacher

This synopsis enables one to see the four volumes (1–4), the fourteen parts (1.1–4.4 and index), the thirty-one volumes of the study edition (1–31), and the paragraphs (§ 1–73, plus the fragment and index).

## PART 2

CHURCH DOGMATICS 1.1

Engaging the God of the *CD*

Karl Barth	Church Dogmatics	I/1	1932 (1936 ET)
Karl Barth	Church Dogmatics	I/2	1938 (1956 ET)
Karl Barth	Church Dogmatics	II/1	1940 (1957 ET)
Karl Barth	Church Dogmatics	II/2	1942 (1957 ET)
Karl Barth	Church Dogmatics	III/1	1945 (1958 ET)
Karl Barth	Church Dogmatics	III/2	1948 (1960 ET)
Karl Barth	Church Dogmatics	III/3	1950 (1961 ET)
Karl Barth	Church Dogmatics	III/4	1951 (1961 ET)
Karl Barth	Church Dogmatics	IV/1	1953 (1956 ET)
Karl Barth	Church Dogmatics	IV/2	1955 (1958 ET)
Karl Barth	Church Dogmatics	IV/3.1	1959 (1961 ET)
Karl Barth	Church Dogmatics	IV/3.2	1959 (1962 ET)
Karl Barth	Church Dogmatics	IV/4	1967 (1969 ET)

CHURCH DOGMATICS, CHAPTER 1

"The Word of God as the Criterion of Dogmatics"

🗺️ **CHAPTER 8**

PREPARING TO TRAVEL THE MOUNTAIN LOOP TRAIL

§ 1. The Task of Dogmatics

👀 **FOCUS STATEMENT:** Get out your map and compass. This is the orienting point of this chapter as we summarize *CD* § 1, "The Task of Dogmatics."

🖋️ **INTRODUCTION:** This first paragraph launches us into how the persons within the Church might be faithful to the living God by making sure our speaking is a clear reflection of what God has given to be known.

In Robert McAfee Brown's essay "How to Remember What's Where in Barth, or Mnemonics for Mprofessors," he playfully begins, "I/1—In English, 'one-one' means a tie; no satisfactory conclusion has been reached. I/1, therefore, is introductory and methodological, and points the way to future volumes."[1]

📚 **CONTEXT:** *CD* 1.1
Pages in Paragraph: 22 pages (pp. 3–24)

Note: Sometimes there will be a reference to the original German edition, for example [*KD* pp. 3–24]. Also, the study edition has different page numbers. The references in this guide are to the English translation in its thirteen-volume format.

Subsections

1. The Church, Theology, Science
2. Dogmatics as an Enquiry
3. Dogmatics as an Act of Faith

---

1. Robert McAfee Brown, "How to Remember What's Where in Barth, or Mnemonics for Mprofessors," in *The Collected Writings of St. Hereticus* (Philadelphia: Westminster, 1964), 94.

📖 **TEXT: § 1. The Task of Dogmatics**

OPENING SUMMARY:[2] As a theological discipline, dogmatics is the scientific self-examination of the Christian Church with respect to the content of its distinctive talk about God.[3]

✠ **SUMMARY:**
1. The Church, Theology, Science (pp. 3–11)

In this section, Barth deals with the shared ways of working in the Church, theology, and science.

The Church talks about God. But in order for what it says to be truthful, what it says must always be a response to what God has said and done first.

2. Dogmatics as Enquiry (pp. 11–17)

When the Church talks about God, it is doing theology. But the words must all be scrutinized and carefully considered to confirm that the words and ideas refer to God and not to human conjectures or illusions.

The Church reflects on God. In the actions of each person and in the acts of the Church in teaching, worship, love of neighbor, and witness to the actuality of God, the Church is a scientific community. This understanding follows because it has a focus of study (God), clarifies and corrects its words (observation and interpretation), and seeks through its research to act more faithfully in reflecting the God from whom its life is derived (developing a research community). By following this methodology, the Church and theology are scientific in nature.

3. Dogmatics as an Act of Faith (pp. 17–24)

Science is properly conceived as the human pursuit of knowledge. It begins with a particular focus of study (in this case God), follows a definite path, and must give an account of how the path has established an appropriate trail for others to follow.

The truth of theology is personal. Theology studies a personal God who addresses humanity as persons. In each age of history, humankind must learn to hear and respond to divine and human persons as a scientific community who properly knows and lives in the light of this foremost living reality who is God come to us.

---

2. Barth includes opening summaries at the head of each chapter.

3. Karl Barth, *Church Dogmatics: The Doctrine of the Word of God, Part 1*, ed. Geoffrey William Bromiley and Thomas F. Torrance, vol. 1 (London; New York: T&T Clark, 2004), p. 3. Henceforth *CD*.

The transformation of our beliefs and the correction of our orientation, from self-focus to this personal revelation, is called faith. A scientific task of the Church is to so clarify the reality of this Living God that transformation (penitence), living connection (obedience), and participation (prayer) become our response to God's self-revelation (grace).

Therefore, the Church is a scientific community who gathers before the living God and prepares to be nurtured and developed as those living in the light of this discovered, disclosed reality and to interpret for others this transforming personal presence.

The Church is a scientific community who gathers before the living God and prepares to be nurtured and developed as those living in the light of this discovered, disclosed reality and to interpret for others this transforming personal presence.

COMMENTARY:

- Theology is a reflective task for the Church to make sure its talk about God is true to God's self-revelation.
- The task of the Church is to explore the adventure of living in light of God's self-giving.
- This primary task of the Church is not to reduce God to an object like other objective, natural sciences but to know the True Subject, God, in a true and faithful manner that orients our thinking and living to reality as all good science should do.

CONCLUSION FOR THE CHURCH: The Church must speak faithfully by listening to God and staying true to what God has said.

INSIGHT FOR PASTORS: The primary calling of pastors is to bring the church's attention to the living God, not to themselves. As you lead, think about how you can let God speak to bring His concerns through you. This reorientation lets God be known freshly each time you are together.

INSIGHT FOR THEOLOGIANS: Science that comes preformatted with categories and definitions will always warp our view of reality. We need to approach theological study with open eyes and ears to apprehend and reflect on reality. We must let encounter shape belief. This is especially true with God, who will not be gift wrapped to fit our boxes of preconception about God.

CLARIFYING QUESTIONS: Does your theology seek to be more faithful to God or more understandable to humans and their interests?

A NOTE ON THE PREFACE TO CD 1.1

Barth begins this volume with a brief account of why he is writing this volume. He started the project before but made a misstep, and he is committed to correct that, to make everything simpler and clearer.

Barth recognized "gourmet theologians" as readers and formatted some parts in small print for their refined palates. The primary text is intended for nontheologians to take with a normal stride.

His approach will be one of listening to voices of the past: God, the Bible, and theologians of note. Then there will be a long journey of commenting, listening again, and further commenting. That becomes our listening journey so that we too can comment and serve the Word spoken.

Barth makes some key modifications from his earlier form:

- Focusing on the Church rather than an individual Christian
- Excluding philosophical foundations and listening exclusively to Jesus
- Rejecting *analogia entis* (thinking from human experience of being) and adopting *analogia fidea* (faithful listening to Jesus)
- Beginning with the early Church and not the Reformation

We would do well to note Barth's comments:

The community in and for which I have written it is that of the Church and not a community of theological endeavour.[4]

And

I have found by experience that in the last resort the man in the street who is so highly respected by many ecclesiastics and theologians will really take notice of us when we do not worry about what he expects of us but do what we are charged to do.[5]

---

4. *CD* 1.1, p. xv.
5. *CD* 1.1, p. xvi.

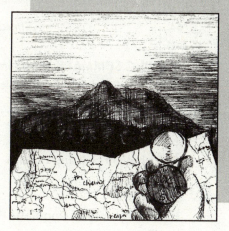

CHAPTER 9

GETTING ORIENTED FOR THE MOUNTAIN LOOP

§ 2. The Task of Prolegomena to Dogmatics

FOCUS STATEMENT: Now you need to get out the map and compass and see which way you are facing. The point of this chapter is to summarize § 2 in the *CD*, "The Task of Prolegomena to Dogmatics," to become oriented to the task.

INTRODUCTION: This second paragraph clarifies why we must talk about truly coming to know God. We must beware the dangers of thinking it is necessary to build our knowing of God on proofs and defenses from experience and traditions that purport to speak for Jesus.

Prolegomena here is not creating a framework in advance for what to believe. It is not laying down foundational theories or rules to conform to human reason. Think of it more like getting pointed in the right direction—to study God and not look in a mirror. Think of letting the other speak instead of giving the other a set of questions to see how they measure up to our expectations. Prolegomena is preparation for discovery without the baggage of only looking for what interests us or makes sense to our limited way of thinking.

CONTEXT: *CD* 1.1
Pages in Paragraph: 20 pages (pp. 25–44)

Subsections
1. The Necessity of Dogmatic Prolegomena
2. The Possibility of Dogmatic Prolegomena

TEXT: § 2. The Task of Prolegomena to Dogmatics

**OPENING SUMMARY: Prolegomena to dogmatics is our name for the intro-
ductory part of dogmatics in which our concern is to understand its particular
way of knowledge.**[1]

It is worth noting that the Thompson translation ends that synthesis:
". . . our business to explain its particular path to knowledge."[2] This may add
some vision of charting a course.

SUMMARY:

1. The Necessity of Dogmatic Prolegomena (pp. 25–36)

Barth now turns to what we need in order to begin engaging in God-
talk and explains how God-talk is even possible.

We do not need to prove or defend the possibility of talking about God.
We do not need to show that we are being relevant to the needs of contemporary culture. There are many ways to get distracted from our task, all of
which we should avoid.

We must be especially wary of a "point of contact" in humans. This was
Barth's point of disagreement with his contemporary Emil Brunner. If we
look at morality or conscience as a human point of contact with God, we end
up merely elevating human capacities and missing God. Human experience
is a seductive starting point in coming to know God, but in doing so, we
make experience rather than God's self-revelation the lens for conceptualiz-
ing God.

Barth wanted his readers to learn to distinguish between true and false
claims about God. We constantly need to be realigned with a right knowing
of God made available in Jesus by the work of the Spirit.

> Any path to knowing God other than God's self-revealing has a bait-and-switch agenda; it promises God but delivers human imitations.

In an attempt to be practical and specific, Barth discussed two modern movements
that had error in need of correction: Roman Catholicism and liberal Protestantism.

Some church people focus too much on humans when talking about
God. In fact, many liberal Protestants try to talk about God by looking at
humans and human history. They want to appeal to human interests to validate the need for theology.

---

1. *CD* 1.1, § 2, p. 25.
2. Karl Barth, *Church Dogmatics: The Doctrine of the Word of God, Part 1*, trans. G. T.
Thompson, vol. 1 (New York: Scribner's, 1936), 1. Thompson only translated the first volume of the
CD. T. F. Torrance and G. W Bromiley started over and oversaw the whole of the project, including
reworking *CD* 1.1.

Some church leaders look like they are talking about God but end up with a confused mixture. For example, Roman Catholics are better at including discussion about God, but their errors are more complex. They build on the Bible, Church traditions, and beliefs of the Church. On this foundation, they subtly merge the action of God and human actions. Jesus is restricted to operate within the Church's forms of belief and not with a free existence.

2. The Possibility of Dogmatic Prolegomena (pp. 36–44)

The reason we can speak of God is because Jesus, as God, speaks to us and we hear.

As the Word of God, the Bible serves in making the living Word, Jesus, available to embrace and address the Church. Jesus provides the way we know God, whom we come to encounter and subsequently talk about.

The Church of Jesus Christ must both learn to listen to Him and be prepared to talk about Him.

COMMENTARY:

This paragraph begins the process of discernment between a proper theology, which begins by listening to God, and the many paths of error, which begin with human capability (individual or Church) and make human beliefs, ideals, or experiences the means to know God.

- Any path to knowing God other than God's self-revealing has a bait-and-switch agenda; it promises God but delivers human imitations.
- We need preparation for this journey before we start. We must follow our guide, not what seems beautiful, easier, or more efficient, nor follow any other intuition that we think will lead to our destination.
- Those who say, "This works for me in my experience" (liberal Protestant), or "We have always believed this and try to keep things under control for Jesus" (Roman Catholic), will miss the free and loving encounter with Jesus as living Lord. That encounter is the task of *Church Dogmatics*.

CONCLUSION FOR THE CHURCH: The Church must clarify how it knows where it is going and how to avoid getting lost.

INSIGHT FOR PASTORS: In a world that blurs our ideas about God, we must clarify our task to understand what it means to know God. We can start in the wrong place and merely give a thousand pictures of beautiful things that remind us of God. To start in the right place for hearing God, the Church must open the windows and let in the wind to bring fresh air. We must allow the Bible to speak anew as Jesus and the Spirit bring a fresh message through ancient words that now speak to our place and time. Start with the voice of God, and then elaborate with human words that make those words present and active. And think beyond words. Words are great, but what could a picture, a song, a story, or a poem do to bring fresh insight to what Jesus is saying to you and those you care for? Search the internet for images, poems, and songs on key words in your study, and see what opens up to clarify what God is saying this week. But start with the right focus, or you will skip the prolegomena and head down the wrong trail.

INSIGHT FOR THEOLOGIANS: The scaffolding that constructs an edifice of theology may actually become a fortress that keeps out God. The task of seeing God in the wild is a grand and terrifying life-changing experience. There is a huge difference between objectifying and studying a person as the object of your study. To objectify a woman or man is to see that person as meeting your needs, not as a person to be known. To have that person as the object of your study could be to marry that person and spend the rest of your life learning and exploring who they are through the seasons of life. The first is impersonal; the second is a form of personal knowing.

CLARIFYING QUESTIONS: Does your theology stay true to the task of preaching Jesus so that He is the priority in all your speaking, acting, and leading, *or* do you prefer sermons that speak to human needs, interests, and inspiration?

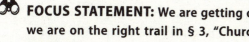**CHAPTER 10**

CHECKING TO MAKE SURE WE ARE ON THE CORRECT TRAIL SYSTEM

§ 3. Church Proclamation as the Material of Dogmatics

FOCUS STATEMENT: We are getting our sense of direction to make sure we are on the right trail in § 3, "Church Proclamation as the Material of Dogmatics."

INTRODUCTION: In the third paragraph, Barth begins with what is spoken in the Church. We must communicate the origin and clarity of what God is saying so that it is not hijacked by human interests or religious obstacles that distract us from hearing the living Word.

CONTEXT: *CD* 1.1
Pages in Paragraph: 41 pages (pp. 47–87)

Subsections
1. Talk about God and Church Proclamation
2. Dogmatics and Church Proclamation

TEXT: § 3. Church Proclamation as the Material of Dogmatics

OPENING SUMMARY: In the Church, talk about God seeks to be proclamation to the extent that in the form of preaching and sacrament it is directed to man with the claim and expectation that in accordance with its commission it has to speak to him the Word of God to be heard in faith. Inasmuch as it is a human word in spite of this claim and expectation, it is the material of

dogmatics, i.e., of the investigation of its responsibility as measured by the Word of God which it seeks to proclaim.[1]

✠ SUMMARY:

1. Talk About God and Church Proclamation (pp. 47–71)

So, what should the Church talk about when it does dogmatics? It should speak of God!

What is said of God must truly be of God, meaning from God's self-proclamation, so that its talk is faithful to what God has already said.

What God has said is *a posteriori* for us. *A posteriori* refers to reasoning that proceeds from our reflection on God's speaking (versus having assumptions about God before listening, which is called *a priori*).

Dogmatics is based on an actual utterance by God. The Bible is the primary witness to this speaking of God. The Bible echoes God's speaking to address us with what God is saying now.

The Church is to act as those who receive and share what God has said. Those who do dogmatic work are called to clarify the accuracy of what is said to make sure it reflects God's intent.

We cannot talk about God from our own wisdom for the simple reason that we are fallen creatures. Only one human truly can speak for God. That is Jesus.

The message of the Church is to be spoken as clearly as possible, as if from God's mouth. Having come to know the One who articulates personally, the Church continues to serve as God's witness, addressing particular humans. The Church, as it is alive to the Word, is a site of active encounter.

> The message of the Church is to be spoken as clearly as possible, as if from God's mouth. Having come to know the One who articulates personally, the Church continues to address particular humans, serving as God's witnesses. The Church, as it is alive to the Word, is a site of active encounter.

Liberal Protestants misunderstand the task of proclamation and replace it with action instead of preaching God's Living Word. Barth gives Paul Tillich as a prime example of starting in the wrong place, which is with human sensibilities. Humans end up speaking to themselves and about themselves. Unfortunately, it is quite compelling for readers to start with their own needs. But in the end, they just answer their own questions and dismiss or miss the Word addressing them.

---

1. *CD* 1.1, § 3, p. 47.

Roman Catholics focus on the sacraments. Consequently, the sermon intended to facilitate the address of God to humanity gets lost or minimized. In any tradition, the ministry of the divine Word, planned to embrace humans, can be obstructed.

Tragically, church activities can obstruct the path leading to Jesus. Activity replaces companionship. We can end up experiencing a profound silence as we miss Jesus.

Barth explains the manner of God's address to us as follows: "Proclamation is human speech in and by which God Himself speaks like a king through the mouth of his herald, and which is meant to be heard and accepted as speech in and by which God Himself speaks, and therefore heard and accepted in faith as divine decision concerning life and death, as divine judgment and pardon, eternal Law and eternal Gospel both together."[2]

Dogmatics is concerned with the pursuit of the truth of the words we *claim* to be God's. Having clarified, proclamation is sharing the truth without forgetting the dogmatic clarifying. Proclamation provides plenty of room for creativity but not at the expense of clarity or faithfulness to God's self-giving.

2. Dogmatics and Church Proclamation (pp. 71–87)

We preach as servants, never as those lording authority over others or usurping God's authority.

We must see God as stepping forth boldly in the Church speaking; the Church functions as servants in this event.

Preaching and the sacraments must be held together as manifestations of the life of God present in the Church.

In dogmatics, we look carefully at the pitfalls of error so that we may boldly walk the royal path that is full of life with God. Then we can run, take pictures, or share our journeys as we proceed with free and open ears.

Dogmatics is the Church's task to do the laundry and ironing so that all is fresh and original to its purpose when proclaimed in the Church.

COMMENTARY:

Note that after the preparation in the prolegomena, paragraph 3 is the beginning of chapter 1, "The Word of God as the Criterion of Dogmatics."

---

2. *CD* 1.1, § 3, p. 52.

- Dogmatics has a corrective and a constructive role. It calls out error that misrepresents God's speech and opens the way to encounter God afresh. These must be held together in tension.
- The role of dogmatics can sound very concrete and judgmental. On the contrary, it is more like making sure we are not getting counterfeit money or being scammed by a con artist.
- Dogmatics is better than most forms of systematic theology. Dogmatics is a clarifying conversation that is in inquiry mode. Systematic theology generally presupposes some human system of thought (like Thomas Aquinas did) and then fits theological formulations and claims within it. Barth has a starting point of Jesus and then follows his theology from the starting point. He refuses to try to fit Jesus into our preconceptions.

Proclamation is not just about telling theories and principles. It is clarifying the voice of God in God's Church.

When we really want to get to know a person as a person and not as an object, we let that person tell us who they are. If we merely fit them into our categories of gender, age, education, and so on, we are not getting to know them; we are fitting them into our boxes.

Engaging persons personally requires speaking and listening, which inform the logic of proclamation and obedience (as attentive and responsive listening).

CONCLUSION FOR THE CHURCH: The Church must clarify how it knows where it is going. It must be all ears before it is a mouthpiece for God.

INSIGHT FOR PASTORS: Leaders love to talk, but the question here is whether we can help our people learn to hear God's voice. We need to become competent to help everyday people know the living God. This requires abandoning the desire to be congratulated for our fine presentations. After a sermon, people should forget our names and voices as they are engulfed by the voice of God and go to share in God's grace. Try asking people as they leave the church what they heard God say to them today.

INSIGHT FOR THEOLOGIANS: Discernment, in what constitutes good theology, must begin by distinguishing what we might say about God and what God has said and is saying today. This is a preliminary task of the theologian. As we begin to write, we are making truth claims that need to be valid to the being and actions of God as lived out by Jesus. Thus, to start a theology of ministry, hospitality, evangelism, politics, or any other study, we need to begin with Jesus as revealed, not as we can fit Him into an existing field of thought. This may be confrontational or corrective. We may see things we never saw before. If we were to write a theology of persons, would we start by looking at humans or at Jesus? One gives us a study of humans, and the other a theological investigation with implications for humanity.

? **CLARIFYING QUESTIONS:** Does your theology consistently begin by listening to the voice of the living Jesus, *or* do you begin by asking yourself what people need to hear (and become a persuader, apologist, or corrector of false beliefs in those with whom you interact)? Is your preparation to speak about God focused on Jesus or on your sense of the needs of others?

🗺 **CHAPTER 11**

FIRST STEPS IN FINDING OUR WAY WITH THE APPROPRIATE TOOLS

§ 4. The Word of God in Its Threefold Form

👓 **FOCUS STATEMENT:** We are getting focused with a map, compass, and binoculars, ready to follow the guide in § 4, "The Word of God in Its Threefold Form."

🖋 **INTRODUCTION:** This section focuses on the harmonious work of the Word of God as revelation (Jesus), Scripture (Bible), and proclamation (preaching) as all necessary for scientific theology.

📊 **CONTEXT:** *CD* 1.1
Pages in Paragraph: 37 pages (pp. 88–124)

Subsections
1. The Word of God Preached
2. The Word of God Written
3. The Word of God Revealed
4. The Unity of the Word of God

📖 **TEXT:** § 4. The Word of God in Its Threefold Form

OPENING SUMMARY: The presupposition that makes proclamation proclamation, and therewith makes the Church the Church, is the Word of God. This attests itself in Holy Scripture in the word of the prophets and apostles, to whom it was originally and once and for all spoken by God's revelation.

✠ SUMMARY:

1. The Word of God Preached (pp. 88–99)

There is an event in the life of the Church where the Word of God is preached—this is the actual preaching that brings to reality the life of God in the Church as a revelation.

Revelation means an unveiling of what is veiled.

Revelation is an act.

The act of God includes the incarnation of Jesus, the writing of the Bible, and events of preaching.

The Church is commissioned to preach.

The Church's main theme is the Word of God.

The Word of God is the criteria for the judgment of the truth by which all claims are measured.

The Word is preached so that human words resonate and make audible God's Word.

The Word of God preached is a remembering of what has gone before in the revelation of God.

Revelation involves a recollection of the self-giving of God in Jesus as the living Word of God.

2. The Word of God Written (pp. 99–111)

Jesus has called the Old and New Testaments into existence and they point to Him.

Revelation is God's Word, and the Scriptures are a record of this as human words that give priority to God.

> Barth holds the highest regard for God, the Bible, and the Church as a community together making the Word come alive.

When we speak of the Word of God, we speak of God's revelation in personal action, in the Bible, and with the proclamation of God's action as mediated through the Scripture. These three are mutually interdependent. We cannot have one without the others.

When we say "God said," we refer to God speaking in the Son, through the Bible, and as declared in the preached word of the Church; humans listen to Jesus through the Bible in congruence of the three together.

3. The Word of God Revealed (pp. 111–21)

When we say the Bible "becomes God's Word," we are not defaulting to human reception in order to affirm this status. We are affirming that it is

God's speech, not ours. God's speaking must be heard ever freshly—as God's Word to which we must submit ourselves.

The Word of God refers inseparably to the living Jesus, who communicates the being of God to us: the Word comes in human form, in the written witness to Jesus, and in the preaching of the Church that listens to Jesus through the proclamation of the Bible.

We must not concretize interpretations but instead learn to listen for God's voice as we come to know Him.

4. The Unity of the Word of God (pp. 121–24)

The Word of God is Jesus, the Bible, and preaching in revelatory consistency and consonance.

There are not three separated Words of God, but one Word spoken thrice: incarnate, written, attesting.

The three forms of the Word of God are like the triunity of God—no part can be removed, each points to and informs of the others. It is a symphonic Word.

COMMENTARY:

The three forms of the Word move our thinking away from any abstract revelation of God, bibliolatry, or legalism in words detached from the living person.

- We do not believe propositions; we believe in a person. Truth-claims can point us to Jesus but ought never to replace Him.
- Barth holds the highest regard for God, the Bible, and the Church as a community together making the Word come alive.
- Barth never departs from this threefold Word in the work of scientific theology.
- The Church is a laboratory where the past is made present, the Bible illuminates the body of Christ by letting the Voice of God be heard, and the primary task is to know the God who meets us in person through His Word.

CONCLUSION FOR THE CHURCH: The Church must identify the mode, moment, and movement of encountering God in person. The life of the Church is in coming to hear and know Jesus, to live in response, having heard.

INSIGHT FOR PASTORS: Words can be a fountain of froth that spouts every week, or they can sprout in the lives of persons. We must orient our words so that they are pollinated by the Bible. Growth comes when we have a deep connection with the living Word, Jesus, who brings life to His Church. This is realized when we hold our words, the Bible's words, and this living Word in consonant harmony. Think about three different modes of communication that you could utilize and bring into harmony to let the message of Jesus address those you are leading and teaching.

Scientific Theology: The human discovery of the revealed God understood in reflection and clarification that calls forth responsive living in light of God's self-giving.

INSIGHT FOR THEOLOGIANS: If we choose *between* study of Jesus (theology), the Scriptures (biblical studies), and preaching (practical theology), we will lose the full dynamic of God's address to humanity. We will develop either as gnostics (elevated ideas), legalists (tied to text), or performers (sounding good, but saying little). We need the harmony of all three to hear and respond to the loving freedom of God.

CLARIFYING QUESTIONS: Does your theology include a mutually informed understanding of "the Word of God" that holds together Jesus as the living Word, the Bible as the written Word, and the sermon as an exercise in knowing Jesus through the Bible, *or* do you think of the Bible as the authoritative Word of the Church to be maintained by its leaders?

CHAPTER 12

PREPARING FOR THE TRAIL BY SURVEYING THE TRAIL

§ 5. *The Nature of the Word of God*

FOCUS STATEMENT: In this section, we consider the nature of the trail ahead as we begin exploring § 5, "The Nature of the Word of God." The point of this chapter is to summarize paragraph 5 in the *CD* on the Word of God as active speaking rather than set words about God.

INTRODUCTION: This section clarifies the dynamic of understanding the place of God in speaking through His Word, and the nature of this Word taking on human form to address us with mystery as well as connection.

CONTEXT: *CD* 1.1
Pages in Paragraph: 61 pages (pp. 125–86)

Subsections
1. The Question of the Nature of the Word of God
2. The Word of God as the Speech of God
3. The Speech of God as the Act of God
4. The Speech of God as the Mystery of God

TEXT: § 5. The Nature of the Word of God

OPENING SUMMARY: The Word of God in its three forms is God's speech to man. For this reason, it occurs, applies, and works in God's act on man. But as such it occurs in God's way, which differs from all other occurrence, i.e., in the mystery of God.[1]

---

1. *CD* 1.1, § 5, p. 125.

✠ SUMMARY:

1. The Question of the Nature of the Word of God (pp. 125–33)

Barth concedes that he may have made a misstep in his first attempt at an introductory volume, which was called *Christian Dogmatics*. His error would have been to appeal to phenomenological and existential philosophy (read: "human experience") to the point that it became anthropology, focusing on humans rather than on the reality of God. "Christian" can be taken so as to focus on the individual human and miss the point.

To begin with humanity is to elevate a natural theology that misses God in discussing the Word of God.

The idea "but I do not see God" must be met with "but God has made Himself known in Jesus." Therein lies the actuality of God.

Discerning that God speaks not as a metaphor but in actuality is to rightly discern the Word of God as addressed to humanity.

2. The Word of God as the Speech of God (pp. 133–43)

The speech of God occurs in an act that is physical and personal.

"God's Word means that God speaks. This implies secondly its personal quality."[2]

3. The Speech of God as the Act of God (pp. 143–62)

In order to properly speak of God, our contemporary speech needs to be drawing from and looking to God's speech-acts in history.

4. The Speech of God as the Mystery of God (pp. 162–86)

The Word of God is mystery. This does not mean it is unknowable.

We cannot prove the mystery of God's Word. We can learn to listen.

The Bible is veiled in human language so that it is available for humanity.

The Bible is wholly God's and wholly human.

God is the source of the speech made known in the Word, as well as the Lord of its hearing. He gets to confirm what He meant. To twist the words to make sense to us is not to listen. It is a rebellion.

God does not show up (physically) in person to address us today, but God is personally present in His speech by the Spirit.

---

2. *CD* 1.1, § 5, p. 136.

COMMENTARY:

- This section reveals the need to see the Word of God as a true expression of God for humanity.
- The Word of God is not to be collapsed into human pursuit of God; the Word is God coming to humans, resounding today as His own speech.
- Mystery is not a hidden form of communication with God; it is the form of God's coming that maintains presence, as well as distinction from us, maintaining both withness and difference at the same time.

CONCLUSION FOR THE CHURCH: The Church must learn to apprehend the address of God as actually manifested by God. We acknowledge that God speaks, not that we have it all figured out. That is the journey of faith seeking understanding.

INSIGHT FOR PASTORS: God has spoken, but do we let God speak today? In our pastoral work, we must become translucent so that Jesus shines through. Then the light of His Word might bring His meaning and focus our attention on what is needed to be said today by Jesus. What would it look like to read the passages of the Bible as though they are spoken by Jesus or His Father or the Spirit? Thus, instead of "God so loved the world" read "My Father so loved you that He sent Me." The living Word and the written Word can speak in a fresh connection when held together.

INSIGHT FOR THEOLOGIANS: We who dwell in the walled places of learning or command a hearing on the World Wide Web must be servants, not masters, of the subject of our study. The academy is founded on listening and learning. When we teach the Word well and lead our students to truth, it must be Truth Himself, who still speaks. Only then can the academy discern what might be added in bringing wisdom for life—especially life with God.

CLARIFYING QUESTIONS: Does your theology focus on "truths" that need to be taught about God, Christian living, and a Christian worldview, *or* does hearing truth require an attentive listening to what Jesus has been and is saying? Do you have an attentiveness to the object of your study, a person speaking today through the Bible as a direct address intended to connect with His people?

CHAPTER 13

STEPPING ONTO
THE TRAIL

§ 6. The Knowability
of the Word of God

FOCUS STATEMENT: We must learn to discern the knowability of the trail ahead. Only then can we astutely see what is there and faithfully respond to it. This will be our task as we become clear about § 6, "The Knowability of the Word of God." The point of this chapter is to hear the Word of God as actual reality and not as an abstract experience.

INTRODUCTION: This section affirms the place of human experience becoming aware of and acknowledging the address of God as real experience. True knowing makes contact with reality; in this case it is revealed to us. God establishes this God-created faith made possible by the actuality of God and not beginning with the human capacity to observe and discover.

CONTEXT: *CD* 1.1
Pages in Paragraph: 61 pages (pp. 187–247)

Subsections
1. The Question of the Knowability of the Word of God
2. The Word of God and Man
3. The Word of God and Experience
4. The Word of God and Faith

TEXT: § 6. The Knowability of the Word of God

OPENING SUMMARY: The reality of the Word of God in all its three forms is grounded only in itself. So, too, the knowledge of it by men can consist only in its acknowledgment, and this acknowledgment can become real only through itself and can become intelligible only in terms of itself.[1]

SUMMARY:

1. The Question of the Knowability of the Word of God (pp. 187–90)

God has spoken, acting in this world so that we might humbly enter the mystery that encounters us.

2. The Word of God and Man (pp. 190–98)

Within the Church, contact with reality is made as God's gift. Not all have this contact, but in the Church we encounter the living Word, who acts so we may witness to His reality.

God has acted to restore relation to humanity, all those who do not know Him without His initiative.

3. The Word of God and Experience (pp. 198–228)

By the Spirit, certain persons know God and thus speak. Not all have this immediate experience (no natural theology).

Knowing God can only happen on the basis of reality, not speculation.

We know God because God has actually spoken, not because of the human capability to know.

The nature of knowing needs to be appropriate to the nature of what or who is known.

Barth is not a theologian who builds on human experience to talk about God.

We cannot let human experience dominate our knowledge of God; that will be the outcome if we start with human experience.

> In learning to know God, we must listen to the Word of God.

Yes, we can know God, but only because God wants to be known and makes His way known to us.

We cannot make claims about God "from the outside looking into God's life." We can only enter into God's life in that manner and mode because of God's address to us. Having heard God, we can make claims from that provision.

The meaning of God's words must be determined by God. They are not authorized or approved by preconceived or natural human meanings that have not first listened to God.

---

1. *CD* 1.1, § 6, p. 187.

We come to acknowledge God's words as God's act and thus are addressed by them. We confirm them by being obedient to them.

Barth wants to avoid experientialist theology that builds from human concepts, experience, or a felt "point of contact"—anything based on a human "yes, that makes sense to me" that has not listened to God speaking.

4. The Word of God and Faith (pp. 228–47)

Faith is an acknowledgment of what God has said and is saying, not an attribute or ability worked up by human beings. It is a recognition that God has spoken directly. The personal God creates faith in us as a response to the Word spoken to us.

Faith is a response to personal reality. This reality encounters us to shape us. Jesus addresses us and attunes us to this personal God who is faithful to us.

God is never grasped naturally by humans. Rather, because God has created and grasped us, we can understand ourselves as those made and held.

Faith first occurs when we experience being embraced as the gift of God.

A life of personally responding to the address and love of God is the human experience of faith.

COMMENTARY:

- Barth was concerned that when we speak of the Word of God, we must acknowledge God as providing the meaning and personal content of those words. Dictionaries cannot give us the meaning of God's use of human language.
- It is easy to refer to human experience that is beautiful, feels good, or makes sense to us when we try to fill in our understanding of knowing God. This is an error. These ever-ready capacities for experience can easily become idols, unconsciously creating a false image of God.
- Faith is not a human creation or capacity. It is always an acknowledgment of reality that is attentive to listen to that reality we encounter.
- In learning to know God, we must listen to the Word of God.
- As in all science, we discover reality and then learn to live faithfully in light of that reality. If our study of reality is focused only on how to meet our needs and desires, then we end up creating illusions, facades to satisfy our egos and appetites.

CONCLUSION FOR THE CHURCH: The Church must learn to acknowledge the address of God as the call to faith which engages us to live in the light of God's actuality.

INSIGHT FOR PASTORS: As servant leaders, we have to ask, "Do I know the One who is the Word before I speak for Him?" Do we speak with confidence, believing that we have it right? We are privileged to be those who stand at the door and invite people to enter the dwelling of God. The welcoming place we stand is not so much a location as an invitation to awaken to the mystery that surrounds us. God's speaking arouses faith because humans hear this new reality and are compelled not to think otherwise. Take a word like *love* and consider what it means in regular usage. Then contemplate what *love* (or any other word) means uniquely in the mouth of Jesus. How does that change and give meaning to the word?

INSIGHT FOR THEOLOGIANS: Good science is *a posteriori*, engaging from what is already established as given. Faith comes as we come to know and attune our thinking and acting to what is there—preeminently the living God. The disciplines of theology call us to keep clarifying in light of what God has said, not what fits neatly within human logic.

? CLARIFYING QUESTIONS: Does your theology build on traditions and interpretations of famous preachers and theologians, *or* does it habitually begin at the beginning by listening to Jesus afresh?

 **CHAPTER 14**

CHECKING TO MAKE SURE WE ARE ON THE RIGHT TRAIL

§ 7. *The Word of God, Dogma and Dogmatics*

FOCUS STATEMENT: On exploratory treks, we must make sure we are on the correct trail and facing in the right direction. Then we must be prepared to indwell the path, to conform to its way of leading us forward. Rightly oriented, we will be able to participate in the beauty that surrounds us and not be distracted into danger. Our theological concern as we wander into § 7, "The Word of God, Dogma and Dogmatics," is to focus on following the Word of God in an appropriate discovery mode, to actually arrive at knowing God in this investigation.

INTRODUCTION: This section completes the first of the seventeen chapters of the *CD*; that is to say, we have been traversing "The Word of God as the Criterion of Dogmatics" to find our way to know God. This way engages a threefold Word. By now, we should have a sense that the person of Jesus, the Bible, and the teaching of the Church form a symbiotic relationship so that we may actually know God as God wants to be known. From here on, Barth will talk about the Word of God in unity but attend to the particularity of the living Word, the written Word, and the Word preached. This threefold Word of God is the object of the science of theology.

CONTEXT: *CD* 1.1
Pages in Paragraph: 45 pages (pp. 248–92)

Subsections
1. The Problem of Dogmatics

2. Dogmatics as a Science
3. The Problem of Dogmatic Prolegomena

📖 **TEXT: § 7. The Word of God, Dogma and Dogmatics**

OPENING SUMMARY: Dogmatics is the critical question about dogma, i.e., about the Word of God in Church proclamation, or, concretely, about the agreement of the Church proclamation done and to be done by man with the revelation attested in Holy Scripture. Prolegomena to dogmatics as an understanding of its epistemological path must therefore consist in an exposition of the three forms of the Word of God as revealed, written, and preached.[1]

✝ **SUMMARY:**

1. The Problem of Dogmatics (pp. 248–75)

God has spoken to humanity. This is incomprehensible, yet God's self-expression is our starting point.

One huge question regarding hearing a witness faithful to God concerns how we are able to test the dogmatics of the Church using the criterion of the Word of God.

Some approaches to knowing God must be cut off—for example, the attempt to be relevant to modern concerns. That is the method of tyrants looking for power, not servants who submit to the king.

The Bible meets us on its own terms. No other authority can judge its validity, as though it must answer to philosophy, politics, or ethical norms.

The Church is not a surrogate for God's Word, as though its teaching offices have a final authority over the Word. The Bible is not a tool for the Church to use for its own purposes.

Rather than *dogmas*—truths of revelation—the task pursued is *dogma*—the agreement of proclamation with the truth of revelation. It is not about establishing truth statements; it is about ensuring that human words are consistent with and convey the address of God to humanity.

Dogma guides dogmatics as a present listening to the voice of God so that our statements about God may be true.

Dogma is a dynamic hearing, creating a personal relation as God speaks and we hear and respond in obedience.

---

1. *CD* 1.1, § 7, p. 248.

2. Dogmatics as a Science (pp. 275–87)

Dogmatics is a science as it investigates and instructs, either in the academy or in the Church.

Dogmatics must fulfill its task to facilitate proclamation. Dogmatics must prepare for proclamation.

Dogmatics must not merely explain what is said; it must clarify and correct. Repeating what has been said is not enough. Dogmatics must unsettle past errors and create lively engagement.

The sole responsibility of dogmatics is to represent clearly the revelation of God. Thus, it is bound to hear the Word of God, the Bible.

Holy Scripture cannot be measured against any philosophy, psychology, history, or political theory. We cannot judge Scripture by cultural norms or wisdom; we judge cultures by the Word of God.

3. The Problem of Dogmatic Prolegomena (pp. 287–92)

Theology is corrupted when it is asked to abandon the task of revealing God and is used to meet the needs of some other human quest for knowledge.

We must study theology in a proper order, beginning with the living Word of God, Jesus. This entry point will open for us the triune life as the objective, actual basis of the revelation of God. Through Jesus, the Spirit will open us to comprehend subjectively, enabling us to hear what is revealed.

Second, we must study the written Word to apprehend its task of pointing to the living Word.

Finally, proclamation must point to Scripture as it points to Jesus and the revealing of God's address to humanity.

Dogmatics clarifies God's Word to humanity.

God reveals Godself.

The Bible reveals God revealing Godself.

Proclamation makes present and active the Word of God as speaking to reveal Godself.

> Dogmatics must not merely explain what is said; it must also clarify and correct. Repeating what has been said is not enough. Dogmatics must unsettle past errors and create lively engagement.

 COMMENTARY:

- Dogmatics is a science in that it does not foist human knowledge onto God. Instead, it lives in the clarifying conversation in which God is heard and human chaff is sloughed off.
- When we do theology, we must begin at the beginning, which is with the living God. Only then do we have a proper context when reading the Bible to judge in a manner consistent with God's self-revealing.

- Dogmatics lives in service of God and only then in service of the Church.
- When we stand and speak in the Church, we speak with no other authority and seek to please no other audience than the God who has spoken.
- When properly spoken, God's Word opens the love within Godself and allows humans to know that they are beloved. We who are addressed are intended to hear His voice, which aims to engage us.

CONCLUSION FOR THE CHURCH: The Church must enter the dogmatic task by encountering the living Word of God, pointed to and clarified by the written Word, and be shaped in its preaching to provide an unpolluted hearing for God's people, so that what is spoken is intrinsically true to God's self-giving. In this way, the personal God is met on God's own terms through the service of the Church.

INSIGHT FOR PASTORS: The task of the Church is to make known the speaking God in clear and compelling communications. Those pronouncements must echo from within God's heart and bring us to know God's very self. This requires reflecting on false statements made in the past and present that claim to speak for God but are not aligned with God's self-revelation. It is best not just to tell people that others are wrong in their opinions. Let them see and hear Jesus so clearly that it casts doubt on twisted ways of using God's Word. Let the truth be healing and clarifying, not defensive and judgmental.

INSIGHT FOR THEOLOGIANS: Theology is a science, which properly means that we must have our thinking and reflections grounded in the reality we come upon. The academic task in dogmatics is to constantly clarify human speaking of God so that it takes on the character of God's speaking. Human articulation must begin with a groundedness that clearly listens to God and consequently penetrates the hearer's heart with God's intended impact.

CLARIFYING QUESTIONS: Does your theology assume that your church and tradition pretty much have everything right, *or* do you come as a disciple, believing that Jesus continues to develop His people to follow His lead?

CHURCH DOGMATICS, CHAPTER 2

"The Revelation of God"

CHAPTER 15

BEHOLDING THE MOUNTAIN TO CAPTURE OUR ATTENTION

§ 8. *God in His Revelation*

FOCUS STATEMENT: Once we are on the trail, we want to make sure we are facing the right direction, heading toward the destination we hope to discover. This is especially true in the case of discerning "God in His Revelation." The big picture should always be kept in mind as it brings forth wonder and delight that make us feel alive.

The point of this chapter is to summarize and clarify the focusing task within the *CD* on the revealed God. This process is hinted at in the grandeur of the mountain, not as a natural theology, but in simply acknowledging the magnificence of what is there. In the *CD*, theology begins by acknowledging the God who is known as Father, Son, and Holy Spirit, and whose revelation opens the way for our discovery with wonder.

INTRODUCTION: This section begins chapter 2 of seventeen chapters of the *CD*, and is called "The Revelation of God" because it begins our investigation with God holding a unique place in all theological discussion. Only God's self-expression can properly inform our words and reflections. Especially, we will see that we can only use the word "God" in its Christian sense by talking about the God who is revealed in history as Father, Son, and Spirit.

There are three parts in chapter 2. We are in part 1: "The Triune God." Stop and see how this frames the conversation to follow as the basis of a helpful and faithful theology.

1. **The Triune God (in *CD* 1.1),**
2. The Incarnation of the Word (in *CD* 1.2), and
3. The Outpouring of the Holy Spirit (in *CD* 1.2).

This is the only chapter in the *CD* that breaks a chapter into parts. Chapter 1 is long and will finish *CD* 1.1 and take us halfway through *CD* 1.2. This discussion on the triune God is essential to grasp in order to see what follows as the proper science of theology.

CONTEXT: *CD* 1.1
Pages in Paragraph: 53 pages (pp. 295–347)

Subsections
1. The Place of the Doctrine of the Trinity in Dogmatics
2. The Root of the Doctrine of the Trinity
3. Vestigium Trinitatis

TEXT: § 8. God in His Revelation

OPENING SUMMARY: God's Word is God Himself in His revelation. For God reveals Himself as the Lord and according to Scripture this signifies for the concept of revelation that God Himself in unimpaired unity yet also in unimpaired distinction is Revealer, Revelation, and Revealedness.[1]

SUMMARY:

1. The Place of the Doctrine of the Trinity in Dogmatics (pp. 295–304)

Question 1: How do we understand revelation with respect to its object (that which we are studying)?

What does God's revealing do in opening our ears to hear the speaking God?

Question 2: How does it come about, how is it actual, that God reveals Himself?

In what way do we say that we hear God and know it is God?

Question 3: What is the result of beginning with revelation? What does this event do in the man to whom it happens?

How will hearing God transform us when we encounter God speaking?

Answer: *God* reveals Himself. He reveals Himself *through Himself.* He reveals *Himself.*[2]

---

1. *CD* 1.1, § 8, p. 295.
2. *CD* 1.1, § 8, p. 296.

1. How do we understand revelation? As *God* revealing Himself.
2. How does God reveal Himself? He reveals Himself *through Himself.*
3. What is the result? He reveals *Himself.*

We must learn to approach God with reference to the doctrine of revelation—that is, God's choosing to be known. Our doctrine of the triune God is possible specifically because God has made Himself available to us.

If we are going to talk about a Christian understanding of God, we must begin with the Trinity as the encountered reality. There is no Jesus without His Father and the Spirit He promises.

2. The Root of the Doctrine of the Trinity (pp. 304–33)

Theology derives from meeting God, who is speaking in person.

Revelation is a new thing for humans. It is not merely part of our experience of the world. Rather, it is God's unique, inbreaking address.

God freely gives an irreplaceable, personal presence in revelation. He comes as Lord over this freedom to be known. We cannot grasp for Him. His coming to be with us is unconstrained and full of loving self-giving. We find ourselves as those who are met and embraced, but we recognize that encounter is about Him.

> Theology derives from meeting God, who is speaking in person.

God comes with unimpaired unity and indivisible distinction, one God in three persons.

The words of the doctrine of the Trinity point to the reality they reveal. The words and images are not an end in themselves. Through them, we meet God.

Proper speaking of God will humbly acknowledge the way God has already spoken. Improper speaking will deny that God-resourced speaking can even happen.

Dogma is a necessary analysis of revelation. It informs our interpretation so that we might ever more deeply pursue the personal truth to which we are directed in God's self-giving.

Dogmatics is corrective for the purpose of making God's communication as clear as possible.

The validity of the doctrine of the Trinity is confirmed in that it is faithfully grounded in God's revelation.

The term *Trinity* reflects God's disclosure seeking adequate human expression. A tri-unity acknowledges three and one simultaneously.

The Son is displayed in the Bible as the visible revelation of God who shows us the Father and the Spirit.

In the Bible, God self-unveils before humanity in a way that is not natural to human experience.

God has become unlike Himself in the person of Jesus; He has taken on our humanity.

The revealed God shows us the hidden God. The mystery is made available but not entirely comprehendible. We see that the universe is there, but it is incomprehensible. So much more the One who made it.

God is the Lord in Godself, both in becoming human and in coming to us.

To hear through the Bible is to perceive the heartbeat of God's presence in history.

Revelation means not created by humans; it is communication by God imparted to humans as a witness and encounter with God.

Exegesis is the Church's affirmation and acceptance of the revelation of God to be heard in its midst.

3. Vestigium Trinitatis (pp. 333–47)

Vestiges are likenesses improperly conceived as traces of the Trinity that we can identify as having an analog to God's being. These are deemed "fingerprints" of God, but they are deciphered by humans who see what they want to see.

People see triads and triplicates and think they reflect God's being, but this is problematic. Metaphors of water, three-leaf clovers, and the like will lead us astray from knowing God, even though they may have a logic of how one thing can be three in some sense.

God does not have three parts or sequential, conditioned forms. God is always one God in three persons. No impersonal illustration can replicate this unique being of the personal God.

Proposals that build on vestiges of the Trinity can be seen as Trojan horses opening the way for foreign concepts to be snuck into our thinking and ruin our understanding in relating with God.

Augustine left the door open for all manner of later invasions of thought. Each of these paid initial attention to human experience. This inadvertently departed from a beginning focused on God as the source of our knowledge of God.

Do we look for traces of the Trinity in the creature or for traces of the creature in the Trinity? No.

Human reason can end up subsuming revelation so that what is visible is diluted to mere human concepts. But God came into the world to become available as God in the world, available for our inequity and biased misreading. God's actuality is usurped regularly by human investigation that finds only what it is looking for and misses God.

The only proper vestige of the Trinity is hearing in our own ears the thrice single voice of the Father, Son, and Spirit.

Our work in theology is begun by listening to the Bible (exegetical) in order to hear the Son (dogmatic) and finally to act in response to God who encounters us (practical).

 COMMENTARY:

- The work of theology is to come to know and understand God as God has given Godself to be known.
- Jesus never depicts Himself as alone. We find that His identity is connected essentially to His Father and the Holy Spirit. He is because they are.
- Theology must avoid other forms of speaking of God that begin with sets of threes, whether in nature or in the human forms of being and thinking. This is the basis of mythological thinking that projects from human perceptions and patterns and assigns them to God.
- God revealed is God in triune self-giving; all theological investigation begins with this affirmation.

CONCLUSION FOR THE CHURCH: The Church must steadfastly attend to the personal God who intends to be known. For this purpose, God gives God's very self to be known, in a manner only God can ensure. God is apprehended in the unique act of personal self-giving, which is a gift to the Church for the world. Only in the act of encountering God can we know God and complete God's intended connection—this is the vocation of the Church. Knowing about God is insufficient; we are to know God personally in a manner faithful to God's actual being as the One who is with us and for us.

INSIGHT FOR PASTORS: We are called to bring our churches to participate in the life of God. This requires that we inform our activities of worship, witness, service, and mission by opening to what God is already doing so that we do not create alternate idols and miss the authentic connection. The Church is especially called to share in God's self-giving as a body. It is constituted by those who are moved by the heart of the Father, who abide in the active love of the Son, and who are empowered to serve by the Spirit's focused, impassioned life of expressing God's restorative love. Any attempt to be relevant to a contemporary audience through analogies derived from human experience, business models, psychology, or other natural experiences are doomed to distract from knowing God or sharing God's life. These create churches that are empty echoes of the culture.

INSIGHT FOR THEOLOGIANS: The science of God must provide focus and limits on claims that refer to God. Only the Trinity provides an accurate reflection that can be the root of the logic and life of God. Understanding the interrelations of the Trinity helps us explore the Bible's expansive vision of knowing God. With all due respect, God's freedom must not be domesticated by human sketching. That methodology can only hint at the grandeur of God while missing it or, worse yet, emphasize something that is not God. When our study begins even slightly amiss, we become misguided. What may have been a good intention becomes a weak investigation. It can only thinly approximate a form of God that distracts from the real God.

CLARIFYING QUESTIONS: Does your theology embrace the Trinity as the place to discover the nature of God's life, thus informing and inviting you into the mission of God, *or* is the Trinity a difficult problem you would like to avoid?

CHAPTER 16

ATTENDING TO THE GRANDEUR OF THE MOUNTAIN

§ 9. *The Triunity of God*

FOCUS STATEMENT: A good guide will awaken our attentiveness to the nature of the mystery to be discovered ahead, to see what we otherwise might miss. In this case we will behold "The Triunity of God." Glaciers, waterfalls, wildflower meadows, and fresh air are all there waiting to be noticed and enjoyed. This chapter summarizes § 9, which explores the heart of what God reveals, the One God in three persons or ways of being.

INTRODUCTION: This section continues chapter 2 of 17 of the *CD*, explaining how the unity and triune nature might be considered a triunity. The term *Trinity* encapsulates the personal and proper life of God in the mutual relations of three persons. We are faced with the actuality of who this God is, the One God with whom we are coming to have personal engagement as we know the Father through the Son, facilitated by the ongoing work of the Spirit.

CONTEXT: *CD* 1.1
Pages in Paragraph: 36 pages (pp. 348–83)

Subsections
1. Unity in Trinity
2. Trinity in Unity
3. Triunity
4. The Meaning of the Doctrine of the Trinity

TEXT: § 9. The Triunity of God

OPENING SUMMARY: The God who reveals Himself according to Scripture is One in three distinctive modes of being subsisting in their mutual relations: Father, Son, and Holy Spirit. It is thus that He is the Lord, i.e., the Thou who meets man's I and unites Himself to this I as the indissoluble Subject and thereby and therein reveals Himself to him as his God.[1]

✠ SUMMARY:

1. Unity in Trinity (pp. 348–53)

The biblical witness to God is that there is one God named Yahweh in the Old Testament and Kyrios in the New Testament.

There is one divine name, not three, in the baptismal formula.

Three persons does not mean three Gods.

God is Trinity, not triplicate.

God is One in threefold repetition.

God is not three individuals.

The unity of God is not a collective, which means not formed by the addition of three separate parts.

There are not three personalities in God, that would be Tritheism—three gods.

God must not be seen as an *it*—that means impersonally. God, as object, is a personal subject who speaks.

Revelation is God's presence, which means the Son and Spirit are revealing God the Father in person.

2. Trinity in Unity (pp. 353–68)

The unity of God is not to be confused with singularity or isolation.

Affirmations regarding the communion of Father, Son, and Holy Spirit govern our understanding of divine singularity and solitariness. God's being is unitary and interpersonal.

With the doctrine of the Trinity, we step onto the soil of Christian monotheism.[2]

Person for Barth is a mode of being, but this is difficult to understand. There are not three sequential modes of God's being; that would be modalism.

The word *person* can mean mask, which would be misleading if we apply this use to God. We must be carefully clear.

---

1. *CD* 1.1, § 9, p. 348.
2. *CD* 1.1, § 9, p. 354.

To refer to the distinctive beings in the Trinity, western theology clung to the word *person*, and eastern theology to *hypostasis*.

A juxtaposition of human persons with one another denotes a separateness of being, which is completely excluded in God.[3] For God, person is an inseparable, interrelated way of being.

Theologians have wrestled with the term *person* because we easily default to human perceptions projected onto God. That is like looking into a room with three mirrors and thinking it reflects God when in fact we are only seeing ourselves.

Boethius offered a persuasive description: a person is the individual substance of a rational nature.[4] But this is not descriptive of God. It is also problematic if we try to use it for humans.

Augustine, Aquinas, Anselm, Calvin, and others were challenged to find a meaning of person that worked in depicting the one God in the particularities of Father, Son, and Spirit. They were not the last to struggle with finding the right word or definition.

In the nineteenth century, the idea of personality added the concept of self-consciousness.

God must now be carefully understood as personal, not just as power or an impersonal lordship over creation.

This God meets us as an I.

We do not want to stop using the term *person*, but it must be as an abbreviation to a larger discussion of what the term means.

God is threefold without tritheism, and so the Father, Son, and Spirit are three ways of God being God as a unity. This refers to a concept of persons that must be determined by God and not by humans.

God is revealed in the Bible as Father, Son, and Spirit, and we must respect this portrayal of the personal God.

God has specific, different, and distinctive ways of being that cannot be exchanged with each other and are together the one God.

The personal God revealed in Scripture is irrevocably three and inseparable.

All that can be said of God is said of the Father, Son, and Holy Spirit.

Distinctions in the revelation of God are not a separation in their essential life together.

---

3. *CD* 1.1, § 9, p. 355.
4. *CD* 1.1, § 9, p. 356.

There are distinctions in the relations of origin, but this in no way separates the three in their unified personal being.

There is a personal source of revelation (Father), there is personal revelation itself (Son), and a personal being revealed to humanity (Spirit) that opens us to the revelation of God.

The threeness in God's oneness is grounded in relations.

"The relations in God in virtue of which He is three in one essence are thus His fatherhood (*paternitas*) in virtue of which God the Father is the Father of the Son, His sonship (*filiatio*) in virtue of which God the Son is the Son of the Father, and His spirit-hood (*processio, spiratio passiva*) in virtue of which God the Spirit is the Spirit of the Father and the Son."[5]

> God is revealed in the Bible as Father, Son, and Spirit, and we must respect this portrayal of the personal God.

There are three of what in the Trinity? Our language points to a reality it cannot capture finally, but it is reality in spite of our inability. Language submits to reality; reality does not submit to language.

3. Triunity (pp. 368–75)

Triunity is a conflation of the threeness within God and the unity to hold them together in the unified manner in which they exist.

There is a unity in God's life, without separation. No one person may be known without the other two.

God always acts freely in the life of the three together.

God's revelation allows us to differentiate the three persons in their particular and shared actions.

> Discussion of the Trinity needs to stand at the head of theology as it is the proper form of God as given in revelation.

"From creation by way of revelation and reconciliation to the coming redemption it is always true that He who acts here is the Father and the Son and the Spirit."[6]

4. The Meaning of the Doctrine of the Trinity (pp. 375–83)

All of God's being is always present to us in His acts.

The Trinity reveals the threefold otherness of the one God as Father, Son, and Spirit.

The biblical revelation is an unveiling of God to humanity in this threefold personal manner.

---

5. *CD* 1.1, § 9, p. 365.
6. *CD* 1.1, § 9, p. 375.

The Church today stands in continuity with the Church of the past to discover the God who self-reveals.

Discussion of the Trinity needs to stand at the head of theology as it is the proper form of God as given in revelation.

In the doctrine of the Trinity, we say that God is the Revealer, and we submit to the reality of that revelation.

There is no above and below in God, no hierarchy of power.

There is no before and after, only a simultaneous life together.

The Trinity reveals how much God wants to and can be *our* God.

God is ours in advance because God has given Godself to us as Father, Son, and Holy Spirit.

COMMENTARY:

- The Trinity is the gateway to theological conversation. All questions regarding the being and work of God begin here. Any other starting point will have a methodological problem, collapsing into human interests, not listening to God's self-giving.
- God is a unity, so Christianity is a monotheistic faith. God exists in three persons who constitute in an inseparable manner the unity of the one God. Thus, God can never be an *it*, an impersonal being, nor can God exist as a solitary being rather than a relational being.
- God does not progress from being the Father, to Son, and finally to Spirit. God is not a shape shifter.
- Theology must wrestle with the meaning of being persons. This is first true of God. All human discussions must follow lest we create God in our own image. The fear of those against social views of the Trinity is that we will make the Trinity merely reflect human sociality and relationality.
- The unity and particularity of the persons of the Father, Son, and Holy Spirit are to be held together to reflect the active self-giving of God in the Bible. God's active being fills out our understanding of personal being. If you want to know what God is like, look at Jesus.
- To lose the triunity of God is to follow an idol that approximates God but loses the way God has shown Godself to us.

CONCLUSION FOR THE CHURCH:
The Church must begin by believing God is self-giving. This is faith seeking understanding. This happens in a manner best described through discussing God's dynamic way of being identified in the persons of the Father, Son, and Holy Spirit. This uncovering of

God portrays a personal way of being the Lord, specifically in meeting us as God who is known as One who is with us and for us. If we want to get to know God, we must meet God where He comes to us.

INSIGHT FOR PASTORS: The task of the Church is to know Jesus and the One who sent Him. The Spirit enables our continued knowing of God both through the Bible preached in the Church and in theological reflection on who God is. God is a community of three-ways-of-being-God who are not three Gods but exist as the life of shared love that intends love, acts in love, and fulfills God's love in our time and place. This section has revealed both the history and elements of the discussion of the Trinity. It also begins to discuss the beliefs to avoid while attempting to maintain faithfulness to the God of the Bible. The Trinity is not a lofty doctrine to be avoided but the personal being of God, who meets us as we gather and is the host to our gathering as we grow as God's family and eat at His table. We do not mimic, measure, or meditate on the Trinity in worship. We come to meet with the Trinity and be transformed as we hear the persons speak and invite us to share God's life and love. Think about shaping your community as a participation in God's family and see if that creates a new way of being.

INSIGHT FOR THEOLOGIANS: Theology in the modern era has rediscovered the importance of the Trinity for theology. In this section, we see the beginning of the challenge and the opportunity to engage God as personal, as well as the need to use the word *person* with humility. We are to ask what we mean by referring to God as person so that God uniquely fills that meaning. If students are going to avoid reducing God to definitions, descriptions, arguments, and confessions that are spoken but not believed, they must learn the personal nature of God as Father, Son, and Spirit.

The being of God alone can continue to inform the task of theology by not being reduced to human words. But words are used by God to serve human understanding. However, we are challenged to align our words to God's reality and not vice versa. The God of the Bible is a triunity of persons who come to address us. We must learn to listen as theological scientists. Together, they act on our behalf as a presupposition of our life together. Proper theology must be rooted in this dynamic life of God, but also invite a participation in God's life extended to be with us and for us. Otherwise, academic theology is an abstract distraction instead of engaged connection.

? **CLARIFYING QUESTIONS:** Does your theology emphasize the existence of God, the unity of God, or the threeness of God, *or* does your theology humbly submit to the way Jesus reveals His Father and Spirit in a manner that is best described as Trinitarian?

🗺 **CHAPTER 17**

COMPREHENDING THE WHENCE OF THE MOUNTAIN

§ 10. God the Father

👀 **FOCUS STATEMENT:** One might wonder about the whence, the source of the majestic spectacle before us, seeking to understand the origination of the grandeur of the mountain in its shared being. This leads us to consider "God the Father." Hence, the point of this chapter is to summarize § 10 in the *CD* to consider the unseen but available depths of the God revealed as Father.

🖋 **INTRODUCTION:** This section, focusing on the Father of the Son, begins at the beginning. It pays attention to God's initiating point in providing personal connection. Jesus is a visible unveiling of the inexhaustible being of His Father and the visible making known the preexisting, invisible God. This is a short section but a significant unpacking in the ordering of God's coming to us.

📚 **CONTEXT:** *CD* 1.1
Pages in Paragraph: 15 pages (pp. 384–98)

Subsections
  1. God as Creator
  2. The Eternal Father

📖 **TEXT:** § 10. God the Father

OPENING SUMMARY: The one God reveals Himself according to Scripture as the Creator, that is, as the Lord of our existence. As such He is God our Father because He is so antecedently in Himself as the Father of the Son.[1]

---

1. *CD* 1.1, § 10, p. 384.

SUMMARY:

1. God as Creator (pp. 384–90)

Humans make two major errors regarding God the Father:

1. Thinking that God is of the same kind and order as us. We make an idol of God fashioned in our own image.
2. Thinking that God remains within God's order separate from us. We make God distant, abstract, and disconnected from us.

Revelation dispels the errors of projected idolatry and abstract cutting off.

God is absolutely different from humans and at the same time completely engaged with them as their Lord.

This God, as Lord, makes Himself available to the awareness of humans as an "I to a Thou." This the Bible calls revelation.

Jesus is the Lord who approaches humanity; this is the presupposition of the Christian Church.

The New Testament ascribes a sending, preceding Kyrios—the Father—who is expressed in Jesus as another Kyrios—Jesus as Lord.

We must ask what (or whom) is the goal to which Jesus is the promised way.

It is worth asking what we see in Jesus as the reflection and mirror of the Father.

Jesus' sense of revealing His Father is at the same time a radical questioning of our human use of *father* as for human fathers.

This Father will deal with death: quickening, blessing, and creating a life that has passed through death—an eternal life.

The Father does not will the specifics of our life or death. His will in our life leads us through death to eternal life.

2. The Eternal Father (pp. 390–98)

God the Father is the Lord of our existence.

The real Lord of our existence must be the Lord over both life and death.

Human existence is sustained by Him and by Him alone above the abyss of nonexistence.

Human existence has a Creator. It is as the Creator that Jesus shows the Father to us.

It was the will of the Father that nailed Jesus to the cross. We all are carried in that death and then into Jesus' resurrection for life.

Using the word *Father* in no way denotes natural human fathers.

The meaning of human fatherhood acquires its meaning from the Father, not the other way around. Only the Father can provide content as to what it means to be Father. Human fathers do not provide insight to fatherhood in God. We can only question whether human fathers approximate the One who appropriately is called Father.

Through revelation, we know the Father of Jesus Christ as our Creator.

The word *Father* takes on a meaning it cannot have by itself. Its connotations come to us in the revelation of Jesus, who interprets it and gives it the meaning that His Father is our Creator.

The Father is revealed first as the Father of Jesus Christ; only in this way is it the basis of our knowing Him as Father.

God can be our Father because that is an eternal mode of His being. From this way of being is established the context for human existence as He is our Creator.

In humility, we must state that God is unknown as our Father whenever and in whatever manner that He is not made known by Jesus.

All natural theology of fatherhood must be ruled inadequate and false in that it introduces alien claims as to the nature and being of the Father on the insufficient basis of human experience.

The Father is not the First Cause, the Most Perfect Being, or any other philosophical name or cozy identification that is given subsequently to make Him more acceptable. He is the Father of Jesus, revealed by Jesus as our Father.

Any idea projected onto God the Father is an idol.

Jesus revealed His Father as the unknown Father, not the philosophical God who has now been given a name.

We learn about the fatherhood of God by seeing the will of the Father revealed in Jesus. This concretely excludes any abstraction that might be applied to the Father. We are focused on that which corresponds to the Sonship we see in Jesus, through whom we come to know the One who is His Father.

God does not exist only in the person of the Father but also in the Son and the Spirit, who have revealed the content of God's being. They personally refer us back to the eternal Father, whom they make known in their particular ways of being God for us.

From the proper name of the Father, as well as the dignity associated with it alone, comes the possibility of "intracreaturely originating relations."[2]

---

2. *CD* 1.1, § 10, p. 393.

This human form of relatedness is the result of God's creative work. Only when seen as God's creative work can the fatherhood derived from the Father's being be seen as working out in heaven and on Earth.

Human fatherhood is to be regarded as a true but improper appellation. The proper meaning is dependent on the power and dignity of God's intra-Trinitarian name of Father.

God's Trinitarian name of Father denotes His personal being in which He is the author of His other modes of being: He begets the Son and sends the Spirit; God exists eternally in these relations.

There is no superiority or subordination within the Trinity. God is firstly Father and in no less a way exists also as Son and Spirit, who are the repetitions of His being.

Because of the eternal relation of Father, Son, and Spirit, we can never say that the Father alone is Creator.

When we begin the creed with God the Father, we also include the involvement of the Son and Holy Spirit as expressed in the creed.

God is undivided in His being and His work as Father, Son, and Spirit.

We cannot call God our Father apart from the Son and the Spirit, nor can we call the Son *Savior* or the Spirit *Comforter* without also having the Father in view in both cases.

God is distinct in His unity and unified in His distinctions. So too is creation unified in its distinctions and distinct in its unity.

Each divine person works in the triune life in the manner and sense that is appropriate to them.

The creative work of God is to be understood within the communion of the three persons in a manner called perichoresis, "according to which all three, without forfeiture or mutual dissolution of independence, reciprocally interpenetrate each other and inexist in one another."[3]

> God's Trinitarian name of Father denotes His personal being in which He is the author of His other modes of being: He begets the Son and sends the Spirit; God exists eternally in these relations.

The unity of God does not mean there is a fourth "essence" of God that is shared by the three persons.

There is no sequencing of God where God transitions from form to form.

All statements about the work of God can be made about all three of the persons of the Trinity. Still, the Father is not the Son who is not the Spirit.

---

3. *CD* 1.1, § 10, p. 396.

We must not see perichoresis merely as an involution, a turning in on the being of God within Godself. That makes for a convolution in the image, focusing on the independence of the persons of the Trinity—this misses the Father's, Son's, and Spirit's personal being in unity together in eternal communion.

There is no separation nor fusion in the relation of the Father with the Son and Spirit.

Our particular knowledge of the Father as Creator within the unity of the Trinity must never threaten the unity nor deny the persons working together. Rather, it must affirm the uniqueness of the Father.

COMMENTARY:

- God is known through Jesus to have a Father, who is the One with whom Jesus wants humans to be reconciled.
- We cannot see the Father as the unmoved mover of Greek philosophy. That view is an abstract idea. It assumes that "way back in time" there must have been a point where a god set a ball rolling to create. That is merely a logical conclusion that there must have been a first mover who originated all the movement of things that move now.
- Philosophical readings of possible gods are based on conjecture and projection; they have no revealed knowledge. If we think every action must have a cause, we are likely to make up a personal cause of some sort. But this is excluded and unnecessary when we know the One who actually created.
- It is convenient to have a made-up god who asks nothing of us. On the other hand, it is likely to be an interruption to have the One who made us speak and want to connect.
- In Jesus, we come to know we have a Father who is alone properly called Father. Our human fathers can only approximate the relation of father as an echo of the eternal Father.
- The creative work of the Father is always a particular activity within the shared creation by the Father, Son, and Spirit.
- Barth leaves room for mystery when speaking of the Father so we do not claim too much. He also does not want us to say too little of the Father, whom Jesus came to show us and to whom He brings us home as His ultimate goal.
- Barth is also attempting to narrow the conversation so that valid claims are made by God's self-revelation in Christ.
- *CD* volume 3 is all about God the Creator, so much more is to come!

CONCLUSION FOR THE CHURCH: The Church must find its life of discovery as one leading to God the Father. The personal way of being known in the Father is as the Lord made visible and vocal through the Son and the Spirit. The Father is the origination of their revelation to be for and with humanity. Together they each share in creation while maintaining their particularity. The Church finds meaning within this personal life of relation to God and, subsequently, to God's creation.

INSIGHT FOR PASTORS: "Who" God is as Father is significantly important for Jesus. Yet we often quickly pass over the Father in our talk about Jesus. We then miss the One with whom Jesus came to restore relationship. If our churches are to participate in the Church of Jesus Christ, we need to learn how to accept our adoption back to the Father who sent Him and with whom He made the world that we occupy. As pastors, we often come across people with issues of abandonment by fathers.

This Divine Father is the ever-faithful one, whom many sufferers have never known. We must learn to know the Father of Jesus if we want to deal with the Jesus of the New Testament. His Father must become our Father, to whom Jesus directed us. The Church needs to rediscover its true north to find its way home. This goes beyond attachment issues; it involves dealing with a loss of identity. We have forgotten who we are as we have convoluted both God and humanity into tragic disfigurement. The poverty of love we imagine can leave our souls withered or twisted, neither trusting others nor valuing the self as beloved. In not knowing the Father, the dignity of being a beloved child is vanquished or suppressed into a shadow of what could be.

INSIGHT FOR THEOLOGIANS: In the science of theological investigation, we can be Christ-centered in our scientific discovery only through focusing on Jesus. But if in the investigation we miss the One whom He came to reveal, we are like those who discovered the ocean but never entered the water. Jesus came to show us His Father so that He would be *our* Father and we would abide in Him. A fatherless theology creates a multitude of orphans. The science of discovery must attune us to God's reality as Father—"our Father," as Jesus taught us to pray. Only then can we understand how the will of the Father undergirds all of the creative, reconciling, and redemptive work of Jesus and the Spirit. Any proper theology must penetrate through Jesus to encounter the Father's heart. Then we can see Jesus, maybe for the first time, as the outworking of the Father's love and activity. Any definition of God's justice, wrath, or judgment that misses the Abba of Jesus will be based on a mirage of human, controlling, fear-based sensibilities that have little to do with Jesus' Father.

? CLARIFYING QUESTIONS: Does your theology depict a Father who is male, judging the nations for their imperfections, terrifying, unavailable, silent except to scold, distant to the point of abandonment, or just playing a game with your life? *Or* do you have a theology that sees Jesus through the Father who lovingly sent Jesus while we were sinners, unaware of our sin or selfishness, and unworthy of a love that was freely bestowed anyway? Does your theology acknowledge that you are a cherished child of this Father as your core identity?

CHAPTER 18

THE VISIBLE STRUCTURE OF THE MOUNTAIN AS IT CAME TO BE

§ 11. God the Son

FOCUS STATEMENT: The mountain not only has a source; it also has a form that shapes its beauty. We see both the ancient structures and the current form as it lives in action; its fiery birth, its glacial sculpting, and the rivers that carve and nurture are all manifestations of this living masterpiece. Its form sustains all that dwell within its habitat.

We now come to regard the revelation of the Mountain's structure and ordered life, and to look at the visible God known as "God the Son." The point of this chapter is to summarize § 11 in the *CD* by exploring how God is visibly known in history through the very revelation of God in the God-human, Jesus.

INTRODUCTION: This section continues chapter 2 of 17 of the *CD*, focusing on "The Son." This is not an abstract discussion of natures and attributes that apply to Jesus; it is a clear depiction of Jesus as He came to be with and for humanity.

CONTEXT: *CD* 1.1
Pages in Paragraph: 49 pages (pp. 399–447)

Subsections
1. God as Reconciler
2. The Eternal Son

TEXT: § 11. God the Son

OPENING SUMMARY: The one God reveals Himself according to Scripture as the Reconciler, i.e., as the Lord in the midst of our enmity towards Him. As such He is the Son of God who has come to us or the Word of God that has been spoken to us, because He is so antecedently in Himself as the Son or Word of God the Father.[1]

SUMMARY:

1. God as Reconciler (pp. 399–414)

Our starting point: Who is the One with whom we have to engage in God's self-revealing as Lord?

Jesus is the answer as the One who reveals. How He reveals cannot be separated from who He is as the Son of God and as the One revealed in the New Testament. Jesus first reveals His Father but in the mode of the Mediator with alienated humanity.

While we must distinguish Jesus from His Father, Jesus exists in communion with His Father.

If Jesus is to be seen as unified with the Father, then Jesus' being, identified as God, is definitive, authentic, and essential. You see Jesus; you see God.

Jesus cannot be seen as a human that was exalted to being God or only appeared as if He were a divine person.

Jesus is Lord; this we must agree on with the early Church. If we cannot affirm it, we deny it and propose some other Jesus of our imagining.

We cannot prove or deduce that Jesus is Lord. It is His givenness and must be affirmed in order to begin any subsequent discussion about God.

Jesus reveals His Father, and this Father is God. Thus, He who reveals Him is God. Who can reveal God but God?

If Jesus were only a creature (human), He could not reveal God, only creaturely work.

If Jesus reveals God, then irrespective of His creaturehood, He has to be God. Any reduction would deny His deity.

To confess Jesus as the revelation of the Father is to acknowledge His being equally God with the Father.

Where Jesus revealed the Father who is Creator, He now is revealed as Son of the Father—this is something different from the activity of God (creation); it proclaims that God comes to us, speaks to us, and desires to be heard by us. He hopes to arouse a response from us (relation).

Jesus establishes an intimacy of interconnection between God and us.

---

1. *CD* 1.1, § 11, p. 399.

God does not work in the dark, hidden from us—He discloses His work. In Jesus and by the Holy Spirit, He seeks us as those who are capable of hearing and responding.

"He deals with us as the Creator, but as a person with persons, not as a power over things."[2]

We know that we are God's enemies because He had to come looking for us.

Jesus comes to tell us that we have abandoned the fellowship between the creature and Creator, but He has set Himself in a place to make reunion possible where it would otherwise be impossible.

Every human wants to be their own lord—this is to choose to be against God, closed off from God. Thus, it is understandable that humans cannot hear God because they will not listen. This is a refusal to hear what God is saying, but God is not silent.

There is a Nevertheless[3]—God's grace for the miracle of hearing that we cannot prepare for or find by our own efforts.

Hearing God is possible. The subjective side of this possibility is enabled by the Holy Spirit.

Restoration means to regain fellowship.

Jesus is the Son of God who has spoken to us.

2. The Eternal Son (pp. 414–47)

Jesus reveals the Father to us, and as the Son, He reconciles us to the Father.

Jesus reveals Himself as the one He was before the event of revelation—the eternal Son.

Jesus did not receive His lordship but has it as His nature.

The fact that Jesus is already the Lord denies untheological speculation; the one who thinks otherwise is exercising untheological speculation.

If we do not listen to God, we will come to think that God is needy. We will believe that humanity is indispensable to God, that it is God's job to forgive us and our job to accept. In that scenario, God is not free in His grace toward us. We wrongly think God is bound to serve humanity—this is untheological speculation.

If we think that God is only known for His benefits in Christ and forget that Jesus is the very speech of God to us that begins in God and is God's encounter, then we have become untheological with a narrow and selfish vision.

---

2. *CD* 1.1, § 11, 407.

3. Barth uses *Nevertheless* as God's gracious act in the face of our stubborn resistance.

If we judge the benefits of Jesus in His revelation and limit our discussion to that focus, we are proposing human judgments that interrupt our listening. We deny true reflection, which listens with humility to what is actually said.

If we judge, evaluate, estimate, and interpret Jesus, are we not being untheological in speculating logic that has forgotten that the Lord reveals and calls into question our judging?

When we do not listen to the grace of God given in freedom, we create another faith that is not a science but limits God by human thinking.

> When we do not listen to the grace of God given in freedom, we create another faith that is not a science but limits God by human thinking.

Those who speak out of human judgments about God do not speak a different language; they speak out of a different knowledge. They usually lock horns over different forms of human knowing that entirely miss God's self-giving.

The Nicene Creed is the most important document established for the Church.

1. The creed begins by focusing on the significance of Jesus as Lord for us, grounded in His being, not in our need: He does not become Lord when we confess. We confess because He is Lord and because we become attuned to this reality.

2. Jesus has an exclusive claim to being the Son of God. No other person can make His claim or reveal what He reveals. Jesus is a unique revelation of God, not a second God.

3. Jesus was begotten of the Father before time but is revealed as the Son in our time as the Lord of history. Jesus was the Son of God before time and encompasses our time within the scope of His creation and concern.

4. In Jesus, we have to distinguish light from light. The source of the light and the rays that emanate are both a unity and distinguishable. We can notice the distinction, although we may not be able to define it. The eternal being of Jesus has His source and dependence in His inseparable relation to His Father.

All of our terms and definitions will be inadequate to capture the being of God.

Jesus is granted deity in that He is exclusively the Word of God. This both separates and unites God as speaker and one spoken inseparably.

5. Jesus is one being with the Father. In His personal nature and with all that makes Him God, He is totally like the Father. Jesus is not only equal to the Father; He is of the same nature inseparably.

   a. Jesus being one with the Father is a safeguard against the Arian view, which holds that Jesus is a superman who is like God.

   b. Jesus being one with the Father guards against the Origenist view of Jesus holding Him as a God of a lesser quality.

   c. Jesus being one with the Father also safeguards against views proposing multiple gods, those confused with the distinctions of the persons within the Godhead. This is a stand against polytheism.

   "Distinction in unity and unity in distinction is the point in all trinitarian theology."[4]

   All lines of deliberation about who Jesus is must converge at the point of affirming that Jesus is one being with the Father.

6. Jesus is the One through whom all things are made; Jesus has a share in the work ascribed to the Father in the first article of the creed. All the works of the Trinity are shared in a manner appropriate to each person, yet always in unity.

"The One who in revelation calls us out of our enmity against Him to Himself, who calls us out of death into life, is the One who in so doing also makes Himself known as the One who previously called us out of nothing into existence."[5]

The Revealer is also the Reconciler who was first the Creator.

Jesus comes and shows us that we are sinners, separated from God, whose revelation is the exposure of our distance.

Jesus shows us in His revelation that He is the Creator and therefore the Lord over all humanity, but His power as Creator is not limited to His revelation.

Recognizing Christ as Lord depends on going to the facts and not speculative conceptions.

Creation and revelation are not mere truths to discuss; they are the reality unified in Jesus Christ, who as the one God is with the Father behind all createdness.

---

4. *CD* 1.1, § 11, p. 440.
5. *CD* 1.1, § 11, p. 444.

The reality of revelation is seen in the mirror of the Bible, beginning and ending with the united creativity of Father and Son.

COMMENTARY:

- The creed begins with the creative work of the Father but goes on to imply that Jesus is involved inseparably in the scheme and outworking of Creation.
- To understand Jesus is to see that He has always existed as the Son of the Father, and His activity in history fulfills what He already was in eternity with the Father.
- Jesus is God and nothing less than One who exists with the Father in unified distinction.

CONCLUSION FOR THE CHURCH: The Church must find its life through God the Son. He has His very being as the One who has eternally lived a unified life with the Father. He shared in creation and has become the Father's revelation. As the reconciling Creator, Jesus comes to bring home what was lost. This is the constituting movement of God establishing the Church. But we are ignorant regarding who Jesus is as our true home. Nevertheless, He has always been at work, preceding our attempts to fit Him into our lives. The Church finds its meaning in connection to its Head, who was already at work.

INSIGHT FOR PASTORS: While many sermons explore the benefits of Jesus for the persons in the pews, here we see that Jesus must first be known for who He is as the very presence of the Father and as the One through whom we were created and who never abandoned humanity. We need to see who Jesus is in relation to the Father before we see Him as being for us. This allows us to understand the triune life of mission preceding our existential benefit. Knowing Jesus does not cause God to act differently; it opens us to the gift already given. Jesus is not an individual like any other human. He is uniquely related to the Father as our Creator and as the One who brings the Father to us that we may once again be His.

What would it look like to make every gathering a reunion of family with all the joy of being together? What if it was about creating joy and connection, inviting friends and those without families, and creating events where people awaken to belonging to Jesus as His beloved and accept their place in their Abba's family?

INSIGHT FOR THEOLOGIANS: Jesus may be concretely described by His earthly ministry and yet abstractly missed in recognizing His eternal identity as the Son of the Father. If we miss the eternal dimension, we make Jesus more human than divine. But Jesus is the very God who is the expression of His unity with the Father. All heresies begin by missing the essential relatedness of Jesus and His Father.

Also, searching for what Jesus has to offer humanity distracts from the deeper reality, focusing on who Jesus is and how that identity reveals what we really need—to know the depths of God who knows and loves us. Only by entering this mystery with humility can we approach God. When we reduce God to our definitions, descriptions, and conceptions, or when we forget that Jesus opens the door for us to know God, it is like we are loving and cherishing a picture of our beloved while ignoring our beloved standing right in front of us. As theologians, we must let God be God, and in knowing Jesus we unexpectedly find home in the Father's arms.

? CLARIFYING QUESTIONS: Does your theology focus on what Jesus has done for you and humanity in His sacrifice for sin, His model of obedience, and His giving you meaning for life? *Or* does your theology cause you to sit humbly in silence waiting to hear what Jesus is saying to guide you, to speak through you, to share in His ministry, and to serve those for whom He cares? Does your knowledge of Jesus help you to know His Father?

CHAPTER 19

EXPERIENCING THE MOUNTAIN

§ 12. God the Holy Spirit

FOCUS STATEMENT: In this section, we come to experience the wonder of this mountain. The presence of what is majestic begins to transform us. We come to see the mountain as an invitation. The mountain calls us to scale it, enjoy it, and explore its heights together. We are compelled to experience its awesomeness. So also "God the Holy Spirit" is the One who awakens us to the grandeur of God. This chapter summarizes § 12 in the *CD* on the God revealed as Spirit—the One in whom revelation becomes encounter as a life-giving presence. This Spirit is not to be confused with our human spirit. This Spirit is God and enables us to know God in fullness and mysterious wonder.

INTRODUCTION: This section continues chapter 2 of 17 of the *CD*, focusing on "The Holy Spirit." This is a glimpse at what *CD* 5 might have looked like because that final volume would have been on the doctrine of redemption. In an appetizer preview, this topic is introduced here in *CD* 1, which surveys the current expression of the Word of God revealed to us.

CONTEXT: *CD* 1.1
Pages in Paragraph: 42 pages (pp. 448–89)

Subsections
1. God as Redeemer
2. The Eternal Spirit

TEXT: § 12. God the Holy Spirit

OPENING SUMMARY: The one God reveals Himself according to Scripture as the Redeemer, i.e., as the Lord who sets us free. As such He is the Holy Spirit, by receiving whom we become the children of God, because, as the Spirit of the love of God the Father and the Son, He is so antecedently in Himself.[1]

SUMMARY:

1. God as Redeemer (pp. 448–66)

To begin again at the beginning, we confess that Jesus is Lord. But now we add another question: On what basis can we say that Jesus is Lord?

Belief is based not in arbitrary reflection but on fact—the actuality that Jesus comes as Lord. This is not a conclusion based on human considerations, as though He might somehow qualify as Lord based on human standards.

Jesus is not a superman from above or a perfected human who has achieved a status worthy of being called Lord. He is not the idea of a perfect human being. He steps into history as Lord, therefore confronting us as a fact, not a consideration.

The question is not how humans reach this conclusion—Jesus is Lord—but how they begin to encounter the actuality to be explored.

How does the reality of God come to the receptive or resistant vessel of each particular human person?

We meet Jesus in the world of human testing and considerations. Yet we meet Him within this problematic world as One who is to be encountered. He is there to be questioned, explored, and discovered, to transform our response so that our thoughts and lives may be conformed to His reality as Lord.

Revelation in the New Testament means meeting Jesus as God.

Faith can never be in unproblematic knowledge. All science begins by applying a questioning mind. But only an open mind can allow a revelation from what is encountered.

Reality itself creates a faithful response in the process of discovery. We do not force our ideas on reality; we let reality shape our ideas. Otherwise, we are lost in illusions and detached from reality.

Having begun with an openness to learn, regarding what is problematic, one proceeds to a faithful understanding that arises from what or who is known. This is the life of faith—seeking to faithfully understand what or who is there.

We cannot fit what we encounter into our preexisting framework of certain knowledge. The structure of what we comprehend is in fact a small box that cannot contain the Lord who is the source of our knowing.

Unproblematic knowledge is not real knowledge. Reality creates new

---

1. *CD* 1.1, § 12, p. 448.

questions that require new investigations. That is the point of the New Testament's revelation of Jesus.

God becoming available must be an act of the Father and Son.

God is known in a specific act that actualizes for us the realization of God's givenness—this is the event of human knowing that is the work of the Spirit. We know Him because He is there.

God is given to be known. God is not an object to be imagined or constrained to human experience. God can be known only as given in Jesus. We meet Him in the New Testament, which now speaks to us so that we realize Jesus is for us and with us in our present moment.

God is present to us creatures by the Holy Spirit.

By the Spirit, God opens a relation for us with Himself as Father through the Son, who makes Him known as revealing God through this revelation of the Son.

The Spirit, then, is that element of revelation that makes Christ known to us. He does not give any other content in this knowing other than knowing this Jesus in our space and time.

The work of the Spirit is significant for three reasons:

1. The Spirit guarantees our participation in the revelation of God by confirming a "yes" in us that God's revelation applies to us. Thus, faith, knowledge, and obedience are the works of the Spirit, who instills God's love in our hearts.
2. The Spirit instructs and guides us in a way we cannot. The Spirit establishes lordship through being immediately present to us.
3. The Spirit is the only one who enables us to speak of Jesus. We speak and proclaim the lordship of Jesus simply because the Spirit brings a real relation with God that enables our service to God.

The Spirit acts as the Lord who is free. In that freedom He brings us to be and know we are the children of God.

Humans are made for freedom. Thus, the Spirit makes us what we are as those restored to our Creator. We were made to be the children of God, and the Spirit brings us to realize whose we are.

In the giving of the Holy Spirit, the human remains a sinful human, and the Spirit remains God.

The Spirit sets us free indeed. He is the Redeemer who enables us to know we are the children of God. We are liberated to confess who we are and to act in accordance with that confession.

When we receive the Spirit, it is an eschatological moment. This means that we discover our eternal being, the future reflected into our temporal being now.

2. The Eternal Spirit (pp. 466–89)

In the event of revelation, the Spirit does not become God but is God in that event. The Holy Spirit is for us the subjective reality of God.

> We were made to be the children of God, and the Spirit brings us to realize whose we are.

God is the Spirit in the same way that He is the Father and Son already in Himself.

The Spirit poured out at Pentecost is the Lord, just as the Father is also the Lord God Himself.

The Holy Spirit is holy in us because He already was in Himself.

The presence of the human at God's revelation is the problem we face.

A human can be present at revelation as a servant at his master's work, "following, obeying, imitating and serving."[2]

1. We believe the Holy Spirit is the Lord, living in an inseparable unity with the Father and Son. The Spirit is the third mode of being in the life of God.
   a. The Holy Spirit is the breath of God that is the love between the Father and Son.
   b. God the Holy Spirit is the act of communion with God, the act of impartation, love, and gift.
   c. The Spirit sets us free, makes us children of God, gives us God's words to speak, and does in time what He does eternally in God's life.
2. The Spirit is the giver of life, who with the Father and Son is the subject of creation.
3. The Holy Spirit proceeds from the Father and Son.
   a. The Spirit is one being with the Father and Son.
   b. The Spirit's work is differentiated, not separated, from the Son's.
   c. Alongside the proceeding of the Son, the Spirit has His own way of procession from God.

Barth follows the western *filioque*.

---

2. *CD* 1.1, § 12, p. 468.

God is Father from eternity.

God begets Himself as Son from eternity.

God brings forth the Spirit of love from eternity.

God is simple in that He lives for the Other within the triune life.

The *filioque* offers a common source for the Spirit from the Father and the Son.

4. We believe in God the Holy Spirit worshiped and glorified with the Father and Son.

The Spirit is not alongside the Father and Son but "together with" in a shared life.

The Spirit is not a neuter *It* but a *He*—personal.

The gift of the Holy Spirit can never be abstracted from the giver who is God.

COMMENTARY:

- The Spirit is the currently acting God who opens us as subjects to know the Father and Son.
- The Spirit is never independent of the triune life but acts in a particular mode of being to bring us to participate in what the Father and Son offer as gift by the Spirit.
- The creed draws us into the inner dynamic of the life of God as those whom God has addressed and embraced in love—the common shared life of God.
- God, by the Spirit, meets us and calls humans to respond to the whole revelation of God. This response is one of worship and glory that facilitates our reception of the gift of God and the life into which we are inaugurated.

CONCLUSION FOR THE CHURCH: The Church is gifted by God the Spirit, whose act makes subjective and experiential the revelation of God to us. This Spirit is not separate in any way from the Father and Spirit but finds a common source in them to be breathed on us. Thus, we are able to find new life in the One who is the giver of life and who develops the fruits of love in us.

INSIGHT FOR PASTORS: The Spirit is the acting life of God as personal presence to fulfill God's intent to be the Lord of our lives. In this act, we discover we have been made new as children of God. We are not called only to teach others about God. We are to hear the address that comes from God and then tell others about God's coming to us in revelation. The life of a Church is only as vital as its ability to depend on God, to actually share in the knowing and being of God, facilitated by the Spirit. This does not lead us to grow a worship service bigger and better. This participation in God's life transforms the community by bringing us back to live nourished by Jesus, our Head. Only in helping people hear Jesus Christ by the Spirit can churches be empowered for service. This means we need to attend to the Spirit, speak and affirm the Spirit's presence, and make space for listening to what the Spirit is saying to the Church gathered.

INSIGHT FOR THEOLOGIANS: The Holy Spirit is often seen to be missing or scanty in the work of Barth. In this section, we see that the Spirit does not exist in a separated life but is the differentiated way of God who comes to bring to life our encounter with God. As scientists, we need to test the words we hear attributed to the Spirit and see if they correspond to the speaking Jesus. In this way the academy serves the Church. The academic life is never an abstract pursuit alone, but it focuses the Church on the sources and means of empowerment. This provision of insight is a gift to be received and distributed in acts of love and service. The object of God as Trinity has become a subject who speaks. We listen and respond in the most scientific manner possible. This means we open up to the inner structures of God shown to us. In this way, our knowledge is not merely reflective and cognitive, from our own resources. Our knowledge is truly the knowing of persons; God's identity is acknowledged to arrive from God's own initiative, and we come to recognize that He is always dynamically going with us. This is the basis for a science of God as the meaningful context of our existence.

CLARIFYING QUESTIONS: Does your theology seek to define and describe the person of Spirit for doctrinal propriety, *or* are you open to know the present, living Lord who speaks and calls you to follow and whose call is consistent with the voice of Jesus and the heart of the Father?

## PART 3

CHURCH DOGMATICS 1.2

Revelation and Freedom in the God-Human Relationship

Karl Barth	Karl Barth	Karl Barth	Karl Barth	Karl Barth	Karl Barth	Karl Barth	Karl Barth	Karl Barth	Karl Barth	Karl Barth	Karl Barth	Karl Barth
Church Dogmatics	Church Dogmatics	Church Dogmatics	Church Dogmatics	Church Dogmatics	Church Dogmatics	Church Dogmatics	Church Dogmatics	Church Dogmatics	Church Dogmatics	Church Dogmatics	Church Dogmatics	Church Dogmatics
I/1	I/2	II/1	II/2	III/1	III/2	III/3	III/4	IV/1	IV/2	IV/3.1	IV/3.2	IV/4
1932 (1936 ET)	1938 (1956 ET)	1940 (1957 ET)	1942 (1957 ET)	1945 (1958 ET)	1948 (1960 ET)	1950 (1961 ET)	1951 (1961 ET)	1953 (1956 ET)	1955 (1958 ET)	1959 (1961 ET)	1959 (1962 ET)	1967 (1969 ET)

## CHAPTER 20

FINDING THE ACTUAL MOUNTAIN FULL OF POSSIBILITIES

§ 13. God's Freedom for Man

FOCUS STATEMENT: Standing fully aware of the sweep of the mountain's free self-giving to us, we are awakened to the vibrant sustaining of life that is available for human participation. That kind of breathtaking revelation is presented in "God's Freedom for Man." God showing up in human form establishes the basis of what constitutes human freedom. As God's Word freely addressed to us, God is making Himself available for humanity. This enacts God's free revelation for us.

INTRODUCTION: This section continues chapter 2: "The Revelation of God." This chapter overlaps *CD* 1.1 and 1.2. Thus, we are still in chapter 2 but moving into *CD* 1.2. Notice that we now begin part 2 within chapter 2, which has been discussing God's self-disclosure. We move from the sources of God's self-revealing to the specifics of that revelation for us. That means we focus on Jesus, who, without abandoning being God, comes to us as a human. This is called the incarnation. This event logically connects the life of the triune God and God encountering us today by His Spirit.

1. The Triune God (in *CD* 1.1),
2. **The Incarnation of the Word (in *CD* 1.2)**, and
3. The Outpouring of the Holy Spirit (in *CD* 1.2).

It is worth noticing that each of these three parts serves as a context of meaning for the others that follow. We see the triune God revealed in the act of taking on flesh in Jesus as God *for* us, who then is poured out to humanity through the Spirit as God *in* us.

As we begin a new volume (*CD* 1.2), it is appropriate to note the playful phrase in Robert McAfee Brown's "How to Remember What's Where in Barth, or Mnemonics for Mprofessors" with his memory device for *CD* 1.2. "I/2–'One, two, buckle my shoe.' A shoe is something on which you stand, i.e., the authority of Scripture."[1]

CONTEXT: *CD* 1.2
Pages in Paragraph: 44 pages (pp. 1–44)

Subsections
1. Jesus Christ the Objective Reality of Revelation
2. Jesus Christ the Objective Possibility of Revelation

TEXT: § 13. God's Freedom for Man

OPENING SUMMARY: According to Holy Scripture, God's revelation takes place in the fact that God's Word became a man and that this man has become God's Word. The incarnation of the eternal Word, Jesus Christ, is God's revelation. In the reality of this event, God proves that He is free to be our God.[2]

SUMMARY:
1. Jesus Christ the Objective Reality of Revelation (pp. 1–25)

We must begin by noting that Barth does not discuss *possibilities* about Jesus, as though there is any human reasoning that will help us to arrive at knowing Him. Hearing God cannot be through our pursuit, employing human capacity.

When Barth says that Jesus is the *objectivity* of God, he is saying that Jesus is the concrete form of God, who stands as a real person in human history. On the other hand, we cannot just study Jesus as an object who silently stands there for our "objective study."

Jesus has the first and final word on who He is and what He is about. He is a real person who came and still comes to us. Our thinking is objective insofar as it is shaped by His reality.

When Barth says that God is the *subject* of His revelation, he means that

---

1. Robert McAfee Brown, *The Collected Writings of St. Hereticus* (Philadelphia: Westminster, 1964), 94.
2. CD 1.2, § 13, p. 1.

God speaks as a person, as a speaking subject, who always has the authority to say what He means and mean what He says. It will not do to have us humans put words in His mouth.

Thus, we must begin with the *actuality* of Jesus, who is presented in the flesh. We must focus on Him on His own terms as one coming to be known. This we call objective reality, encountering a real person who meets us.

The Word of God has become a man. God comes as a human, not as an abstract, distant idea.

The man Jesus is this Word of God, who is given so God can be known. There is then a particular human to study; we are not dependent on our ideas of humanity or the best of humanity. We are coming to know the God who created humans. We engage this human-creating God in one person, Jesus.

The actuality that God reveals is in the human form of God, who proceeds from the Father who is for us, is present as the Son who is for us, and is fulfilled in the Spirit's work in us.

Barth finds it a significant question to ask how freely God is able to be revealed as Lord. Is God prevented from communicating with us in any way because of His deity? Does being God keep Him from speaking to humble and fallible humans?

On the flip side, it is also important to ask: How free are humans in their knowing processes? God has taken a risk manifesting Himself to us. Who knows how badly we might abuse what He gives to us? Can we think of any ways that God is prevented from being known by us because of the problems associated with our alienated humanity?

Barth affirms that the grace of God is His freedom for us, unhindered in any way.

But how can God reveal Himself? The actuality of God answers this question.

God is free for us and in us. We are free to the point that we let Him be for us and work in us.

The grace of God is known in His unhindered way of being for us and in our unconditional way of living in this freedom, which is His gift.

> But how can God reveal Himself? The actuality of God answers this question.

The doctrine of the incarnation means the Word of God made flesh as a human.

Jesus is not just a perfected statue for us to look at. He is the speaking, engaging person of God, who is overtly for us in active affirmation—freely God and freeing us.

Jesus is revealed and then interpreted; we must keep this order in our investigation. Otherwise, our interpretations will usurp and cast a shadow over Jesus' revelation.

We cannot come to God thinking we can tell Him what our needs are and demand how He needs to meet us. We cannot provide the bridge God must cross to meet us. That would be a bridge to nowhere.

It is easy to create a god from the divine convictions in one's heart. Grasping at big ideas, we will miss the living God. This is like looking for the perfect spouse and not learning to love the one we are with. Possible ideal persons become mirages distracting us from the flesh and blood before us.

The writers of the Bible do not argue for the possibility of God. That course of thought ends up projecting from our experience of human conscience, goodness, or some other potential attribute being utilized to create a logical bridge to the existence of God. God is not an idea, although we can have our ideas formed by God.

In the same way that one does not argue for the existence of the sun because of warmth in our human body, so we do not argue for God because we think and feel. No, because the sun is there, we become witnesses to what is seen and felt, but it cannot be touched.

The sun itself is the actuality that allows for the possibilities of apprehending and seeing, not only it but all it touches.

Jesus is the actuality that precedes all possibilities for human knowing.

In all science, one must first acknowledge "what is to be studied." One must believe that the object of study is there, or one cannot go on to interpret what is studied. Mythical creatures are made up by human minds and are not interpreted as fact. All actual beings are available at some point for study as subjects. These subjects act meaningfully in contexts and can be interpreted.

Jesus is the subject who is the face of God with humanity and for humanity. We can explore the possibility of understanding Jesus because He has actually come. In this way, actuality informs possibility in knowing.

The Bible is not the revelation of "ideas about God" but of "God in the flesh" as a person who speaks to us. We have a vocal God.

God is revealed in the simplicity of Jesus; this one human is the straightforward presence of God.

The reality of Jesus is the once-for-all reality of God. In Him, God is definite, unrepeated, and comes as an event in human history.

The God who exists eternally as the Son is known as Jesus Christ in history.

The Word of God is known in the man Jesus of Nazareth.

The New Testament contains the content of God's incarnation, witnessing to His taking on human flesh.

Jesus of Nazareth is God's Son. We need to look at this from two directions:

1. God's Word is identical with a human, the man Jesus. We have a human person who shows us God.
2. The man Jesus is identical with the Word or Son of God. We actually get to know God when we look at this human.

Jesus does not and should not be fit with any prior human ideas about divinity. In Him and Him alone, we discover the Godhead.

Jesus does not just seem to be human (Docetism) while showing us God; He is God in His unique manifestation in this man.

Jesus does not just seem to be God while acting in some heroic form of humanity (Ebionite); Jesus takes us into the actual inner life of God as God.

The early witnesses in the New Testament could only stammer, "We have met God, we have heard His Word."

Jesus was not seen as just a great man. He was and is the presence of God's Word, the Word made flesh.

That God's Son is Jesus of Nazareth is the one christological thesis of the New Testament. This is the correlate of the fact that the human Jesus is God's Son. Both are necessary as one true reality. This is the double basis of doing theology that is true to God and humanity.

When we say Jesus Christ, we speak of this person who is not a synthesis but a person who is the fullness of God and human in one reality: very God and very Man.

In Jesus, we have an objective focus for our study of God's reality.

God's freedom is not an abstract concept; it is the very fact that Jesus is for us.

2. Jesus Christ the Objective Possibility of Revelation (pp. 25–44)

The actuality of Jesus being the freedom of God for us allows us to discuss the possibility of God's freedom being experienced by us humans.

Because God has been revealed as being freely for humanity, we can focus on discussing a reality that actually concerns us instead of musing about what might be possible as human imagination or logic.

The fact of the freedom of God for us in Jesus enables us to ask what this means for us humans. Not only *might* we ask what this means for us; we *must* ask what it means so that our actual life is conformed to the reality of God. We ought not to become like those who claim another reality, born of human fancies, upon which to build their lives.

There is a good way to go on in life, using our best knowledge and conscience. This is the scientific way; it is a path of discovery attending to God's revelation.

There are many bad ways to go in thinking about God: speculating, popular opinion, or intellectualizing. All those attempts aim at conforming our thinking about God to human categories and arguments alone.

> God's freedom is not an abstract concept; it is the very fact that Jesus is for us.

The question now is: How is it possible for God to reveal Godself to humanity? Scripture tells us it is possible because it happened. How far can God's revelation take us in truly knowing God?

If we let ourselves be told that Jesus Christ is the revelation of God, we are faced with the objective possibility of divine revelation.

Either God is completely hidden. Or God is freely revealed in the humanness of Jesus, and we see that the Godness of Jesus discloses that He is for us. Hiddenness is not eliminated, but is addressed by the One who reveals.

While the fullness of God's revelation is available in Jesus, God limits His freedom to be for us in Jesus alone and in no other way.

Humans can live with a self-chosen blindness to God and assume the hiddenness of God is God's problem. However, that sightlessness is a denial of the actuality grounded in the factuality of God's self-giving and God's specific way of being free for humanity.

God is not free to be possessed, conformed to human thought, or denied. These stances can only lead to forms of human unfreedom or illusions.

In revelation, we see that God, who was hidden, is seen. This establishes the qualitative difference between God and humanity and the pressing need to bring us together. We were blind; now we might see.

What we discover in God's revelation is that God is freely for us, and beforehand we could only live in blindness. Therefore, God provides freedom for humanity in seeing who He is for us.

When we look from our place of blindness, there is a boundary; God is hidden. But God has crossed that boundary.

God has freely come to us to give us freedom that only God can and has given.

To speak of impossibilities—or other possible ways of knowing God's free giving of Himself to us—is to bypass the actuality.

Our task is only to deal with reality, and that is given in Jesus.

We must discuss possibilities only from actualities for engaging realities:

1. God has come to us in the form of a reality different from Himself. God has crossed the boundary from unknown to known and remains Himself in coming to us. We know it is possible for God to become human because He actually has. In this free act, God has desired to be our Mediator, and only God could bridge the gap to fulfill our freedom in person.

2. *God* has become human in Jesus. The Father and Holy Spirit are not human. In spite of this distinction, Jesus is fully God as a human. The person of the Son became flesh without losing His essential being in relation to the Father and Spirit. The Father is the divine *who* (is revealed), the Son is the *what* (of God revealed), and the Spirit is the *how* (God is revealed). Jesus becoming human is a work of the whole Trinity. But only the Son is human. God's nature is not solitary, but it shares the harmonious work of the three modes of this one God for us. But there is also a similarity between this human and our humanity so that, through Him, we become God's children.

3. God has come as one of us to be for us. Jesus freely comes in a form that is recognizable to us as humans. Jesus could have remained foreign to us, but instead He comes in a form perceptible to us as a fellow human. He forms the basis of analogies that are appropriate to our created nature. Jesus is also God visible, revealing the hiddenness of God. God bends down to us not as a stranger but as the restorer of our original connection. Jesus demonstrates God's love for us; this is grace enacted unconditionally to restore what was lost.

4. Jesus comes in a form familiar to us. He maintains hiddenness even while revealing that He is part of this cosmos. Jesus becomes a human, but one crucified and resurrected. Jesus united creation to Himself in taking on the body of creation. No one else could have shown us the Father, except for His own Word, His Son. No one else could have spoken to us—only the One who took our existence to Himself for our sakes.

5. Jesus becomes what we are. We are flesh. He became flesh. And we stand before God as flesh, even as our humanity is dying. If we

are alive, it is because we are encountering God's restoring work and verdict on our behalf. Jesus stands as the human for all other humans before the Father. While we were dead in our separation, Jesus has made us alive in His person. He is the one true human acting for all untrue humans.

Nothing is more puzzling to us than our fellow humans.

Conversely, nothing is closer to us than our fellow humans, who are constitutive of ourselves.

To encounter other humans in the flesh is basic to our existence. "To live as a man means to be related to man, to differ from him and to agree with him, to come from man and depend on man."[3]

Our words are human words, and we encounter others through language to see and hear. Acknowledging the objectivity of those who are other than ourselves allows us to converse.

Other humans are near and dear as those belonging to us, or they may be neighbors whom we might desire to know. Yet so much is hidden—we are sinners before each other and God, separated by our flesh. We stand under the verdict of a closed door with God and each other.

> Jesus stands as the door that opens the possibility of our reconnection to God and one another.

Jesus stands as the door that opens the possibility of reconnection to God and one another.

Jesus reveals that much is hidden but not lost. So much is revealed in one specific place or, rather, one person.

Humans have no properties that make them special bearers to reveal God. We are hidden from one another, and God is hidden from us.

The good news is that in Jesus we see God and we see humanity in true form.

Jesus had to become flesh in order that God's revelation would be possible.

COMMENTARY:

- In this section on how humans come to know and hear God's address, we find that there is only one sure way for this to happen, which is in knowing Jesus as witnessed to in the Bible.
- While some may say, "I do not see God," God is there to be seen in the person of Jesus.

---

3. *CD* 1.2, § 13, p. 42.

- If we are going to talk about a vast and hidden God who cannot be known, we would have to silence the voice of Jesus and the testimony of those who heard Him.
- Barth's theology has a scientific character. He will always direct us to the actualities of history. He will not succumb to the philosophies and human experiences that "feel" like what proponents imagine God must be like (conscience, power, goodness, etc.).
- God is free for humanity, and this does not just imply some unbridled choice. Freedom means God's choosing to be with us in a manner we can apprehend. It actually creates a freeing impact. To live in response to the personal embrace of God is to experience God's freedom (and not isolation). To hear "I know and love you" creates a freedom not available in "I do not know you or want to know you."
- Barth does not say Jesus a thousand times merely to etch our thinking, although that may happen. He says Jesus repeatedly because to say His name is to speak of the presence of the true God as made available to us.
- We experience Him as the true human, living the connected life for which we were created; at least that is what happens when we listen to Him. In speaking His name, we pay attention to Him.
- We know God *can* be free for us because He *has* become free for us in Jesus.

CONCLUSION FOR THE CHURCH: The Church must find its mission and proclamation in the God who acts in Jesus Christ. Every other program is an imitation at best and competition at worst. Jesus is the reality of revelation in human history in the form of a human. The fullness of the good news for the Church is that God has freely taken this specific way of being so that He is able to connect with humanity. And as God's Word, Jesus remains God in this form. We get to meet the One who is fully God and fully takes on our nature and speaks our language. And we discover that He has already acted on our behalf.

From now on, the solitary starting point for discussion is the fact that God has fulfilled this act of incarnation. Only in light of this self-giving can we now possibly and properly say anything about God—and that only in response to what He has said to us. We are not in a glamorous theme park or on a shopping spree, looking for our happiness to be fulfilled our way, accommodating to our desires. We are waking up to reality, and it is personal.

INSIGHT FOR PASTORS: In this section, Barth wants to make clear the task of the Church. As a human community, the Church points to the actuality of God in Jesus. We do not invite people into the Church to learn about principles or truths about God to improve our lives or understanding. First, we stand with God, who has come in the person of Jesus. Second, we speak of Him and for Him in our churches. Third, we speak in a human language as Jesus did. Finally, we respond to God as the God who loves us.

In our proclamation as a Church, we adore Jesus when we come to embrace and engage Jesus, who is already available for us. We see that Jesus, as God, meets us as humans who are to be known, embraced, and in the end, to whom we belong. When people ask, "How can I possibly know this God whom I have never met in person?" we can say that this God has come and, by His Word, still comes to speak to us. God has chosen not to be separate from what He created. He has chosen to enter this life to be with us—then, now, and into the fullness of the future. Jesus is the doorway out of our hiddenness into His hospitality.

INSIGHT FOR THEOLOGIANS: This section presents a scientific argument intended to separate illusion from actuality when it comes to talking about God. Any speech or illustration regarding God that begins with "in our experience" or "I am sure it makes sense to you" is a misstep. That methodology will most likely follow human ideals and logic of projection, transference, and bias in an attempt to get to God. We are told that many lenses show us God, but they distort and leave us confused. But Barth commits to remove all other claims for doing theology. He resists all routes that seek to know God other than the way God has freely chosen. For gaining appropriate clarity, God must open the way from hiddenness to being known.

Being known cannot be reduced to mere sentences and propositions. We must know God in person. All true theology and proclamation must pass certain criteria. To make theological claims and proclamations in the Church and world, we must clearly determine the focus of study, even if He is not sitting in front of us. In order to build constructive theology, we must accept that the ascended Jesus is still with us. We must investigate this unique person who is still God, and thus we must study in continuity with what Jesus has said, promised, and is still saying. That is part of the ongoing mission by the Spirit. Theological science must answer to Jesus. Every claim must be tested to confirm it is true to His nature and life. This is verification that looks for falsification not of Jesus but of imposed claims and ideas that are alien to Him.

? CLARIFYING QUESTIONS: Does your theology begin by looking at the orderliness of the world, your interpretation of what is important in the Bible, or following a system of thought? *Or* is your theology daily learning from Jesus, who is alive and asks you to follow Him, listen to His voice, and live in Him as He lives in you?

A NOTE ON *IN PLACE OF A FOREWORD* FOR *CD* 1.2

Barth lays out for us why the church will go on, sustained, into the future. It is not because of us!

Jesus will sustain the church. He was, is, and is to come. We see the past, present, and future in *CD* 1.2, but always with reference to Jesus' revelation and the work of the Spirit through Scripture in the Church.

Jesus is the same yesterday, today, and forever. We are not building a new life and ministry apart from Jesus in order to speak in our time. God speaks now and forever. His Word will not pass away.

Quoting Luther, Barth ends with, "And may there come finally the revelation of the glorious liberty and blessedness of the children of God, for which they wait and hope in patience. To which all those who love the appearing of Christ our life will say from the heart, Amen, Amen."[4]

---

4. *CD* 1.2, p. xi.

CHAPTER 21

TIMES OF PREPARATION, PARTICIPATION, AND REMINISCING

§ 14. *The Time of Revelation*

FOCUS STATEMENT: A mountain is more than a static object. It has a history stretching into the past, pulsates in seasons of the present, and has a future that lives out mountainous possibilities. Ancient strata of rock are shaped by elegant waterfalls. Splashes of rainbows radiate in that graceful flow. This history, past and present, is an event that can be seen as the life of the mountain. That bigger picture will prepare us to think about "The Time of Revelation" and the life of God in which we find ourselves addressed. The point of this chapter is to summarize § 14 in the *CD*, which opens up the context of God's life as the context for our placement within God's event of self-giving in its grand, personal scope.

INTRODUCTION: We are still in chapter 2 on the revelation of God, focused specifically on the incarnation of God in His Son. Barth wants to set the stage of "an event" that is a much larger concept than a momentary occurrence or event within a human era. Barth sets a large stage to bring to bear all the vast, unnoticed, extended implications of what God has been and is still doing in opening our self-understanding in God's context of time and space. Of course, meaning always depends on context, so this is meaningful time seen in the light of Christ, as Barth clarifies for us.

CONTEXT: *CD* 1.2
Pages in Paragraph: 77 pages (pp. 45–121)

Subsections
1. God's Time and Our Time
2. The Time of Expectation
3. The Time of Recollection

📖 **TEXT:** § 14. The Time of Revelation

OPENING SUMMARY: God's revelation in the event of the presence of Jesus Christ is God's time for us. It is fulfilled time in this event itself. But as the Old Testament time of expectation and as the New Testament time of recollection it is also the time of witness to this event.[1]

✠ **SUMMARY:**

1. God's Time and Our Time (pp. 45–70)

God makes time to be with us. God has time for us.

God's taking on flesh in Jesus means God comes to us in time, not in abstract ideas.

Revelation means there is a time of coming, Jesus present with humanity. It is an event of engagement as God's time encounters us in our time on this planet.

Time is not bigger than God, although it has been conceived of as a vast stage within which God appears. Rather, time is the appearing of God as all that God has created for us, as the act of His being to make space for us.

There is no other time beyond the time in which we live. We experience time as God's act of revelation. That we live in time bespeaks that God is for us and has time for us; therefore, time is a revelation that God has made and within which God gives meaning that is acted out as God's revelation.

Revelation alone tells us the meaning of time. The mere occurrence of the progression of days does not give us the meaning of time.

We must listen to God's revelation to understand the time of God's self-revealing, to apprehend it in its event form, intended to unveil the God who has been veiled.

If we think from "my time" and "our era" as the lens to understand time, we will default to our human observation, concerns, and sense of the events we witness.

Our memories, our expectations, and our sense of presence are unsuitable measurements to understand God's time. Those perceptions tell us about ourselves but are inadequate to understand God's revelation in time.

In order to know God, humans cannot merely focus on our self-determination of time—how we plan our days—to frame our existence as creatures in the cosmos. We live within the gift of time but erroneously think we have control over our time.

---

1. *CD* 1.2, § 14, p. 45.

God's good, created time has been ruptured by the fall so that we have a defective sense of time that surrounds us. We experience time as separate beings rather than as those participating in God's time.

There is an original sense of time (created time). Then there is the time we sense as fallen time (lost time). A third sense is to be affirmed in light of Jesus' revelation.

There is this given time of revelation, when God steps into our lost time and, in the event of Jesus Christ, shows us real time—that is, with God's view of the past recollected and the future anticipated.

To say Jesus Christ is to speak of God with a human, temporal presence. As a human, Jesus has a past and a future known only to God but made known to us in his time on Earth.

Revelation means time, implies time, brings significance to time, and refocuses us into correspondence with God in that it is a historical movement of God to act in our time.

The Old Testament and New Testament speak with reference to the time of God as the historical time of God with us. The Bible is not a philosophy book or speculation beyond time.

The time of Jesus Christ is the time of the Lord of time; therefore, it is fulfilled time.

Jesus is the same yesterday, today, and tomorrow. There is no sense that He is not the faithful Word of God, that he is "not yet" or will "no longer" be the eternal Word who speaks what is faithful and true. He speaks as this Word in our time.

As the Lord of time, Jesus is always before us and after us, as well as with us and for us.

The phrase "God reveals Himself" means the same as "God has time for us." To give someone your time is to give them yourself. But God alone has real time to give. And He does not ration out time. He gives us each the fullness of His time.

> As the Lord of time, Jesus is always before us and after us, as well as with us and for us.

We may come to share God's real time. He directs His Word to us that we may become contemporary with Him, free in His time to be with Him.

The light of Jesus is particular, but like light in a dark room, it fills the whole space.

The light can be seen in those places where the light has come. If we look for the light in history, for a revelation apart from this particular light, we will miss the light that has come as fulfilled time.

God's revelation becomes history; however, we must not be confused and think that all history is revelation.

Real time is understood only from the person of the Son, who acts and speaks. All other time is apprehended as human time without God and is therefore lost time, separated from God, an illusion, an opinion, and a non-genuine perception.

"God reveals Himself" means that this Word is the truth, which reveals the Master of time.

"God reveals Himself" is resisted by humans who deny the Lord of time and set in His place their own statements about time as human understandings of history. God's revelation then becomes offensive to our sense of time, and we rebel.

"God reveals Himself" means that the new time breaks into the middle of the old time as a miracle.

Our time will always be in the neighborhood of real time. Our time is a sign and a shadow that points to the real and hidden time. This assessment includes all human perception of the past and future time.

We clarify the relation of our time to real time by affirming:

1. Real time is what nourishes and restores us as the Son reveals our contemporariness to God. He does not point to our lostness in the passing away time of this world.
2. Real time makes concrete the meaning of time. It therefore eliminates the vagueness that we have in understanding time.
3. Real time announces but does not bring to completion the fulfillment of our lost time. This lost time still operates as something limited and somewhat complete. God is at hand but has not ended fallen time.
4. Real time ends the myth of endless time. When our time consciousness is aware of real time, it makes us congruous with God's time. Rather than act in light of the limitations of our time, we are opened to the origin and intention of God's acts in time that call for our participation. We "wait on the Lord" not passively but as the Spirit brings us to actively live in real time, the kingdom coming.

2. The Time of Expectation (pp. 70–101)

Once we see Jesus as defining fulfilled time, we can see that a preparatory time is coordinated with His time.

The time before Jesus' incarnation is pretime that anticipates the revelation of God in Jesus.

This pretime is a witness to the expectation of the coming of Jesus. It is the time of the Old Testament. It is not a separated time; it is bound up with the time of fulfillment.

The Old Testament points to what is coming and so rises above other times as it anticipates what is beyond human history. It signals ahead to the time fulfilled in God's coming in Jesus.

The Old Testament does not just rise to the peak of human wisdom among the religions of that era. It is also a witness to God's inbreaking, preparing humans for what is to come. There is still a hiddenness, even as the prophetic word reveals what is coming. What was hidden could only be recognized after the revelation was fulfilled.

The New Testament recollects all that was proclaimed as it pointed toward its fulfillment in Jesus.

Jesus Christ was already the Expected One in the Old Testament.

Three connections can be made between the Old and New Testament times.

1. The Old and New Testaments are witnesses to the unique, concrete actions of God. They both proclaim to humans, "You are mine," in a covenant of gracious faithfulness extended as self-renewing adoption by God. The expectation of obedience is fulfilled in the person of Jesus as its completion.
2. The Old and New Testaments disclose a hidden God who reveals Himself in the midst of a godless world. The old and the new works of God are seen in Israel and in Christ as the suffering God brings mercy in mystery with His covenant partner. This displays the Crucified One making peace with sinful humanity.
3. The Old and New Testaments witness to the present and coming God. Even in His hiddenness, God is fulfilling the future. For us, there is a waiting that hastens to meet the God who is coming to the door.

We stand before the covenant-making God who is hidden but sustaining. At the same time, we are sustained by the God who shows us the finished work yet to come.

The image of the people of God anticipating the promised land is a meeting of the liberating act of God and the vision of its fulfillment.

The story of the tabernacling God, who exercises lordship for judgment and grace, reveals a redeeming God who lives to be King at a given time for a chosen people.

There will come a day when the King will fulfill all the covenant promises for His people.

The Messiah is the hope of Israel, the breaking in of God. He interrupts all other human histories with a real historical event.

In the Old Testament, God's covenant is revealed but not realized. From the fulfilled time of the New Testament, we can see the expectation fulfilled and standing at the door.

"The mystery of revelation, which is the mystery of free, unmerited grace, includes the Church of the New Testament inseparably with the people whose blessing is attested for us in the Old Testament as expectation of Jesus Christ."[2]

3. The Time of Recollection (pp. 101–21)

The New Testament has a particular task as a witness, a recollection of the fulfilled time of revelation in the person of Jesus Christ.

The New Testament is not a witness to general history but to the revelation of God in person.

To read the New Testament is to participate in a genuine act of recollection. The text must speak and fashion our hearing so that we may respond to Him who is its focus.

The New Testament writers can only offer a subsequent description of what they have witnessed as the revelation of God. Jesus is the revelation; they are witnesses to Him.

1. The New and Old Testaments make known a togetherness of God and humanity freely facilitated by God. God becoming human has been the goal of the Old Testament. The New Testament knows only one covenant, one *Now* that is the person of Jesus Christ who is the same yesterday, today, and tomorrow. Jesus is the togetherness of God and humanity.

> The New Testament is not a witness to general history but to the revelation of God in person.

2. The New and Old Testaments witness to the revelation of the hidden God. The tension between God and humanity is resolved in the God, who Himself experiences and

---

2. *CD* 1.2, § 14, p. 101.

bears the godforsakenness. One has died for all that He may deal with suffering and the evil world. He is risen to speak a "Yes" that is a "No" to human suffering.

3. The New and Old Testaments present the God who is coming to humankind. The Easter Story is the recollection to which all other recollections are related. This time is the pure time of all times. It is the pure presence of God with humanity. This is the time of fulfillment for the coming Christ. The Messiah has come. This time is not only behind us; it is in front of us. He who came is He who comes today.

Revelation remains ongoing. It does not become a past revealed state. It is not a bygone event but lives as the ongoing event of God's time in which humanity partakes in God's fulfilled time.

In our time we hear Jesus say even today, "I am with you to the end of the age" (see Matthew 28:20).

COMMENTARY:

- This section is intended to open our minds to see that God is not to be thought of abstractly and timelessly. Instead, God has provided time for being known.
- We are coached in this section to move away from thinking merely through our own point of view with the filters of our past, present, and future.
- We are invited to see that, from God's point of view, the time of Jesus is the bounding together of all time that exists before Him and after Him. He draws all times into Himself so that He is present to all times and made known in His being as the Lord of Time.
- What was proclaimed in the past—in that person of Jesus, in that place—is still spoken as present to us and still contemporary for us if we will hear.
- We cannot merely say "God has spoken." We must say that "God is speaking." This is true because His Word, who entered and addresses all time, is still addressing us through Him.
- The Old Testament is history but not mere human history. It is historical time that is already aware of Him who was coming as the Messiah. It is history that lives in tension between an expectation of and an awareness of a time that is coming—that would be the time of God's unveiling.

- The New Testament is a witness that is not simply a record of events and sayings but the turning of our eyes toward the revelation of God, who is the person Jesus Christ. His revealing of the purposes of God in time permeates our understanding. He makes available knowledge of all God has been doing. He shows that God's work is still active as we recollect what was promised. This realization happens for us within a time of reconnection, now in focus because of what has been made evident in Jesus being made clear by the Spirit.

- The Old Testament not only proclaims that a train is coming but also is the train. We discover that the train was coming as we greet its arrival. Those who are on it did not fully know its destination, but the conductor knew.

- The New Testament is a witness that the train has come, and it is not just a record that it came and went as a recollection, but that we got on that train.

- We are now still on that train.

- We must understand ourselves in the context of the movement of the train as the kingdom, not merely in the context of the places we live.

- We are going with Him from a place that originates in the past, moves toward His destination, and now is with Him (as anticipated, remembered, entered, and now experienced) as part of the whole event of His being the Lord of Time. (This is only a metaphor and has potential challenges but gives structure to the outlined perspective).

- Proclamation happens in space and time; it is historical. It is personal in that it reveals Jesus in a manner that resets our thinking to personally live within real time, His time.

CONCLUSION FOR THE CHURCH: The Church must find its context for existing through a dynamic encounter in the history of the God who is portrayed in the Bible. God is not to be known as an abstract idea outside time and space. God is known in the creation of time and particularly in the revealing time of Jesus Christ, who gives meaning to all other times and to the Church. The Old Testament anticipates His coming and the New Testament facilitates a recollection that reminds us that Jesus is still present today as the fulfillment of what is revealed of God for the building up of the Church in the world.

If we try to be relevant to our times, we abandon God's time and deflate the meaning of time into the slogans of time management for human agendas. If we think we do not have time for Jesus, it exposes our sense of being lord over our time. A key task of the Church is to reorient to the time of "Thy kingdom come" (Matthew 6:10 KJV) as living within Jesus' fulfillment of time. This cannot be put on the calendar; instead, we must use the time we have to live within Jesus' intentions and to make them our own as we plan and act with Him now.

INSIGHT FOR PASTORS: Congregations can easily think of Jesus as an ancient figure whom we cannot hear today. Barth's conversation here breaks Jesus free from our limited understanding of time. He frees our thinking and hearing to know that the living Jesus is made concrete in human history. The historical record does not provide the full extent of His ability to speak to our time. This section moves us from the "God who has spoken" to the "God who now speaks." This invites a reading of the Old and New Testaments that is less about the literature, author, and recipients (although these are all important) and more about asking us to see the revelation of God in time and space. It is more than a shift to daylight savings time; it is like moving somewhere that thinks in relation to a person, not a clock. That person is Jesus, who is timeless with regard to the extent of His involvement with humanity. If we think He is absent in our time, we are stuck in our own time zone. If we believe He is present, we will align with Him like we are on safari or on a rescue mission. Time yields to the person who leads.

If we can change from thinking only about what is relevant to our time to thinking first of Jesus' meaningful embrace of all times and persons, our perspective will shift from self-serving to God-serving as we attune to His actions and intentions in time.

INSIGHT FOR THEOLOGIANS: This section prevents the theologian from reading our interpretations of history as God's intention. That course is taken by some. This section of the *CD* is resistant to a natural theology of time. Our natural inclination is to see time as past, present, and future as we understand them. Then we see God in our past and future and hope He is in our present. We are coercing God to bless our sense of time.

The affirmation that Jesus is the time that God has for humanity keeps the focus on God's meaning and actions being informed by Jesus. This is the appropriate result of God's being the Lord of time. Barth's method stands against all searches for the historical Jesus outside His revelation. Even the witnesses and writers are not the authoritative interpreters of time. Their task, privilege, and service were to point to the One who fulfills God's purposes for all time.

The Old Testament is not merely a history of Israel. It is the time that anticipates and prepares for the One who is coming. The New Testament is not simply a collection of literature to be mined for insight into how to live. It is an event of recollection that God has and will continue to break into human history. This God will always make time because He has made time in Jesus to be with humanity and will be faithful to His promise and people.

? CLARIFYING QUESTIONS: Does your theology present time as a sequence of human eras into which Jesus comes and points to another time after this life, eternal time? *Or* does Jesus' coming provide for you a fullness of seeing time as transformed into a way of seeing God's purposes fulfilled in Jesus? Is the kingdom of God a place, or is it the space and time where Jesus is present to bring His purposes to fulfillment? If you say, "I do not have time for that," what does that say about who sets the priorities for your use of time?

CHAPTER 22

DISCOVERING THE BEING AND BECOMING OF THE MOUNTAIN

§ 15. *The Mystery of Revelation*

FOCUS STATEMENT: A mountain is a mystery that displays both solidity and dynamic movement. It invites us to climb without a complete understanding. Its being cannot be captured in laboratories. It cannot be understood when isolated to one season. We may be limited profoundly in our ability to understand its history in becoming what it is. We are much less in touch with all it will be. But we can get a glimpse of its invitation and engage the mystery if we pay attention to what it gracefully makes available.

This posture prepares us to engage "The Mystery of Revelation" that is discovered in the person of Jesus Christ. Although He is human, Jesus is not reducible merely to human categories. Hearing who He is as God takes listening that is not normal for us. Nevertheless, Jesus captures our attention as we wonder at the miracle He is revealed to be. The point of this chapter is to summarize § 15 in the *CD*. In it, we come to know the way to enter into the privilege of knowing this unique God-human person. We come to realize that He is the touch point of all our knowing regarding God and humanity.

INTRODUCTION: This section brings us to focus on the epicenter of God's self-giving. Here we will consider the complexity of God as made known. We must resist all desires to fit Jesus into the categories of our thinking. He must teach us the very grammar of what we are apprehending and its meaning in the context of His mission. As we develop a confidence in who He is, we must acknowledge He is beyond our grasp for certain knowledge.

CONTEXT: *CD* 1.2
Pages in Paragraph: 80 pages (122–202)

Subsections

1. The Problem of Christology
2. Very God and Very Man
3. The Miracle of Christmas

📖 **TEXT: § 15. The Mystery of Revelation**

OPENING SUMMARY: The mystery of the revelation of God in Jesus Christ consists in the fact that the eternal Word of God chose, sanctified and assumed human nature and existence into oneness with Himself, in order thus, as very God and very man, to become the Word of reconciliation spoken by God to man. The sign of this mystery revealed in the resurrection of Jesus Christ is the miracle of His birth, that He was conceived by the Holy Ghost, born of the Virgin Mary.[1]

✠ **SUMMARY:**

1. The Problem of Christology (pp. 122–32)

Having established that God is free to come to humanity and that God actually has made time to come to humanity, we now prepare to listen to what this personal revelation tells us about God and what it means to be human.

Theological discussions have lost their way by talking about God. Think about the difference between someone talking about you versus talking to you to get to know you. The "about" conversations falter by looking at the human experience of being human and then derivatively talking about God—this is called Natural Theology.

If the Church is to have Christian knowledge, it must begin solely with the person of Jesus Christ and the Trinity. Any other starting point is a foreign encroachment on our knowledge of God and ourselves.

The Church will only be restored again when it avoids general truths about God, supposedly discerned from creation. Only then can it really listen to God in the person of Jesus.

God chose to take on human form to speak and actualize reconciliation with humanity in Himself.

The goal of God to enact reconciliation comes into focus exclusively through God's intent to reveal and cannot be limited to our capabilities for understanding. It is God's mystery to facilitate and to fulfill in God's way.

In doing the work of Christology, we come to listen and learn the limits

---

1. *CD* 1.2, § 15, p. 122.

of the starting point. Christology focuses us on all that God has exercised for humanity in acting for us.

The early Church had as its central proclamation that God has become one with humanity in the man Jesus Christ, who is fully God and fully human.

The mystery of Christ's incarnation cannot be solved, but it can be recognized. Jesus is not a picture of perfection in the clouds or a system of perfected ethics to imitate.

If we let ourselves be led scientifically to Christ, to know His being by listening to those prepared to witness to His revelation, we will conclude that Jesus is rightly recognized as wholly God and human.

2. Very God and Very Man (pp. 132–71)

Who is Jesus Christ? The answer is given in the phrase "The Word made flesh" (see John 1:14).

As Word, Jesus proclaims God as God.

Jesus as the Word is the "divine, creative, reconciling, redeeming" participation of this man in the divine nature who comes to us as one of us.[2] These four words reflect the four volumes of the *CD*.

Affirmations to clarify the prime fact of Jesus as the Word:

1. Jesus is the speaker, the subject who is the source of what is said. Jesus is not a product of this world. He is the speaking act of God, who addresses His creation.
2. The Word speaking is a free act, not necessitated by any logical demand on God by humanity, to fix what is broken. No, this free Word lavishes unwarranted love as a free expression of God. An alienated creature receives this miracle of love.
3. The Word is God in unstoppable divine action. "The Word speaks, the Word acts, the Word prevails, the Word reveals, the Word reconciles."[3] Jesus is not a word pointing to God; He is God in the process of engaging His creation.
4. Mary can rightly be called the Mother of God in that she was the woman, the mother who bore the Son of God in the flesh. We ought not to worship her, but we recognize the claim made of her is because of who Jesus is as God in her womb enfleshed. Mary is the mother of this Jesus. We honor Mary with a Christological interest.

---

2. *CD* 1.2, § 15, p. 132.
3. *CD* 1.2, § 15, p. 136.

As "flesh," Jesus proclaims His humanity. In both form and nature (embodied and personal), He participates in our fleshly way of being. He shares the same historicity with which we humans live.

All that can be ascribed to humans may be established as true of the divine One who comes as flesh.

This man's life became the theater of the acts of God in the world. He is the Light that reveals God for humanity in this world's history.

God was in Christ in person. He is the active presence of God that makes revelation possible.

> Jesus as the Word is the "divine, creative, reconciling, redeeming" participation of this man in the divine nature who comes to us as one of us. These four words reflect the four volumes of the *CD*.

By becoming flesh, Jesus became a participant in real human affairs and being.

Jesus did not cease to be God when He took on flesh. He became what He was previously not, a specific human in the flesh.

Jesus was never a being other than Himself. He was never a being by Himself. But He was a being as the Son of God, now in the flesh.

Jesus is already the Word of God related to human nature; He is grace related to fallen humanity.

Jesus represents God to us, and He represents humanity to God. As one person, He reveals God to us and reconciles us with God.

Jesus not only takes on the material form of our existence, our fleshly being, He also takes on our alienated, guilty existence, worthy of death.

It is humanity's fallen existence that Jesus embodies. He personifies our nature, originally made for communion but now destroyed. He indwells our being, as those opposed to God and otherwise inaccessible to His grace. Jesus takes on all of Adam's separated being when He comes to share our flesh.

Jesus took on the body of our sin to take away the sinful nature that needed to be addressed.

Jesus did not come to merely teach us, pronounce a judgment over us as a perfect judge, or model what perfection looks like. He took on our sinful humanity to crucify it and give us a new humanity in Himself.

As God, Jesus takes on sinful human form. In that state, He shows the meaning of reconciling action in this world.

Jesus embraces our unholy human existence to draw near to us.

Jesus' obedience was seen in the fact that He took on the burden of human sin and all its consequences that must be borne by humanity in its alienation.

Jesus does not take on a prefall form of humanity. He takes on the bent and twisted character of Adam to deal with the burden and consequences of human violation against God.

Jesus completely bows before the grace of God with the sinner's verdict upon Him. In conceding all rights to God, He draws the world out of its rebellion to be reconciled to God. He acts as one on behalf of the many.

Jesus "became," not as a surrendering of His divinity but as a proper expression, a miraculous act of God's mercy.

Jesus becomes, as a human being, the present and audible Word of God addressed to humanity.

To say Jesus "assumed" human flesh is helpful in affirming that He never lost his divinity.

The fact that Jesus became a man is not a change or transformation in His being as God.

Once and for all, God became human so His Word would reach the ears of those He intended to reconcile to Himself.

What is said about Jesus is said about the actuality of what has happened, once for all, achieving union between God and the humanity assumed by Jesus.

The miracle of the incarnation reveals that God freely came to us without becoming unlike Himself in assuming our likeness as a human being.

Every question to be asked of God and His being known in the world must be directed to this one human who is the Word of God. Any other avenue that evades this focus will be a nonexistent and meaningless shadow.

The "coming to be" of the birth, death, resurrection, and ascension of Jesus is the actuality that allows us to recognize the reality demonstrated to us.

God's personal action is the basis of human faith. We respond to the actuality made known in Jesus—God's act is the basis of human faith.

To say Jesus became flesh is to work with a completed event. That occurrence established the actuality of the God-human who brings union through reconciliation.

The incarnation is the prime mystery and gives us the content of our comprehension in experience.

God does not fit into our experiences as a conformity to our perceptions. Rather, He takes us beyond what we thought was possible. We attune to His reality; He does not conform to our belief systems. Jesus interrupts human reason to jar it back to reality.

Jesus is the new focus of our attention who will not comply with any former point of connection upon which we build our knowledge and thought.

The knowledge of God is not ours to grasp but is one that unexpectedly comes to us, dynamically gifted to us, meeting us in person.

We do not master this knowledge of God but come to submit to its reality.

3. The Miracle of Christmas (pp. 172–202)

In the incarnation, God has become present in this world, a member of it.

In the Christmas message, we find this inconceivable possibility: God has become one of us and remained God.

The miracle of Christmas is the conception of Jesus by the Holy Spirit in Mary's womb.

The importance of connection with the person of Christ compelled the inclusion of the virgin birth narratives in the New Testament.

In the virgin birth, all questions are answered with the acknowledgment that God has acted with a miracle. It is not a human enterprise. God takes full credit for this event.

The virgin birth is an event in the creaturely world that unifies the physical (material) and psychical (intentional) in space and time. In this drama, God takes the initiative.

The miracle of the virgin birth parallels the miracle of the empty tomb. Together they designate and mark out the existence of Jesus Christ in history.

The virgin birth denotes the mystery of revelation. Hiddenness acts in revealedness. The Savior is born.

The empty tomb denotes the revelation of the mystery. The mystery has become knowable. God has reconciled humanity.

The virgin birth is the sign of the thing signified: God has come in the womb of a woman (sign) to share our humanity as God (signified).

1. Jesus was born of a virgin. This signifies that it was a divine act. Thus, Jesus is born sinless. Virginity is not required for God's grace, but God's action determines the free grace of self-giving signified here.
2. Saying Jesus is born of a virgin is the negative side of the story—what is withheld from this birth (not of a human). Affirming that Jesus is conceived by the Spirit is the positive side of the witness (born of God). Mary's virginity signifies that God's other, with whom He interacts, is specifically humanity. The Holy Spirit is God's freedom to give us Himself.

Jesus is the Son of God not because He was conceived by the Holy Spirit but because He is the Son of God, and thus we acknowledge the mystery that He is born of a virgin and conceived by the Spirit.

"The mystery does not rest upon the miracle. The miracle rests upon the mystery."[4]

COMMENTARY:

- Up to this point, we have prepared the way for engaging the God who has come to us. Now we "stare Him in the eyes" and see that He is God speaking to us. We also see that He is fully a human who has become like us to fulfill His mission of bringing us back home.

- Barth feels that most theological conversations have lost their way in trying to be relevant to human concerns and experiences. That direction turns the eyes and hearts of humans away from the mystery and majesty of God who is speaking to us. This kind of theological distraction is so normal that we do not know what or who we are missing.

- In Jesus coming to us, we observe a temporary mission. God invests all He has to restore the lost relation with the world He has created. God reveals God doing something in His self-unveiling. God steps into our skin to reboot humanity in an act of reconciliation.

- Jesus is God in the form that fulfills His love for His beloved. We cannot know Him apart from His assuming the form of a human. The humanity of God is the love of God made present and available without abandoning being God.

- To say Jesus reveals the mystery of God is to say that the hiddenness has come to be known and loved, not that we will comprehend all that could be known. We behold the One who loves us and hear Him speak to invite us into that love that is foreign to us.

- Encountering Jesus is like stepping out of the senseless side of Alice's looking-glass world and seeing a world set straight for the first time.

- We cannot explain the logic of the love of God by trying to fit Jesus into our irrationality. We begin to find the logic of the God of love as He opens for us the actuality of love in action that may change all we have thought in the realization of freeing love in action.

- The virgin birth of Jesus is the event of God's intervention as God doing what only God can do to be God in human form. It does not prove that Jesus is God. It is the act of God that becomes our starting

---

4. *CD* 1.2, § 15, p. 202.

point even though it is not "reasonable" in our natural thinking and experience. We begin with actualities, not with conformity to our limited, natural thinking that denies God's possibilities.

CONCLUSION FOR THE CHURCH: Now the Church can talk about God if it will only remember where to direct its attention. It must talk in terms of the mystery of God's self-gift in the person of Jesus Christ. Spreading the news of the unveiling must never be a conversation about a God who is less than completely engaged with humanity. The compelling focus must be on who God is and how God has fully assumed our humanity. The Church is virtually defined by an expansive disseminating of this invitation. This creates a thankful answer to the invitation. The Church lives to share in Jesus' life, a life together with God. The Church can talk about the human Jesus but never without seeing that He is God in the flesh. Jesus is the dynamic data that speaks and embraces in person. There is no Christian life within the Church apart from engaging the mystery of this unique person who is the touch point between God and humanity.

INSIGHT FOR PASTORS: One of the greatest challenges for the Church is to find its focus without becoming attached to the messenger or the potential self-interest to be gained. This section is a clarion call to fix our eyes on Jesus. All the attempts at "success" as a Church that miss the Godness of Jesus and the humanity of Jesus are theological failures. To miss the face of God in Jesus is to neglect becoming a people who live in relation to God. It is not bad to be good people, care for the needy, and to provide for our families and countries. But when these good things become our focus, we lose our footing and become preoccupied with ourselves. This section of the *CD* is significant for the Church not merely for the sake of good doctrine but also so the Church might experience the dynamic relationship made available in Jesus—to know God and to see ourselves as the beloved community.

INSIGHT FOR THEOLOGIANS: There is no shortage of writings on Christology. But Barth is unique. He moves away from descriptive modes of theology that intend to create certainty through human logic and investigation. Instead, he enables theologians to humbly investigate the mystery of the interactive person named Jesus. Only He can lead us to a confident knowing of God, with a Christology fixed on who Jesus is and what He is up to.

Barth's move is simple and monumental. We go from seeing Jesus as the object of our discussion, like a display in a museum, to engaging a subject who is able to open our exploration to know the living God. This is radical, in the sense that He returns to the center. Every theological discourse that attempts to fit Jesus into existing human philosophies or to meet our existential needs is doomed to become a tainted and illusory glance. Much of the *CD* will take a stand against those outcomes. Only by seeing that God is known uniquely and particularly in Jesus can we do proper theology. Not only that, but Jesus is also the only one who can make clear what was hidden about who we are as humans. It is only natural for the many forms of human thinking to look at humans. But those modes primarily seek to give security and direction. They are instigated by human control and amount to mythologies—projections of ideas onto the divine. But Jesus opens a mystery to invite us into the reality of God. We are called to submit to the provision of God as one personally involved today. This awakens hope for theology. It is once again in a position to become a discipline that seeks to study God.

? **CLARIFYING QUESTIONS:** Does your theology depend on human experience, apologetics, looking for God in the goodness of humanity, or in the ideals of divine perfections? *Or* does your theology cause you to look undistractedly at Jesus and ask Him to speak to you and inform your thinking and, even more than that, to awaken you to the meaning of all He is up to?

CHAPTER 23

FREEDOM TO EXPLORE THE WONDER BREATHED INTO US

§ 16. The Freedom of Man for God

FOCUS STATEMENT: While beholding the beauty, majesty, and availability of the mountain set before us in all its grandeur, we are also invited to experience the freeing delight of indwelling its wonders as it invites us to play.

We are not passive in this adventure, as we see that "The Freedom of Man for God" is an opening of our horizon. We come to see that we are participants in what God discloses. Our part begins by listening and responding to the freedom that comes from discovering we are already loved and embraced. The point of this chapter leads us to understand the part that the Holy Spirit plays in activating our human response to God and the new vision of freedom that brings.

INTRODUCTION: This section finishes chapter 2, "The Revelation of God." Notice, we are still discussing God's self-disclosure. We have moved from the sources of God's self-revealing through the specifics of that revelation for us in Jesus Christ. Now we explore the work of the Spirit, who enables humans to acknowledge the approaching of God. In our response, we are freed to be the children of God as we participate in the outpouring of God's gift.

We are entering part 3 of chapter 2.

1. The Triune God (in *CD* 1.1),
2. The Incarnation of the Word (in *CD* 1.2), and
3. **The Outpouring of the Holy Spirit** (in *CD* 1.2). This part contains three paragraphs (§ 16–18), and we are looking at the first on how the Spirit establishes our freedom for God.

CONTEXT: *CD* 1.2
Pages in Paragraph: 76 pages (pp. 203–79)

Subsections
1. The Holy Spirit the Subjective Reality of Revelation
2. The Holy Spirit the Subjective Possibility of Revelation

TEXT: § 16. The Freedom of Man for God

OPENING SUMMARY: According to Holy Scripture God's revelation occurs in our enlightenment by the Holy Spirit of God to a knowledge of His Word. The outpouring of the Holy Spirit is God's revelation. In the reality of this event consists our freedom to be the children of God and to know and love and praise Him in His revelation.[1]

SUMMARY:

1. The Holy Spirit the Subjective Reality of Revelation (pp. 203–42)

How has the Bible displayed the revelation of God to humanity?

1. God has revealed Himself as Father, the Revealer, known in His act as the Revelation of God in Jesus, and God acts as Himself in the Spirit who is the Revealedness (the completion of hearing the revelation) in the Holy Spirit. God is known in triune form.
2. The reality of the revelation is provided in the incarnation of the Word; His place in history is a fact already completed and available for response. God is known in Christological form.
3. Now we must ask regarding God's revelation as to how God is active in an event of confirming His revealedness of Himself to us. How does God enable a faithful hearing? God is known in a pneumatological form.

In the person of the Holy Spirit, we are given to know God as a gift completed by the Holy Spirit, not by our capabilities.

When we talk about the Spirit as the subjective side of revelation, subjectivity is not a matter of mere human opinion. This is the experience of reception, an acknowledgment that we, as persons, are beneficiaries of what is other than ourselves. We are "knowing subjects" who apprehend and

---

1. *CD* 1.2, § 16, p. 203.

reflect on the objects that surround and encounter us. Since in this case the other is a person, we focus on their self-revelation to know them.

Our question here focuses on how humans are enabled and free to be reached by the revelation of God.

By the work of the Trinity, human hearing becomes possible. This happens through the objectivity of Scripture. This is possible because the freedom of God to speak precedes the freedom of humans to hear.

What is real is the actuality of God speaking, not the mere possibility of human hearing.

Faith and obedience can be seen in the dynamic between God's work and the freedom of human response. We do not hear out of the possibility of human capacity but out of the actuality of God's active revelation.

In the Bible, we see that God has trodden all the way to humanity's location. The impassable has been traversed by the only one capable.

The reality of the revealedness of God is the starting point of human reception. The reality of God's revelation is made complete in the hearing and obeying of the revelation in Jesus as we humans acknowledge and respond to the Word that encounters us.

God and humans together constitute the Word of God—but in one direction, from God to humans. In this, the Holy Spirit is God acting upon the human through the Holy Scripture.

Within the life of the Church, God transforms humans into listeners. This transpires through the address of the specific Word made known in the Son. People are made believers as those who hear what is made available in Jesus.

> In the Bible, we see that God has trodden all the way to humanity's location. The impassable has been traversed by the only one capable.

The Church is that community of persons who have heard, believed, confessed their belief, and acknowledged that in Christ they are God's. What was *invisible* in those whom Christ calls His own is subsequently made *visible* in this community of hearers. Their hearing completes their belonging as a confirmation of the call extended to them.

The Church can never be considered independent of Jesus, as a community of autonomous interpreters who come to seek God.

The Church has its head in Jesus Christ, not in its own ideas and structures. Only in submitting to Jesus' headship can it be the Church of Jesus Christ. It cannot function as a headless body that talks about Jesus from human resources that are severed from God.

In clarifying what we mean in stating that the Church has its origin in Jesus, we affirm:

1. The Church lives because the Word became flesh. This Word was spoken to be heard in our world. In hearing, the children of God become the subjective reality of revelation, those met and embraced through the Word of grace that claims them.
2. The Church is the community of the children of God for Jesus' sake. Humans are reborn in response to Jesus, not as a society with a liberated sovereignty in thought and action to do their own thing.
3. The Church is the life of a community who finds common existence in dependence on the living Word. We do not merely have familial love. Rather, "by belonging to Christ we belong to all who belong to Him."[2]
4. The Church lives the life of the children of God as the subjective reality of revelation. As a historical reality, the Church is hidden in God's life. Therefore, it is divine and human, eternal and temporal, visible and invisible. As the children of God, the Church is visible in the events of coming together to be gladly held together by their head.

There is a coherence between the incarnate Christ and the Church.

1. As the children of God, we are raised by Christ into His life together.
2. Jesus' lordship is His grace for His Church to sustain us.
3. Jesus, as creative and ruling Word, is the unity of His Church held together.
4. In the Church, the coherence of God and humanity may be encountered by humans in reality.

The Church is not a human production. Its existence does not depend on the resources of this world.

After becoming human for us in Christ, God adopts us so we will be ready to hear His Word to us. He enables both the speaking and the hearing of His Word.

The mystery of Pentecost is that humans who are not Christ are gifted to share in Him. We are standing with and for Christ, who has been with and for us in His incarnation and now holds us as His own.

---

2. *CD* 1.2, § 16, p. 217.

How does revelation come to humanity? How does the revelation come to indwell us?

1. God gives definite signs of His reality through events and relationships in this world. Not only are these relations meaningful within our world's sense; they are also proactively intended with meaning as the Word speaks incarnationally into our world.
2. God leads humans to the conviction that they are made for connection with God and cannot be understood outside of this relation to the God who draws them as hearers and doers in response.

The experience of revelation can only exist as we become hearers. The actuality of the speaking and acting of God in Jesus makes this possible. That we recognize this is the work of the Holy Spirit.

The Holy Spirit opens our blind eyes so that we are able to acknowledge the One who has come to us and to gratefully say "Amen" to His Word to us. God acts in grace:

1. He acts not for His own need or fulfillment, but to enrich those who are impoverished and needy. The Father sends the Son, and by the work of the Spirit we participate in this life with enjoyment.
2. He acts so that the work of the Spirit is the Work of Christ. The grace of Jesus exists only through the fellowship of the Holy Spirit.
3. Grace is portrayed in the many ways the Spirit is depicted uniting us to God, enabling us to become one with Him.
4. Grace is the work of the Spirit by which we acquire what we need to have our eyes opened, to become participants in what God has done for us. This is baptism in the Holy Spirit, whereby we are made new creatures, the dwelling place of God.

2. The Holy Spirit the Subjective Possibility of Revelation (pp. 242–79)

The subjective, personal experience of revelation comes as we hear ourselves addressed by God in the Church. We are aroused as those who hear that Christ has called us His own. We are awakened to our true being as those known and addressed as the children of God.

The actuality of God always precedes the possibility of our knowing. Understanding follows encounter.

Reality insists on being understood in its own light, not to be filtered by our selected focus. We are free for God as an engagement with the reality of God enclosed in the work of the Spirit, who brings us out of our darkness into the light.

As we discover the reality of God by the Spirit, we also discover who we are as those who have stood apart from God. The Spirit both comforts and convicts as we see ourselves before God.

If it is said that God cannot be known, it is stated from the side of human possibilities. But from God's life, it is not only possible but actual. The Spirit wakens us to that actuality.

1. It is possible for humans to hear God because His Word is given by God to humans through the outpouring of the Spirit in the Church.
   a. The Spirit is the location that corresponds with the incarnation as a particular place where the Head has His body as His own place of revelation.
   b. In this place and by God reaching out to us, speaking to us, expressing His love, we come to hear and see only by looking to Jesus. The Spirit draws us to understand what is said to us by Him.
   c. In the outpouring of the Holy Spirit, the possibility of hearing becomes actual; that is subjective reception. The revealedness comes to us as the Lord extends free grace to facilitate our hearing.
2. Through the outpouring of the Holy Spirit, God can meet humans, who hear that they have been addressed with a Word that sets them free to hear. A deaf person who heard the words "be healed" would both, in one particular instance, hear anew and be impacted by the transforming intent of those specific words.
   a. In acknowledging the freeing words of Jesus, we become free as those who can finally hear.
   b. The Word can only come as freely given; it cannot be taken or grasped.
   c. The Word can only become our own as God speaks, encounters, and penetrates our very selves with His Word.
3. By the Spirit we are free as we are met by God's unavoidable Word.
   a. We are freed as this Word addresses us. We gain a freedom not realized out of our own capabilities. It comes as the

miracle of being awakened to God's possibility. It is pure gift, not achievement.

b. The divine possibility is given to us, and we participate in it. As a subjective response, our living is placed within the act of God's coming to us.

c. When we are met by God, we do not abandon ourselves to God without responsibility. We are opened fully to responsible possibilities as we stand before the immense possibility. God opens this way for us within a life of participation. We are not enclosed in a prison; we are embraced within the miracle of unconditional, unlimited love. We are newly birthed into a previously unimaginable freedom as the revealedness of God envelops and delivers us to love anew.

Freedom exists for humans where Jesus is Master, Teacher, and Leader. We are servants, pupils, and followers.

Only in this One, who has died and been resurrected, is it possible to be free. God becomes man to free us. Humans become freed in Jesus to be who we are created to be. This is the divine possibility that becomes the actuality of freedom.

We find Jesus unavoidably our Master:

> Through the outpouring of the Holy Spirit, it is possible for God to meet humans, who hear that they have been addressed with a Word that sets them free to hear.

a. He is one whom we cannot avoid. He is an accompanying presence. Jesus brings a specific, enduring relationship so that we cannot leave, even in rejection. He abides in us; we may abide in Him correspondingly.

b. He is our supreme authority. With regard to all other authorities, we may remain independent—with them we may choose. But this Word speaks to us as God, who is the Lord, and we may disregard, disobey, or confirm the reality. We cannot be rid of the reality of the One who sustains us, the One whom the outpouring of the Spirit reveals.

c. Jesus has given us a command by which we mark our existence. The order is to love and obey Him, and we are defined in our response. If we cannot fulfill this command, our guilt and failure define us. We live in response and are capable of hearing His revelation—that makes us free. Or we can resist, bound in unfreedom even with freedom knocking at the door.

d. He is Master, yet we exist in profound and ultimate irresponsibility. He claims our response, our will, and our action. We are presupposed to be able to respond, but we are unable to accomplish a loving and obedient response. We can only respond in participating through the work of the One who adopts us into His life as children. In Him we participate in the freedom of the One who cares for us.

e. Jesus is Master as the One who is a specific image into which we are formed. All other images are imitations. As those conformed to His image, we are sinners in whom the Word may be found at work. This is accomplished through our participation by grace in His life. We are, by His Spirit, reborn into His life. We follow Him as a gift; we do not imitate Him as a replication. We are not left on our own.

f. With Jesus as our Master, we have no concerns of our own; His concerns are our concerns as we are led by the Spirit who enters us. That limitation becomes our liberation. There is a revolution from our separated, broken selves. Made anew, we are filled with a love that creates His goodness in us.

COMMENTARY:

- Because Jesus has come and left His Word, we have the possibility of divine-human connection.

- Most often, humans look from their own point of view. This vantage lacks insight into the possibility of being open to the Word of God speaking. That human limitation is dispelled when it is acknowledged that the Son has already spoken. What is required is a recognition that here and now we are addressed.

- The Spirit brings the actual to be the experiential; the objective becomes the subjective. What was other as God's mystery becomes together as address and reception are grasped.

- The Holy Spirit is never an independent actor. He is the One sent to bring to fruition all that Jesus says and does. The Spirit comes to actualize, working in us and compelling us to life. We are invited to inhale and exhale the breath of the freeing Word that transforms us into the children of God come home.

CONCLUSION FOR THE CHURCH: The Church is intended to be a community of hearers who know that Jesus has spoken to them. This confidence comes only by the Spirit. As the actuality of Jesus is spoken, there is an actual possibility for hearing. This hearing is not by human potential but by the outpouring of the Spirit accomplishing the work of bringing the body into union with the Head. Instead of asking where someone goes to church, we might ask whether they go to a church where Jesus' voice is heard and the Spirit is making a new community of love. This is a question of alignment. Does the community drink from the well of Living Water or from prepackaged bottles?

INSIGHT FOR PASTORS: The Church can easily focus on the preaching of the pastor, its programs, or the fruit of the people who are part of the community; however, the focal point of the Church as the body of Christ is to be enamored with the Head, who loves, guides, and empowers people to be led by the One who can give them life.

This love story is only accomplished when we recognize the work of the Spirit, who allows us to extend beyond our self-limitations in thinking and self-interest. By the outpouring of the Holy Spirit, we are embraced in the Word of God, who revolutionizes us from existing as separated sinners into imperfect sons and daughters who know whose we are. A Church that submits to the Spirit's invigoration will be made anew into Christ's likeness. Leaders must assess what the Spirit is saying every day and week. Rather than develop programs and productions, ask how to arrange the time together as a table talk. There, the Spirit brings the spiritual feast. That might include food, but it definitely leaves us walking away feeling as though we have been with Jesus, heard His voice, and are filled and overflowing with love in action for those we will encounter as we hit the streets. This is the life of freedom in action.

INSIGHT FOR THEOLOGIANS: As theologians, we are directed to deal with primary data in our investigation. This means to deal with Jesus Christ. Yet we are to acknowledge each aspect in our investigation as a process of coming to know. We submit to the object of our study—that is, to Jesus—to inform our conclusions. This also means that in studying the revelation of God we submit to the Spirit as the One who guides our scientific investigation in knowing Jesus. The Spirit illuminates the Bible so we come to know Jesus. We listen to the fathers of the Church to gain their wisdom and insight.

The Spirit provides access to God so that what we say and claim is consistent with and opens us to understand what has been spoken and who said it. Thus, we cannot merely speak of Jesus as an object of our investigation. We must acknowledge the outpouring of the Spirit, who enables us to know and hear dynamically and thus be transformed in the hearing that claims our lives. This is not a science with objective distance; rather, it creates a transforming moment. It brings personal knowledge to shape theology as a form of worship. There is a pneumatological control regarding our claims about Christ. We must ask whether our claims about Jesus are consistent with the Spirit's revelation in the Bible, with the faithful community of God through history, with the fruit of our claim in its contemporary context. The Spirit is the One who confirms and opens the way to an authentic investigation and conversation.

? CLARIFYING QUESTIONS: Does your theology keep the Church in line, managing the beliefs and actions of all members so they appear pure? *Or* does your theology seek to live in liberty, which is evidence the Spirit of the Lord is present and active? If your Jesus does not create a freeing connection in relationships, it is not the freedom God made for us as humans.

CHAPTER 24

DEFENDING THE MOUNTAIN AGAINST HUMAN ATTEMPTS TO EXPLOIT IT

§ 17. The Revelation of God as the Abolition of Religion

FOCUS STATEMENT: Some people can only see in the mountain resources for their own ends. All self-seeking agendas to either utilize these resources, tame the mountain for human entertainment, or in any way disrespect its dignity must be contradicted. While we may enjoy the mountain, we must question all attempts to co-opt its resources for human ends.

Thus, we come to see in "The Revelation of God as the Abolition of Religion" that we partake in an agreement with the Spirit. We share in God's resistance to imposters and false forms of religion that miss the living God. The point of this chapter is to clarify the problems associated with human attempts to replace the work of the Spirit with human endeavors.

INTRODUCTION: This section continues the discussion regarding the outpouring of the Holy Spirit. Barth has established that we are free for God by the Spirit, who brings us to experience the freedom to be God's people. We now turn to see the forms of unfreedom that attempt to usurp the place of God in the God-human relation. As we continue chapter 2, part 3, "The Outpouring of the Holy Spirit," we explore the second of three subsections, identifying how human religion subverts our freedom for God.

CONTEXT: *CD* 1.2
Pages in Paragraph: 82 pages (pp. 280–361)

Subsections
1. The Problem of Religion in Theology
2. Religion as Unbelief
3. True Religion

📖 **TEXT: § 17. The Revelation of God as the Abolition of Religion**

OPENING SUMMARY: The revelation of God in the outpouring of the Holy Spirit is the judging but also reconciling presence of God in the world of human religion, that is, in the realm of man's attempts to justify and to sanctify himself before a capricious and arbitrary picture of God. The Church is the locus of true religion, so far as through grace it lives by grace.[1]

✠ **SUMMARY:**

1. The Problem of Religion in Theology (pp. 280–98)

There is a limit that must be set in place to do the work of theology faithfully.

The crucial limitation in our study of God is that we must begin with the actuality of God and not with the supposed capacities of humans in knowing God from their own resources.

Proper focus in theology stays true to God's self-revealing, the whole history of God that has been and continues as an event which encounters humans.

The problem of religion is that it makes it appear that we have a viable choice to either listen to the revelation of God as it comes to us, or we may choose some other way to make claims.

True religion listens; false religion walks away to self-create.

The sphere of religion is a real human phenomenon. We can study all the ways humans seek to find God or find psychological fulfillment from religious activity. Alternate forms of religion are inadequate to facilitate an encounter with the God of revelation—they actually perform a study of an entirely different character.

Religion lays and looks within the world of humanity. It is a human activity that includes Christian activities.

One can observe and compare all manners of religious activity. This investigation can help us understand human experience across the ages. That does not make it theology.

---

1. *CD* 1.2, § 17, p. 280.

Throughout our history, humans have felt that there are forces beyond nature that influence their existence. Religion points to these human perceptions.

The world of spirits is discerned by humans as a "reality" related to humans. It is deemed to be something ultimate and powerful so as to influence and call for reverence. It is a form of the personal other conceived as transcendent of the physical. This is a human proposition, not revelation.

Humans see what appears to be striving, dedication to a life that comes from beyond the known. This human devotion shapes the practices of life here, both individually and corporately.

Each religious group holds respect for leaders and holy books. Those tangible witnesses are the evidence of the realities and possibilities to which humans give their dedication.

God's revelation has entered a sphere that is populated by more or less adequate possibilities for human modes of grasping the divine.

The question must be asked as to how the Christian form of religion, existing among all the other forms of human striving for divine life, might be the form of religion where God has actually hidden Himself.

Christianity has the possibility of being just a human religion, based on human additions to or mutations of God's revelation.

The first question to be asked is whether theology and the Church will take seriously their basis of the revelation of God in Christ.

The Church can either abandon their basis in the revelation of God or keep to the task of hearing the revelation of God. Both have a human element; in the second case, however, God is taken seriously.

The crucial task for humanity has been to determine whether to have a religion based in revelation (from God) or a revelation of religion (from humans). One attends to God's self-giving, the other to human forms of pious living.

Depending on the "light of nature" to reveal God leads humans to reject revelation and to pursue dependence on human reason. This approach becomes a natural ethic. It directs the actions of human interaction in a manner that has no need for God. In this scenario, all that remains of God is His bestowing of human capabilities for religious activities.

The key methodological commitment for proper theology is to keep revelation prior to religion and never to reverse the order.

Free inquiry into the things of God must be pursued for the sake of truth. Conservatism that will not question is a function of fear. It builds walls to protect religious beliefs through appealing to human reasonableness.

The proper ordering of theology for the Reformers was that Jesus is Lord and humans belong to Him.

We cannot ignore the anxieties of our day. At the same time, we most certainly must not attach ourselves to the certainties of human knowledge in our time.

The modern Church did not so much go astray in allowing itself to be charmed by modern forms of education, science, and free investigation of the truth. The catastrophe was that it lost its object of faith, the God revealed in Jesus. It exchanged revelation for religion.

> The crucial task for humanity has been to determine whether to have a religion based in revelation (from God) or a revelation of religion (from humans). One attends to God's self-giving, the other to human forms of pious living.

If we try to equate religion and revelation, we do not understand revelation. If we give priority to human evaluations to reasonably explain the divine, it can only be an unhappy reminder of the war that was lost as darkness excluded the true light.

Revelation is denied when it is regarded as open for discussion. We then default to human reason and religion as our lenses. God is reduced to fit our schemes, and we are left with a mirage.

In His revelation, God is present to the world of human religion. To perceive how God is present for us is our task in theology. This distinguishes theology from religions who look for God in their own ways apart from God's self-presentation.

By pursuing a path which comprehends revelation first, we can then see ourselves as those adopted and loved by God.

When religion responds to Jesus, it may be seen as a response in the God-human relationship. Consequently, appropriate human participation functions as a form of religion in a proper relation. However, this negates all prior human claims to truth in knowing God.

Theological evaluation of religion begins with an actuality, not with conjecture.

Whether or not they know it, every human stands in an actual relation to their Lord, to Jesus Christ.

If belonging to Jesus is the actuality, then both religion and nonreligion are forms of unfaithfulness to this reality. Thus, these activities are already judged problematic as denials of reality.

The evaluation of religion cannot begin with an assumed nature in human experience. We do not have a spectrum of capabilities that get us to God.

When the Church receives the revelation of God, can there possibly be a critique of divine truthfulness? Only in knowing Jesus can we discern that which is faithful or unfaithful to Him as the One who creates the possibility of true religion.

All false religion is a form of unfaithfulness to Jesus and thus a human-created idol.

The Church is the locus of true religion but not by any intrinsic nature. Only by grace does the Church exist as the location of God's chosen revelation.

The evaluation of religions must have a patience that echoes the patience of Jesus, who has demonstrated grace for all humans and their religions. This is even true of Christianity, which needs just as much patience from God as other religions.

2. Religion as Unbelief (pp. 297–325)

We must begin by identifying the concern that religion is unbelief in the form of faithlessness to the living God.

People are godless when they seek what is other than God—that is the nature of false religion.

Human attempts to purify and perfect oneself for God, as well as trying to reason our way to God, are an affront to God. They deny and disregard the already won acceptance completed by Jesus for humanity.

Divine judgment on religion does not referee levels of quality in thinking or behavior. Religion simply has chosen to pursue a course other than that of responding to the revelation of Jesus as its ground.

We are addressing a basic problem of the human heart before God. Religion can never provide tools that measure us appropriately. Religion points to human standards and prevents us from accepting God's gracious embrace.

Religion is unfaithfulness. Two considerations confirm this in light of revelation.

1. Revelation is God's self-giving, a self-presentation.
   a. Human attempts to know God from a human vantage point are void of knowing God.
   b. The truth of God, that He is the God of every person, is missing—that is made available only in revelation.
   c. Religion is a humanly manufactured replacement of God's work.
   d. Humans do not believe in God or they would listen. Instead, they talk.

2. God's act of self-giving is the grace-motivated act whereby God reconciles humanity to Himself. In the same act, humans are shown that they are unable to help themselves.

   a. Humans were created to have a joyful, obedient response to God, not one of alienation and unfaithfulness.

   b. In God's reconciliation of the world to Himself, He replaces all human attempts, which prove vain in the end.

   c. The practical content of religion is composed of attitudes and activities that contradict the revelation of God's grace. Sin is always humanity's belief in itself, not God.

Only by starting with the revelation of Jesus Christ can we characterize religion as idolatry and self-righteousness.

Religion is called into question by two forms of a common human quest: mysticism and atheism.

Primitive forms of religion develop a concept of deity with patterns of law to relate to that deity.

Rather than trust in the revelation of the image of God, the religious person creates God in their own image. The religious person then acts in conformity with what will make the relationship right with their deity.

Religion can only ever satisfy what humans deem to need fixing. It aims at what is believed will finally bring satisfaction. Unfortunately, those ends are not fixed. They change with each season and culture in unending states of flux.

Religion either tries to be relevant and concedes to the times, or it is behind the times, committed to obsolete doctrines that once held sway.

With the weakness and nonnecessity of religion, attempts to construct religious meaning become uncertain. They are suspicious, contentious, and oppressive, and they find it impossible to be open to God's revelation. Systems of law, dogma, ethics, and other external manifestations of human effort become the externalized artifacts of religious life.

Religion can only ever satisfy what humans deem to need fixing. It aims at what is believed will finally bring satisfaction. Unfortunately, those ends are not fixed. They change with each season and culture in unending states of flux.

Religion is a path of nonsatisfaction, a cessation of the soul in emptiness. There will be no realization of a final cleaning up for an emancipated reality.

With religion, the path that one is on comes to a fork in the road: either mysticism or atheism.

Mysticism is religion liberated from the need for outward forms of engaging the world. It claims friendship with God. But it focuses on the inward and spiritual meaning of religious activity, not externalized forms. These emphases are part of the passing world; spirituality is eternal and ideal.

Atheism is the artless form of the internal turn. It is a mere negation. Its identity is in saying no. It denies the existence of God and moral laws. It is an exercise in denial. Thus, it becomes artless.

Atheism has its own dogmas of truth. Its forms of certainty appear as replicated forms of a religious character. It aims to purify the world for its own vision. It hopes in the potential of humanity to create a better, secular way, allying with political powers and against God.

Mysticism is the negation of the overworld of religion. By denying the world in favor of the esoteric, it lives its own secret.

Atheism aims at the liberation of the world from religion. But this leads to a dead end.

The negation of God, His law, and the world inevitably leads to new religious constructs. These are designed to serve the internal and ideal desires of humans in the vacuum that remains.

If religion dies, it is because of the victory of another religion, not because of the triumph of mysticism or atheism.

Mysticism and atheism are both forms seeking liberation, aimed at the goal of being free of God and His law.

The ebb and flow of religion will come and go in many forms, including atheism. Even purer forms of religion will be unable to change the status of humans who are intent on creating idols and laws.

3. True Religion (pp. 325–361)

When we say "justified sinner," we mean one who is both truly sinner in reality and truly made whole by God's activity. This is the sense we must hold for "true religion."

Religion can never play the role of mediating between God and humanity, but it can be the earthly place God embraces to use in order to make Himself known and loved.

Religion can be a phenomenon of grace when God's action is its sole cause.

Religion, standing on its own, can only be a death trap. But religion as the vehicle of God's address to humanity can be an invitation to awaken to God's revelation.

Christianity can be called the true religion only in the sense that religion may become the redeemed community God commandeered for His purposes.

Christianity has no superior merit on its own. Only within a history of deference to the living God, that submits to God's justification of humanness, can its activities make space for Him.

In essence, there is no difference between Christianity and all other religions. They all have a propensity to practices of human striving. These take on various forms of idolatry and self-righteousness.

One on a humble path accepts God's judgment. We may recognize that we have become self-dependent and finally hear the Word of God's offer of reconciliation.

Only in the acceptance of grace, abandoning all attempts at constructing new stairways to reach God, can we exercise true religion.

Our faith is in the faithfulness of God's promises.

We cannot "attain" right relation with God by our own pursuits and actions. All is gift.

To the extent that Christianity continues as *our* work, *our* efforts, *our* actions, *our* formulations, *our* history, it is on the same level as other religions.

To the degree that *our* Christianity pretends to be a work of faith and pretends to be obedient to revelation, it is, in fact, unfaithful. It is an exercise in unbelief through idolatry and self-righteousness.

We often build Babylonian towers to make our way to God, and in the process we deny His self-giving. When we become focused on being good Christians and exemplary churches, *we* hope to receive the glory.

The history of Christianity is one of contradictions. Foremost is the unbelief that neglects, forgets, or chooses another way.

We get sidetracked from the grace that proclaims God's revelation to the ungodly. This unbelief lives in a distracted state that is the essence of sin: missing God, it chooses countless distressing paths.

Christianity often forgets that it is the religion of revelation and abandons its humble task to seek paths of glory instead.

When standing fully aware that we have contradicted God's grace, we become able to have faith that God is capable of contradicting our contradiction.

We must accept that no degree of pure living or mystical experience can save us or gain favor with God. We are restored by the One who comes to us as embodied grace. We cleave to Him who reconciles us.

Where the face of God is seen as the expression of grace, true religion is found as created by the presence of God.

True religion is an event where the grace of Jesus Christ is poured out by the Holy Spirit. This is an event in the Church living and loving as the children of God.

The free kindness of God is the source that gives rise to knowledge of God, which leads to service, active life together, and restoration amid human corruption.

We must accept that no degree of pure living or mystical experience can save us or gain favor with God. We are restored by the One who comes to us as embodied grace. We cleave to Him who reconciles us.

By the grace of God, the children of God live as participants in God's grace, which makes them who they are.

Only as a gift can there be true religion that goes beyond human creations of religion.

God's self-giving is God's reality of sustaining grace. That grace is what actually bears humanity in the face of their refusal to respond to God's true religion.

Humans become bearers of true religion not by their own resources but because God has intervened with His good pleasure as the only motive.

God's grace is embodied in the person of Jesus Christ. In Him, the divine revelation is opened and the human situation is addressed.

Jesus brings us to receive His grace acting on our behalf. This man is the divine good pleasure being fulfilled unconditionally for us.

True religion is grounded and available in the self-evident basis made real by the coming and revealing of Jesus, who has chosen to be freely for us.

1. Jesus is the root of life for Christianity. Any form of Christianity that neglects Him or creates structures apart from Him is an empty possibility or a decaying system that can only stagnate. In Jesus, humans have peace with God; without Him they are alone in self-isolation from God, creating numbing forms of religion.
2. Jesus is the election of God that accomplishes the goodness and compassion of God. Jesus is the continuous election of God to be faithful and patient with humanity. By the provision of the Spirit, God freely and mercifully turns toward us to be embraced, for us to hear and express what has been received as the fruit of God's gracious choice.
3. Jesus is the establishment of true religion. He makes humanity right with God through forgiving human alienation and separation.

This is accomplished through a transforming act of reconciliation. The light has come to the darkness and revealed what was hidden. He has provided what is needed for life.

"For the sum total of the qualities of even the Christian religion is simply this, that it is idolatry and self-righteousness, unbelief, and therefore sin. It must be forgiven if it is to be justified."[2]

4. In Jesus, God adopts humanity. In Jesus, He gives Himself to us as the only basis of Christianity as true religion so that He might be known and embraced. Christianity can only ever become an illuminated people, never a source of light. We come as those directing others to Jesus by the work of the Holy Spirit.

The Christian religion is the arena created by the Spirit in which the Word who is made flesh continues to speak and where humans hear by the same Spirit.

Christians are moved by the Spirit who calls them. They are directed to the One who established their existence as children of God. The consequence of this movement is a living within the restorative work already accomplished. It comes to be manifested as redeemed life together.

COMMENTARY:

- We often find Christianity pitted against other religions. Barth wants to expose the reality of all the ways humans seek a "spiritual" or "religious" life that are of human creation. In all those pursuits, we miss the living God.
- It is possible to have true religion. But the practice of religion can only be true if it is originated by the God who seeks us.
- True religion answers the call of Jesus as a response in the human sphere of activity. Its trueness lies in its being connected to and given vitality by Jesus rather than by human strategies and efforts.
- *Religion* is a term that can be properly used of the activities of humans in the sphere of human history and existence. But religion can only be *true* when its activity originates from God and facilitates human response. All other attempts are like the tower of Babel, efforts to reach God through human means that employ human capacities.
- True religion can only be a response to grace, the personal gifting of Jesus made complete in humans by the work of the Spirit.

---

2. *CD* 1.2, § 17, p. 354.

CONCLUSION FOR THE CHURCH: The Church must become aware of the many traps of religious experience. So much of what churches do ends up creating programs and structures that focus on human action and performance, all the while neglecting to know the living God. Its life of true religion can only become authentic as a participation in a life that depends on the grace of Jesus made actual by the Spirit.

INSIGHT FOR PASTORS: The great challenge for pastors today is to shape the life of their community as a gathering of those who come to know the living Jesus, as made available to us by the Spirit. When we gather, leaders must not focus on what we do or should be doing. We must come to know Jesus' presence, bathing our being in the company, call, and sustaining of the One who loves us. All else is a form of religion. Ask yourself whether you are more concerned with how you are appearing, or if Jesus is appearing, to flood the space with a penetrating grace that meets those gathered.

We must not pit Christianity against other world religions. Rather, we must clarify the character of a faithful Christianity when it functions as a beacon of redirection back home. All religion and irreligion and antireligion are the same when they seek human management in pursuit of truth apart from the One who made and sustains it all. The Church needs the humility to rejoice, celebrate, and bear the fruit of being enamored with its Beloved. We become irrelevant when we desire to be relevant to the culture or try to meet the perceived needs of the people—we become culturally religious. True religion can only be an intimate acting out between beloved humans who know they live by grace alone. They live within the provision of God's living revelation. They are a community embraced by God's choice to bring life in relation to Himself.

INSIGHT FOR THEOLOGIANS: The science of religions is usually an objective study that is akin to sociology. It studies the historical development, practices, beliefs, and ongoing developments of a set of people. It is assumed that religion is and can only be a human search for the divine or the remnant of human ideas gradually developed.

Barth calls for scientific clarity in distinguishing true religion as being grounded in the actuality of God in the person of Jesus and as shaping the life of a people in Spirit-led response. Any human projection onto God that begins in observing the human need, desires, quests, or any other quest for God is deemed by Barth to be a false religion.

When revelation takes its due course, it will not leave these other attempts unaffected—they will be abolished or brought to find their true source in the living God. This includes Christianity. Much of what passes as being "Christian" is merely another form of religious undertaking to give power to human organizations and achievements. The task of the theologian is to shed light on the actuality of God—pursuing true science—and to correct the myriad forms of misdirected religion to drink from the wells of grace. Theological clarification will articulate both the proper outcome of the work of the Spirit in shedding light on how humanity goes astray and what it means to reestablish true religion in relation to the triune God. Every claim we make will need to be tested as true or false in response to the question: Is this claim true to who Jesus is, what He desires, and what He is bringing to fruition?

?　CLARIFYING QUESTIONS: Is your theology full of truth claims and perfected practices that make people feel better about their improvements? *Or* does your thinking continually loop back to consider whether your life demonstrates the grace of the One who is present and active, who draws you into His love, who is the only path of becoming who you are intended to be in relation to God, others, and an accepting self-care?

CHAPTER 25

THE FREEDOM TO BE ALIVE IN THE FACE OF THE MOUNTAIN

§ 18. *The Life of the Children of God*

👓 **FOCUS STATEMENT:** Although we have just started trekking, we have come a long way. We have come to see that the mountain is there and has a history and reality that precedes us. As we continue the journey we are opened to see who we are as those standing before this mountain. We are positioned to discover how our unfolding recognition shapes who we are and where we are going. We are renewed as we are reframed.

Situated in this context, we are prepared to explore what it means to experience "The Life of the Children of God." We can see ourselves in what surrounds and sustains us. This perspective is not one of turning the camera toward ourselves but of seeing ourselves dynamically imbedded within our context. The point of this chapter is to gain a point of view as to who we are in specific situations, not in isolation: we are those who participate in the freedom of the Son of God, who is for us and with us.

🖋 **INTRODUCTION:** This section completes our discussion on the connecting work of the Holy Spirit, the One who brings to fulfillment the divine-human relation. The freedom we have is not our own but is generated and sustained for us. It is nothing like a quest for independence, as a freedom *from* others, especially God. Rather, it is participation in the gift of the Holy Spirit to engage in a freeing share within the life of God's love. This paragraph (§ 18) completes chapter 2 on "The Outpouring of the Holy Spirit" and prepares us for chapter 3 on "Holy Scripture" and the experience of the Word of God in the life of the Church, where freedom under the Word is lived.

||||| CONTEXT: *CD* 1.2
Pages in Paragraph: 93 pages (pp. 362–454)

Subsections
1. Man as a Doer of the Word
2. The Love of God
3. The Praise of God

📖 TEXT: § 18. The Life of the Children of God

OPENING SUMMARY: Where it is believed and acknowledged in the Holy Spirit, the revelation of God creates men who do not exist without seeking God in Jesus Christ, and who cannot cease to testify that He has found them.[1]

✠ SUMMARY:
1. Man as a Doer of the Word (pp. 362–71)

The Word of God comes in person. The testimony of Scripture points to Him. This testimony about Him is the basis of the proclamation of the Church conveying God's self-expression so we can become doers in response.

We have discovered that God is revealed in self-expression. The expression of His unity is in the persons of the Trinity. Jesus Christ is the concrete expression of this unveiling in which He took on human flesh to be one with us. The impact of this self-expression of God is realized in humans through the outpouring of the Holy Spirit who brings us to share the gift of being beloved.

The freedom that God has for us is the basis of the freedom we have for God. In the Son and by the Spirit, the time and place is made by God for God to act on our behalf in a freeing embrace.

In Jesus, we are taken up into a unity completed by Him. The outcome is one of being joined to His body on Earth. That is to say, His act of gracious retrieval has made us sons and daughters in a manner proper to Him and a pure gift for us.

The reclamation act by God culminates as participation in the life of God.

The faithfulness of God enables our faith that responds as love and belonging. Consequently, we are freed to be and act from love that is not originally our own.

---

1. *CD* 1.2, § 18, p. 362.

No anthropology or psychology can be abstracted from Jesus to make a beautiful or understandable image of humanity's fulfillment.

We must see true humanity in Jesus alone and come to have faith in Him who is for us. We cannot cherry-pick what appeals to us in order to gain understanding.

His act of gracious retrieval has made us sons and daughters in a manner proper to Him and a pure gift for us.

We must hold to the Word made flesh and not merely to Jesus as human example.

We must hold to the Spirit who redeems us in our flesh (which is in conflict with God), not as One who makes us masters of truth in self-sufficiency.

We live in the paradox of being sanctified sinners. We will always be sinners. We will always be those beloved and embraced.

Who we are is defined both by our resistance to Jesus and our acceptance of that personal presence of Jesus as He accepts us as we are and thus transforms us.

Jesus' revelation shows us both who He is and who we are as those who resist Him.

Further, by the work of the Spirit, we become aware of our resistance and our acceptance. We can rest knowing that love wins the day and accept the actuality of our being sanctified sinners.

Humanity does not stand outside the circle of God's concern. The circle of God's self-expression encompasses and gifts humanity. With a change made possible only by the Spirit, God intersects our existence to renew and restore.

In His revelation, God retains the freedom to free humans into a true freedom. This divine freedom is not in competition with humans. In fact, it makes space for human freedom.

A Christian is a free person whose freedom is established and protected by God.

The life of freedom for the children of God is not focused on what we should do. Rather, it pays attention to how we live a joyful obedience with the One who loves us.

Human self-determination, when it is called human freedom, is not human action that simply comes from our own created resources. If it is indeed Christian freedom, with a determination to be who we are in Christ, moved by the Spirit, then it will be motivated from outside, that is, from God.

It is "He and not I" who enables me to live in freedom.

The life of the children of God is a creation of the Holy Spirit. The Spirit impacts our being and doing for life together. This shapes what we call our "internal aspects" as well as our relation to others. They cannot really be separated.

God, in love, claims humans to be His as specific beings; thus, we become truly new beings.

If we see ourselves only in our inward aspects, focused on thinking and feeling, we are left in isolation, curving our attention inward into our being. Inadvertently, we disconnect from others.

If we conceive of ourselves through observing our outward aspects, our acting in the world, then we are dealing in the realm of interaction. This engagement unites us as particular people in community.

We cannot separate or neglect either the inward or outward aspect of our awareness. In truth, we are unified beings who stand before God as new beings. Our human being acts in response to His revelation. We acknowledge His claim to be our God, for us and with us in our thoughts and deeds.

As new creations we hear and believe the Word of God by the Spirit.

Awakened to the God who has come to us, the human intention is transformed. God's love for humans ignites human love for God in response. Whereas we would die in isolation, we are now raised to live in relation to the One who loves us.

We live love outwardly in our acts as testimonies to the fact that the God of love has found us.

Our new identity is as a person found by God. We did not seek; we were sought out.

In Jesus, God was free for humanity. In the Spirit, humans were made free for God.

"In the freedom of God he himself became free and the child of God. This is the irresistible summons to action."[2]

In Jesus, God was free for humanity. In the Spirit, humans were made free for God.

By the Spirit, we are compelled to a life of love. We are then empowered to witness to who we have become because of this freeing God.

The life of the children of God now consists in love and praise. In this relation, the children are what they are and do what they do in discovery of this state as beloved children.

---

2. *CD* 1.2, § 18, p. 370.

2. The Love of God (pp. 371–401)

The love of God shapes our *being*, and the praise of God informs our *doing*.

The Christian life is one of love from beginning to end.

Love from God and for God kindles the faith that is the actuality of our seeking God who has been faithful to us. This faith, born of love, confirms that we do believe and are not delusional.

What is the loving thing to do? This is always the decisive question.

Whatever good we do in life before God, love is what makes it good.

Love cannot be understood in itself; it can only be born in us as we become children of God.

The first thing to be said of humans is that we are loved; we are beloved.

The love of God precedes the Christian life, which follows as a life of expressed love.

The Spirit opens our eyes and ears, sparking in us the faith that is expressed as love of God and others.

Love is expressed in real acts of human self-determination. Divine love does not take the place of creaturely love, nor is it developed by humans.

When the love of God is heard and embraced, that love does its work in the beloved children who are earthly parts of His body. The earthly members are always grounded in the love of God.

The miracle of the Holy Spirit founds the love of the children of God and is not an extension of a human capacity.

There is no master concept from which to deduce love. It can only be the unique love of God for us that displays its reality.

> The love of God precedes the Christian life, which follows as a life of expressed love.

The love of God is not associated with mere opinion, feeling, or sentiment. It exists in definite being, relationship, and action.

Being loved by God, we look into His "heart."

The "heart of God" can only refer to His being as Father, Son, and Spirit. It is overwhelming, overflowing, free love.

Any "inwardness of God" can only be in this shared life, one that is expressed as the result of God's way of being love for us.

The "outwardness of God" that occurs in His revelation brings to light the real nature of God for us.

In the Bible, the love of God is made evident in that He chooses us, guides us, helps us, and brings us home to Himself from our alienation. All this language points to our meeting and meaning in Jesus, who comes to us.

The Spirit makes God's address personal: "I have loved you. I am with you. Do not be afraid" (see Jeremiah 31:3; Deuteronomy 31:7–8).

Any attempt to describe the love of God can only be understood by looking to and listening to Jesus.

God is already complete love in God's triune being. He does not need us to fulfill His love. Free mercy and kindness embrace us in His love.

God's love kindles our answering love.

What is the nature of our love? It can only be a responsive love to the love of God for us.

Human acts of love occur in the light of what has been said and done for us from God's side of the interaction.

There is no "love in general" that can filter or define our thoughts on love. There is only the actual love of God made known in the incarnation of the love of God in human form in Jesus.

The grounding text of love in the Bible is the Great Commandment.

1. The call to hear is given to a specific people chosen to believe, to be the true Israel, the children of God. We hear because we are the children of God. Because we are loved by God, our activity will be love.

2. The God who loves does not belong to any human category. He acts toward humanity in a way that no one else does. He does not demand, claim, and order. He gifts, offers, and promises. As our Lord, He takes the matters of life and death out of our hands and makes them His business.

3. Love can be and is demanded only from those who already belong to God. Real love can only be an obedient response to the command of God. This is a voluntary response of reverence for God. The love of God does not originate in human hearts.

4. Human love finds focus in loving God. He comes and gives Himself. His love becomes the form of His presence in their hearts; there He can and will be loved by humans. In this openness to the otherness of God, love is made real. Where one is alone, there is an absence of love. Self-love as a natural phenomenon is not love; it is aloneness. We are to love God and be as covenant partners.

5. What does it mean to love? To love is to become what we are as those loved by God. To love is to accept that our future is in God's love, to confirm His love for us, and to embrace the God who goes with us into the future. The love of God is an honest confession that in all

things we are granted a love that is undeserved and unworthy—the love of God grasps us. We are held by a love that comes to us, that we allow to do its work in us. In loving God, our autonomy is taken from us. In seeking God, we ultimately rejoice in finding that He first loved us.

6. Humans are to love God with their whole being. In all spheres of human activity, the whole of life is covered as the appropriate actualizing, the making real of God's love. The whole might of humans is to be caught up in one thing: to love God. Love cannot coexist with a fear of unforgiveness, the world, or ourselves. There is a fear of God that is love supreme. But love can never be lost. Christian love cannot be understood as other than the thankfulness of the believer toward God.

To love our neighbor is to act as the children of God. As all our activity is claimed by thankfulness, it returns praise to God from whom all love and blessings flow.

The meaning of Christ's lordship is manifested in our speaking, living out, and showing that we are redeemed children of God.

3. The Praise of God (pp. 401–54)

The praise of God will always be acted out in our love for our neighbor.

In what sense does love of neighbor stand alongside God as the expressed life of the children of God?

Are there two absolute commandments? No, the core command is to love God completely.

Is there one absolute commandment, identical in both forms so that each means what the other means? No, this emboldens religious sensibilities, an inclination to start with love of humans rather than God.

Is there one command to love God and a second that approximates it, the real nerve of its content? Partly yes. God has first loved us, even as sinners, and this breaks forth as love for neighbor, but not as a lesser call.

Humanity does not exist in a vacuum. Humans have no inherent dignity as individuals or as a social group.

Only as God has posited neighbors as companions for us can we see that we are gifted by God with each other. We love as an act of praise to God in gratitude for the gift.

The orderings of our relationships are to be seen in the light of God's arrangement of creation.

We cannot pursue an ideal of perfected, loving humanity (idealism) or a historical study based on the best of human conjectures (realism). These approaches take us back to the praise of humanity.

Humans must be seen as distinct from God as made clear by Scripture.

Humans are creatures made by the Creator.

Obedience to the command to love God is the freedom to love our neighbor.

We live now as justified sinners, made right with God yet still in the creaturely flesh. We watch, wait, and serve him in the light of His reordering of this reality by His resurrection.

There are clarified elements to be explored in the proposed relation between the two commandments: to love God and to love our neighbor as ourselves.

1. To love God and neighbor are two commands.

   One is living before God as a completed child in Christ.

   The second is for a not yet completed walk as God's child on Earth.

   They are two commandments, spoken by one Lord, significant for the human to live as the child of God.
2. Both commandments have the claim of the One God on the one human. In Jesus having come to us, He has claimed us as His children.

   In Him, by the Spirit, we love God and neighbor. The one personal revelation calls for this twofold actualization.

   The Word and Spirit provide the unity of the commands.
3. The two commands reflect both an eternal and temporal context. The greater command encircles and embraces the lesser.

   Love of God is the cause for the love of neighbor.

   The two loves are not equal; the second derives from the first. But it is both in the sphere of God's life and in the life of the world that we wholeheartedly love God and neighbor as a response to the one revelation.

What is the love of neighbor?

1. It is the claim and command of God, who has captured our hearts in love. It is intended for members of both the passing and the

coming world. This is our walk as those found by God, extended to those who need to discover that they are beloved.

Because He loved first, all must discover this as the awakening love. The light of our human witness to love in action is our praise of the God who goes with us.

Our love answers His love with thankfulness. God's love orders our ways.

2. Who and what is this neighbor we are to love? Not someone worthy of love in themselves. Not those required by society's obligations.

If we try to reason why we should love any neighbor, we will not love them. Where God is known and acknowledged, we are called to nurture those put before us.

The God who wills to love us and desires us to love in return also wills us to love our neighbor. It is a miracle we can love God. It is a consequent miracle that we can love our neighbor. This love is not duty; it is gift.

There is not a mutual obligation between all humans to love just because they are human. The neighbor is the particular person who emerges before us as a beneficiary.

The Church is simply about the work of service in loving our neighbor to the praise of God (Good Samaritan). Wherever a church does not offer the service of being neighbor, it is not being the Church (priest or Levite).

Humanity as a whole can take part in compassionate service to a neighbor.

The Church is not just to be a neighbor inwardly but is called to be a neighbor for the world that surrounds us; this call does not oblige us to every person but to the particular people who stand before us awaiting compassion.

To believe in the Church is to affirm that we can see a neighbor and consequently see that person as within the sphere of the care of the love of Jesus here and now.

We do not judge another based on their human nature. Humanity does not have a static quality of its own. The human does not have a capacity which might be developed to fulfillment. We only judge each person as confronted by the love of Jesus.

Jesus has set up in Himself the being as neighbor who is compassionately active for humanity. Jesus made Himself neighbor in the incarnation. Jesus made Himself neighbor in His resurrection.

The world is full of hidden neighbors who stand outside the Church. These strangers play a striking role of offering service. In the resurrection, Jesus is proclaimed as the Great Samaritan who acts with compassionate service. In the light of the incarnation, we see these persons as neighbors who glorify humanity as those embraced in Him.

The Fatherhood of God and the Sonship of humanity is known only in Christ. We are transferred into Him as an act of God. So too are we brothers and sisters because Jesus has made us that way. He has called us into relationship with Himself. Thus, He gives us His Father to be our Father.

Jesus is the first and true Brother. Only through Him can there be other brothers and sisters. In this way we become the beloved family of God.

The neighbor is any person who is a companion in faith, and this extends to all whom we expect to be a brother or sister. Any neighbor can point beyond themselves to the encounter with Jesus as brother.

Meeting the neighbor, the one who needs our service in helping with suffering, calls forth an active love that directs the children of God. Through us, He wills a better world. The true worship of God is to act in love for our neighbor, moved by this love.

The issues that form the plight of humanity are not merely in what is seen. Often, they are hidden behind strength, control, power, security, and other manifestations of human capacities for managing life.

Humans live with a will that may be masked or open, needy or confident, bold or withdrawn, but that will always attempts to live while facing the oppression of life with shame, always hides while seeking something better.

Our neighbor is the one nearest us in misery. In this sense, Jesus is in solidarity with them as the compassionate neighbor who shares their misery and challenges.

3. We must go back to asking what it means to *love* our neighbor.

It means to live into God's future with the neighbor God has given us.

We must accept the benefit of having a neighbor who is a gift to us in not leaving us isolated.

We must exist not as those alone but as those who by God's grace are to be with our neighbor in coexistence, not intent on being separate.

We must see our neighbor with all the misery and needs that do not leave us comfortable and satisfied to leave them alone. We naturally desire to be concerned with our needs and well-being, willing to neglect the neighbor.

The misery of our neighbor comes back as a shadow on ourselves. In the light of what is afflicting the other, we recognize our own issues.

When we truly see the challenges of our neighbor, we see ourselves also as a sinner with a particular form of the challenge of being a sinner.

Our afflicted neighbor is the sinner who reminds us that we are sinners. We would like to see ourselves as better and offer our own form of worship to God under our form of management. But this is dishonest.

The nonconfirmation of our neighbor, not telling them that they are loved by God, is the seriousness of walking in the dark. Jesus confronts them as light who shows salvation, not condemnation. They are loved neighbors, invited to love.

Our neighbor reveals to us that we are sinners in need of forgiveness and grace. In our neighbor we can see that we are the same: we are in need and hiding from what is real.

We are shown that there is no private existence of self-satisfaction, only an acknowledgment that we stand in coexistence with our neighbor.

> We have no superior place to judge or accuse, to blame or to shame the other. We have a common humanity in need of grace and forgiveness.

We have no superior place to judge or accuse, to blame or to shame the other. We have a common humanity in need of grace and forgiveness.

If I know my own need and see another in need, I am driven to bind myself to the other in need of the help of God.

In meeting our neighbor, we are summoned afresh to know the love of God, who has met us in our sin and brokenness.

We always need to hear afresh the love of God for us, but we cannot hear and accept it for the other. They must hear it for themselves, as grace personally for them.

We can only meet the stranger as a brother and testify to our love for Jesus Christ, fulfilling our responsibility to be a neighbor.

There are three forms of this witness:

   a. We do not hold back a word of help regarding both our need and our neighbor's need. We ought not speak only about our sin and need. Nor should we talk about experiences that alleviate our need.

   b. Our help to our neighbor is a sign of the promised help of God. The needs of our neighbor are like ours. Our challenges affect body and mind alike.

   c. We witness as God's love enacted when our attitude confirms our words and deeds. Attitude is a display of the mood with which we meet our neighbor. This is an attitude of being under the lordship of Christ. We engage our neighbor with all the comfort of forgiveness, as an atmosphere that surrounds and touches us. We must be evangelical, not heathenistic or legalistic.

4. In loving neighbors as ourselves, we are not directed to self-love as a focus but to give what is natural to ourselves in a love for the other. We find our neighbor as a person in need.

   a. We are exercising the courage of humility. We serve our neighbor as obedience in love that serves the other.

   b. To love our neighbor is to be called to prayer. We can only love our neighbor by praying for ourselves and our neighbor. Prayer allows Jesus to work in us and through us for our neighbor.

Through it all, we love because He first loved us.

COMMENTARY:

- The concept of freedom is given a clear relational connection in this section. The Spirit connects us to the love of God, and that love frees us to love God and our neighbor.
- The life of the children of God is one of response. We do not generate or develop the ability to love by our own efforts. In the work of the Spirit, we find that the love of God for us transforms our acts, thoughts, and attitudes because of the reality into which we are invited.
- Worship is not a human act to please God. It is a way of responding to the love that encounters us and compels us to love God and neighbor.
- The natural love of humans can never be the basis of the love command. Human love is naturally self-focused. In loving God and neighbor, the love of self is transformed in the outward actions that shape our identity as God-birthed forms of neighborliness.

- Loving God with our whole being is the result of God's revelation, not our concentrated efforts to train ourselves into submission. Obedience is a freeing response to the call to love.
- Loving neighbor is a confession of our human need for companions. We cannot consider the worthiness of the other or the benefit to self. We are compelled by God's love to be an active witness to that love in word, deed, and the atmosphere we bring to each encounter.
- Where the Spirit is received in the power of God's outpouring of love, humble, self-giving, compassionate persons echo the life of God in that particular place.

CONCLUSION FOR THE CHURCH: The modern Church often focuses on Jesus and holding beliefs about Him. It concentrates on the individual experience of the worshiper in gathering and in the development of the self alone on a separate journey that gathers weekly. But the Church is also to live by the outpouring of the Spirit, who reveals and actualizes the love of God. If this love is absent in the body or the neighborhood, then the Spirit is not being allowed to create the freedom of the children of God. This church has a flat tire; it has no freedom to go anywhere.

INSIGHT FOR PASTORS: In the leading of a church, the creation of a loving community is paramount. However, this cannot be a managed program to learn skills and host prepackaged events. If a loving community is to be authentic, it must be developed like a garden nurtured by light and water. In this case, it needs the revelation of the love of God in Jesus and the power of the Spirit to transform how we live together in freedom. In coming to know the personal presence of God and the belovedness that envelops us, we fulfill the great commandment in extending God's love in practical actions in everyday life. In falling in love with Jesus, we become those who act differently as love has its way; that is to say that the Spirit guides our actions. This is first lived in community, gathered to be made new as neighbors who find in Jesus the Great Neighbor, who goes with us into the neighborhood. There needs to be a liturgy in the Church that becomes a liturgy in the neighborhood. In both cases they are rituals of reception and extension at the same time. These become customs, habitually reminding us that we are loved as we reach out to help others.

INSIGHT FOR THEOLOGIANS: In the science of theology, the evidence that God is known may be seen in the attitude and activity of the community who loves profoundly but not self-consciously. The evidence would support the claim that the Holy Spirit has been at work in opening the eyes and enabling action from those who participate in the community—both within the Church and in the surrounding neighborhood. In this, the doctrine of the Church loses any abstract sense of invisibility, and the doctrine of the Holy Spirit comes to be connected boldly. The Spirit informs the active, not theoretical, life of those gathered and scattered within a specific location. The freedom that is evidence of the Spirit's outpouring is a joyful willingness to embrace and act with unconditional compassion for the needs of those within the sphere of influence of that community. This is the empirical data that we are dealing with reality. The Great Commandment is never an abstract wish; it is a description of those who have opened to the reality of God's love expressed in Jesus and made active by the Holy Spirit.

? CLARIFYING QUESTIONS: Does your theology bind people to believe in the freedom of God in theory while lacking authentic actualization of the theory? *Or* does your theology allow the Spirit to shape the freedom of the human who is transformed by the active and empowering love that embraces and transforms humans to be new in thought and deed in a manner not of their own creation?

CHURCH DOGMATICS, CHAPTER 3

"Holy Scripture"

CHAPTER 26

THE GUIDE'S GUIDEBOOK TO ATTENTIVE EXPLORATION OF THE MOUNTAIN

§ 19. The Word of God for the Church

FOCUS STATEMENT: As we approach the mountain, we find we are not alone. Nor are we making a first ascent in our discovery process. We have been preceded by a guide who is the focus of a guidebook that will serve us on the journey. Through the written guide, our personal guide will be referring us to the immensity of what we will be exploring. He will start by helping us get to know Him and His relation to the mountain. Others have been involved in writing the guidebook as well.

All these experienced people gathered by the guide help attune our thinking and enjoyment for the journey. They have learned to guide from the Great Guide. The way forward is opened by this unique Great Guide, who goes with us even as we walk in His steps. Thus, in this paragraph called "The Word of God for the Church," we find that following Jesus, as well as the book that witnesses to Him, serves us in the journey of knowing God. The guidebook, the Bible, functions as a continuation of God's address to humanity. It is part of the current manner in which God speaks, has spoken in Jesus, and will continue to reveal Himself to us by the Spirit. Amid these collaborative voices, we have the all-surrounding context of God's voice infusing our lives as He goes with us.

INTRODUCTION: This paragraph begins chapter 3 of 17 of the *CD*. The chapter is called "Holy Scripture" but is referring to more than just the book. When following Barth, we will come to see that we can only use the term *Word* by talking about Jesus, who is witnessed to in the Bible. The Bible is important. But it must be read to get to know Him. Preaching the Bible is important, but to hear the living Word, that preaching had better focus us on the Bible. Expand your listening to hear the harmonic, threefold Word of God, whose reality we come to hear down the trail in *CD* 2, "The Doctrine of God."

Chapter 3 of the *CD* has three paragraphs (§ 19–21) discussing Holy Scripture. These three paragraphs focus on the Bible, its relation to Jesus as the living Word, and what they together open for human freedom. Chapter 3 is half the length of chapter 2 on "The Revelation of God" (§ 13–18), which focused on Jesus and the Holy Spirit. Now we will take a step closer to the process of our reception, our hearing of God speaking through Scripture, as well as our reaction to this unique manner of God coming to us.

The point of this chapter is to summarize § 19 in the *CD* on the Bible as the place of hearing the living voice of Jesus. Having heard, we will then be able to speak with confidence. We will be prepared to proclaim what the living God is saying. We will be able to work toward the Bible's goal of freeing humans to live within God's freeing word of grace.

CONTEXT: *CD* 1.2
Pages in Paragraph: 81 pages (pp. 457–537)

Subsections
1. Scripture as a Witness to Divine Revelation
2. Scripture as the Word of God

TEXT: § 19. The Word of God for the Church

OPENING SUMMARY: The Word of God is God Himself in Holy Scripture. For God once spoke as Lord to Moses and the prophets, to the Evangelists and apostles. And now through their written word He speaks as the same Lord to His Church. Scripture is holy and the Word of God, because by the Holy Spirit it became and will become to the Church a witness to divine revelation.[1]

SUMMARY:
1. Scripture as a Witness to Divine Revelation (pp. 457–72)
Dogmatics seeks for a faithful recounting of the revelation of God in Jesus by the Church.

---
1. *CD* 1.2, § 19, p. 457.

By acknowledging that the Bible has an authority that precedes its witness, namely the living God, this personal God informs the appropriate reading of what is then proclaimed in the Church.

Hearing God comes when the Bible is heard as Jesus' voice, articulated in human speech under the lordship of Jesus, who reveals the triune God (and avoids any human mishandling).

The preaching of the Church must be in agreement with the signpost of the Bible that consistently points to Jesus. Otherwise, it would speak in vain as it succumbs to an alternate authority with another agenda.

The Bible indicates, prepares for, and facilitates an attentive listening to Jesus. Obedient listening is to submit to His authority.

The Church confesses the witness of the Bible. Further, it never stops clarifying that its revelation rightly corresponds to the One it reveals.

The Church confirms that Holy Scripture is a witness to the living God, who calls us to obedience. To answer with a yes is to live under its authority. To answer no is to continue without God's revelation and call.

The authority of Scripture is to be found in the exegesis of Scripture itself. This happens when preaching moves through the text, but it does not stop there, bringing to us the revelation of God Himself.

In listening to Scripture through the voice of the Church, we enter the history of obedient listening. We accept the responsibility in our own context to confirm the accuracy of the exposition of Scripture to properly hear the One who is its authority.

The authoritative witness of the Bible is grounded on the reality it reveals.

The Bible is written with human words. These words convey in human speech that which enables us to hear the lordship of the triune God.

The Bible is a witness to revelation, not revelation itself. And yet it is not to be distinguished from revelation.

The Bible is revelation insofar as it comes to us, mediating the voice of God in a way that accommodates human listening.

Through the apostles and prophets, we have an immediacy of hearing. They speak to us.

A true witness cannot be identical to what is revealed. But what is witnessed to is to be acknowledged as really set before us.

If we are to take the Bible as a true revelation of God, we must:

1. Note its limitation as a Word in God's revelation distinct from a human word. This is a proper humility.

2. Recognize the unity of the human word with the divine Word, who is its origin, main subject, and gives it true meaning. This is a proper respect.

The Bible is really given to us. It particularly applies to the God-human relation. For that reason, the Bible must be received as written by humans like us, given for us to understand this intended relation.

The Bible is a historical document and points to something quite specific. It is a genuine human word that presents us with God's revealing in person.

To listen to a human word can only mean that we are prepared to show up and try to understand. Words require interpretation and the intention to understand the speaker.

Meaningful human hearing can only come when the words provided are perceived in accordance with their intent. This enables understanding.

There are many unsuccessful attempts at speaking and hearing.

If we do not perceive what is intended by the word that is spoken, then we have not heard at all. In that case, any interpretation is a twisted imitation created by the hearer alone. It fails to be a revelation of the speaker.

It is a great and common tragedy that we have impoverished and isolated relationships because we do not take seriously the address of one person to another with an understanding form of listening.

We have to listen to the Bible as a human word. We have to understand it as a human word intended for us.

The Bible ought not to be read as an object of study, as a philosophy, or through any lens of human wisdom that does not listen first—that is to read unbiblically.

We must learn to hear what is said to us as those addressed by God in human words.

The Bible must be understood, as all human literary works are understood, as the self-gifting of the author and interpreted respectfully so. In the case of the Bible, the human authors witness to God, who is its proper focus. We are not to make of it what we want.

> We must learn to hear what is said to us as those addressed by God in human words.

God's revelation is what is at stake in the interpretation of the Bible. This is a question of either being true to God or putting words in God's mouth.

The Bible must be confirmed by clarifying what it demonstrates and indicates from God.

God, speaking through the Bible, summons us to hear.

The Word of God wants to lay hold of us, to embrace us into God's reality and not leave us to our own sensibilities.

2. Scripture as the Word of God (pp. 473–537)

The Bible is a witness in human words, but it is more than this. Its witness is to the God who speaks and so reveals God's own self-giving in person.

1. The Scripture That We Acknowledge as Witness Refers to the Canonical Books of the Bible

There was a time when the Church was called to recognize what was a true witness to the living God. This formed the process of canonization. The Church responsively affirmed what was given and distinguished as holy and true to the God revealed within.

The Church can only confirm the worthiness of Scripture as what is already formed. It humbly acknowledges what God has opened up for humanity. Canonization is not an act of human authority but a submission of the Church to the call of God to be a true witness in this particular written and gathered form.

In faithfulness, we concur with the Church's affirmation that the Bible is true to the God who is witnessed within.

The authority of Scripture is not in the Church and resides in God alone. "Holy Scripture is the Word of God to the Church and for the Church."[2]

When we are obedient to the Word of God and not the Church, we act truly as the Church.

God's Word to us is true and trustworthy; however, human hearing is not exempt from error or without need for improvement.

Particular persons need not accept the canon of the Bible just because the Church does, but they must be obedient to the way it compels a response by the Spirit. But this also must be lived in the Church and not as a private reading. A private interpretation claims its own lordship and authority.

We cannot speak and act with regard to Scripture without first listening to the Church. Our own experiences do not have authority to usurp the wisdom of those who are the cloud of witnesses that go before us.

The ultimate authority always belongs to the living God, to whom the Church bears witness. Thus, we speak in such a manner that our listening is always to God and not ourselves.

---

2. *CD* 1.2, § 19, p. 475.

2. When We Come to Scripture as Witness, We Come to Listen to Moses and the Prophets and to Hear the Evangelists and the Apostles

The time of expectation and of recollection have prepared the way for the accomplishment of what is to be known in the revelation of Jesus Christ:

1. Law, in the Old Testament, is the calling of Israel.
2. The Prophets speak to provide direction and instruction of Israel.
3. The Gospels glance back at the words and acts of Jesus as they look forward to the resurrection.
4. The Apostles look from the resurrection to the human situation as it is affected by the resurrection.

While there is a unity in what is said by the writers of the Bible, they retain their particularity.

Through the recording and the message of the Bible, the witnesses to the resurrected Jesus gave rise to the Church.

The unity of focus in the Old and New Testaments constitutes the witness of the whole Bible to God's revelation.

The Church exists by making clear what it has found in the Bible for God to speak here and now.

Only God can give Himself in revelation. The unity of the Bible is affirmed in that all the biblical evidence points to Him.

God's revelation shapes perception of God. It brings the promises and compels us to the task of listening so that we can pay attention to this personal Word of God who addresses us.

By listening to the recollection and expectation of the witness of the Bible, it brings us to the peace that is the origin and goal of God's promises and presence.

Revelation is not merely behind us as a proposition, it is alive and with us, and we must follow.

Scripture does not consist merely of its parts but functions as a whole. And it is through the whole that we find the one God, even in the parts.

3. Does the Bible Call Us to Recognize Its Character as Holy Scripture over All Other Writings?

Yes, with the humanity of the person of Jesus as its focus, and its self-witness to His historical reality, the Bible calls us to listen uniquely to the Son of God, who is resurrected from the dead.

Through the confirmation of the Holy Spirit, Scripture testifies to its trustworthiness in that it reveals the incarnate Son of God, who is now resurrected. The actuality confirms the possibility of its trustworthiness.

The Bible is a revelation to all humanity that Jesus comes to encounter and oppose the lostness of the human situation.
Prophets and apostles witness to His coming.

The first witnesses within the Bible allow for the witness of the disciples and all the generations that follow who are promised and given His Holy Spirit.

> The Church exists by making clear what it has found in the Bible for God to speak here and now.

The Church can speak today only because those first witnesses recorded what they saw and heard. They made possible our knowing. The original unique event can be a living event today through those documents.

Scripture not only attests to the anticipation and recollection of the revelation but also affirms the existence of specific human witnesses who enable us to be human listeners in our time.

Those witnesses heard and expressed what came to them as a unique encounter that changed their perception of the world. Their witness expands our perception of the world as we receive their engaged accounts as those who see and hear.

Those persons proclaimed boldly the revelation they encountered—they were sent to speak regarding whom they had met.

The writers of Scripture were only truly exceptional in what they beheld, not in their own capabilities. They were witnesses to revelation, empowered to communicate what they had known firsthand.

To look to and listen to the writers of the Bible is a call to attend most specifically to the One who sent them.

4. The Bible Affirms the Place of Prophets and Apostles

The prophets and apostles created the forms of the documents that consequently attest to their witness of revelation. Revelation always comes through a witness.

We cannot free ourselves from the texts of Scripture. It is the manner of witness to engage God's reality. This availability is made possible through these persons who were called, enlightened, and empowered.

We are free to become content with the Word witnessing to the person who has sought us. Thus, Christianity is a book religion that links us with a living Lord.

5. The Writers of the Bible Are Different from
Others as Witnesses of Divine Revelation

The biblical authors' uniqueness is not in themselves but in what they beheld.

Through these authors and their records of recollection and anticipation, we have a unique opening to what has come to humanity in Jesus. These are not merely wise authors; they are faithful witnesses.

If we are going to call the Bible *Holy Scripture*, it is because it is a witness to the unique revelation of God. It was written by witnesses entrusted with this moment and message.

The Bible is set apart as holy in order to reveal God. It will also confront all our false and twisted understandings of God and our place in the world.

We cannot give priority to the Bible as a book of human wisdom. There is one priority in the witness of the Bible: God is the Creator over all creation and each of His creatures. We learn this from the Bible itself.

The Bible is not merely a drama that we observe as a spectacle. And the drama ought not to take priority in our reading. We enter the drama of the Bible as a faithful opening of our limited reality to God's reality.

The Bible reveals the absolute; our lives are lived relative to its divine drama. God is the absolute, and His creatures are related to Him. It is not a theory; it is about a relationship.

In these distinctions, we find dissimilarities between God and human existence. His is reality, and our conceptions are warped and inaccurate, in need of God's restoration.

The gospel is God's correction of the human situation to bring the promise of life that, by God's grace, encompasses us. It reveals the gracious God and needful humanity restored by His grace.

In Scripture, God makes plain what was hidden and impenetrable in Himself. This word from the Bible is an echo, relative to the presence of God in Jesus' incarnation. Jesus reveals God; Scriptures attests and affirms.

The Bible holds out the truth of Jesus as the concrete reality under whose promise it lives.

Acknowledging the priority of the Bible in the Church does not threaten a proper honoring of the living God or a living faith.

6. Holy Scripture Has Priority over All Other Writings
and Authorities, Including the Church

The Bible is the original and legitimate witness of the revelation of God. Thus, it is acknowledged as the Word of God.

We believe the Bible, which involves recognizing and knowing its voice. This involves a clear hearing, appreciating, and discerning. The validation for the listener is that one has comprehended, and consequently one speaks and acts in a manner consistent with what has been heard.

Believing is not arbitrary, haphazard, or illogical. It is an act of recognizing what is engaged in an encounter. We believe a human is not a wild animal until they prove otherwise in the encounter.

Belief is a free act. It is conditioned only in the sense that we meet or hear that which confronts us, the reality entering into our field of awareness.

Believing does not control that which is encountered. Instead, it recognizes what is already there. Believing acknowledges that the happening before us has real existence.

We must attune our thinking to reality itself in an open manner. This is an act of keeping our thinking and speaking aligned with what can be known.

> We must attune our thinking to reality itself in an open manner. This is an act of keeping our thinking and speaking aligned with what can be known.

We recognize the Bible as already for us and speaking in a manner sufficient for its purpose. It points to Jesus, who is already there, and in a manner recognized as true He claims to be God in the flesh. Thus, Jesus and the Bible are believed as faithful to their claims and revelation.

The Bible is not a direct impartation from God but a witness to God's self-impartation in Jesus.

If we look at the Bible for truth as an oracle, apart from Jesus, we make it an idol.

Truths cannot be abstracted from the Bible in a manner dislocated from Jesus. We miss the one real thing God intends—to know Him.

We may wrestle with the Bible and its authors. It is likely to offend us. But in it we find true humans speaking to us in the name of the true God. The miracle to be acknowledged is that these humans saw and heard and could pass it on to us.

The writers of the Bible were historically conditioned. They used human words and concepts to witness to their experience of divine revelation.

The authors wrote within their limitations. They had a particularity of perspective. They were describing something beyond human capacity, something words and concepts cannot capture. Yet the authors spoke to open to us what had come to be known in Jesus. They said what they could.

What do we mean when we say the Bible is the "Word of God"?

A miracle occurs when we take up the Bible and let it speak to us. When it does, it awakens us and transforms our thinking to conform to the reality that opens to us.

In freedom, we hear the speaking and are grasped by the words that will not let us go. We freely choose to embrace the address that comes from the One who freely loves us.

Jesus is ultimately Lord over the Bible and also in the Bible. The Bible is indebted to and tied to this living Word of God.

The human side of hearing, within the life of the Church, is to grasp at the Bible, to honor it, and to accept its promises. We are called to open the Bible and read, search, and expand on its contents.

The Church must prioritize the preparation of prayer. Specifically, the Church must pray that the Bible be the Word of God in its midst and that the Holy Spirit does a work through the Bible. Finally, the Church must pray that the free grace of God is applied in the lives of humans as an act of living in the very presence of Jesus.

Sometimes the open book is a closed book as if a veil blocks the human heart. Only a return to the Lord by the Spirit could remove the veil and open up access. The Spirit facilitates this unveiling.

Christians are transformed to become an unveiled mirror of the glory of the Lord. This is the work of the Spirit, not our own.

The Spirit knows the things of God. Paul acknowledges the Spirit as the One who has enabled his writing. And by the Spirit we come to understand what is written.

Humans have been entrusted with the mystery of God. It remains a mystery to be freshly revealed by the Spirit for understanding. The Jews, without the Spirit, see the letter of the law but miss what came at Pentecost: the Spirit opened humans to the Word that transforms hearts.

God is the author of Scripture. Its words flow from heaven and are found to be communicated through humans who submit to the Spirit's work.

God is the One who brings humans to faith in His Word. The same Spirit who spoke through the writers of the Bible must penetrate our hearts today.

Honoring the inspiration of the Bible honors the grace of God in speaking to us through it. Therein, we are acknowledging the source, medium, and ultimate impact of God's address to humans.

With the inflow of natural theology in Church history, the doctrine of supernatural grace dwindled and a stricter doctrine of inspiration developed.

Thinking from the human (natural reason) began to exert an influence that elevated the human element and diminished God's voice (supernatural revelation). The conversation became one way—upward.

The nature of the Bible was shifted subtly from a Word from God to a human work inquired into under human control, filtered through human-shaped lenses.

The historical method came to mean that the significance of the Bible was only relevant as a historical record. The free grace of God speaking to humanity was traded in for a human-controlled use of the Bible to facilitate the achievement of human ends and desires.

> God is the author of Scripture. Its words flow from heaven and are found to be communicated through humans who submit to the Spirit's work.

What was lost was a native and intrinsic power implicit in the words of Scripture in its primary task to witness to the Word of God with His authority. The opening of hearts and confirmation by the Spirit was usurped as academic garb veiled the revelation of God.

Rather than the authority of the Living Word and Holy Spirit as the source of its truthfulness, human criteria and human-based attempts at relevance became authoritative in how the Bible might be used—trusting an authority outside the Word.

Certainty in knowledge of the truth came to mean provable by humans, not confidence in God. Human certainty was desired, not God's faithfulness as a basis for trust.

As a weapon against the authority of Rome, some orthodoxies made the whole of the Bible a certain body of truth. This became a petrification, locking down the sense of each word in a manner that stultified the word in legal language. Pursuing abstract, philosophical truth led the Church away from the dynamic of truth in relationship.

The words of the Bible became maxims, axioms, and "truth-statements" separated from the living Word and the work of the Spirit. The Bible became a "paper pope" set against the pope in Rome.

The Bible became an instrument of human power rather than the free and freeing Word of God, whose grace nurtures a spiritual life of relationship and communion.

When the grace of God as poured out in Scripture was handed over to the court of human judgments on truthfulness, the Bible became exclusively a historical document. Its claims of trustworthiness and supernaturality were rejected, deemed invalid for natural reasoning.

With the shift in thinking about the Bible as only a human book, Jesus then was looked at as a human, not as God. The way of the Spirit was consequently barred as not conforming to human reason.

We need to rebuild helpful ways to explore the meaning of the inspiration of Scripture in light of the Word:

1. To call the Bible the *Word of God* means we have to let it be an opening to God as the author and speaker who is lord over its intention. Reading the Bible requires attending to God Himself.

2. The Bible, as a Word of God, is an act of God. It is His work in communicating with us to enable a new thing to happen to us in knowing the One who knows us. Reading is hearing. It is an event that allows us to encounter the God who is present to us.

3. Reading the Bible as the Word of God means to be open to the unexpected possibility that we are not just reading an ancient book, but that a miracle occurs in meeting with God.

4. To read the Bible as the Word of God is to not compromise it with human explanations that remove the wonder of the miracle that it is and that is claimed within. We must acknowledge the miracles and the resurrection. Otherwise, we will be claiming our own authority and "reality." We will not be open to what has come to be in Jesus. This proposal offends our reasonable minds. That stance is a nonreception of the grace and mercy of God.

5. In reading the Bible as the Word of God, we acknowledge that it recollects that the Word of God has been heard in it over the centuries and that we believe we can hear it again. It is not embedded with divine character as much as serving us in hearing the living Word in our present moment as a faithful speaking of God for our listening to the voice of God.

6. God chooses the time and place for Jesus to speak to us. So also, our hearing of the Bible is in God's hands. Through it, He speaks to us now as His Word. If we seek God through the Bible, God decides how and when it speaks. We do not bring about the encounter. We are summoned to the Bible. No mere human-created experience mines its depths. We respond with gratitude and hope.

7. When we speak of the inspiration of the Bible in the sphere of time, there is a twofold reality. First, we engage a commissioned text that is human and can be used by God, if we respect its commissioning

as God's. Second, God shows up with His presence through the text, defining our recollection as thankfulness and our expectation as hope. If we will not listen to the living God through the Bible, we implicitly protest against God and prefer our own authority, missing His grace and truth.

8. The inspiration of the Bible cannot be reduced to our faith in it. Its inspiration is always tied to the once-for-all, original revelation of God to us. To believe in the inspiration of the Bible is to believe in the God whose witness it is. God sees to it that the Word is neither spoken nor heard in vain.

In our act of confession regarding the inspiration of the Bible, we admit to ourselves and others that, as the Word of God, it can have no other authority or proof that stands above it by which we judge its character.

We enter the life of the Bible, willing to hear with open ears, listening as God has already willed to address us.

In entering the circle of freedom that comes with hearing the Bible, we hear what was previously impossible. We hear God speak. We are bathed in His presence and grace as we meet Him.

No outside authority "proves" the Bible any more than an outside authority can prove light and darkness.

The authority of the Bible is intrinsic in that it witnesses to the only one who has authority to confirm its truthfulness. It must be read in a manner true to Him to discover its purpose and intended goal of knowing that God.

Like the Church, the Bible does not affirm its own authority but is accredited by its grounds to speak by the One who is its source and life. Both are sustained by the one ground to whom they point.

All other proofs for the validity and authority in a secondary defense of the Bible beyond God's authority are supports for our weakness.

The internal witness of the Holy Spirit can be taken or rejected as a human verdict that does not trust that God has attested Himself to be the God of the Bible.

Ultimately, the witness of the Spirit gave way to human convictions with human judgments. Reasoning moved readers to bring their own meaning and read by their own knowledge and conscience.

Scripture is recognized as the Word of God by the witness of the Holy Spirit, meaning that God in His free grace has turned toward us and that we are content to listen rather than judge based on our human reason.

At this point of utter dependence on God, the indestructible strength of the Church finds its life in Him by the Spirit and not by a self-generated church life.

🏠 **CONCLUSION FOR THE CHURCH:** The Bible is the means whereby Jesus maintains His position as Head of the Church. If church growth is built on any program other than knowing the God who speaks through the Bible, we are building on another foundation. Barth aims at the Church learning to discover the cohesion in the way God addresses the Church and leads it with communication. The origin of that speaking is in the life of God, manifested in the person of Jesus, made vocal in the Church by attentive listening to the Bible, and heard as the Spirit opens our ears and thinking.

🔬 **COMMENTARY:**

- The Bible is the central text for the Church, the communicative basis for the possibility of the Church having a relationship with the living God.
- The Bible is not a source for preaching helpful sermons merely to prompt humans to live moral lives. It is the dramatic stage that brings us face-to-face with Jesus, who is its author, lead actor, and continues as the present servant-leader in our churches.
- The question of authority is significant for Barth. The authority of the Bible can only be affirmed in that it refers back to the God who is its originating agent. This means that God must be acknowledged as the One who brings it into being.
- The Bible is not an accessory for the Church or a product to be marketed for its good ideas. It is the umbilical cord that connects us to the source of life as we are growing into it.
- We cannot merely confess with our mouths that the Bible is true. We must conform to its reality by falling in love with the One it reveals. Finally, we must act like one who continually rediscovers their first love.

🛐 **INSIGHT FOR PASTORS:** If you want to keep someone who is not physically present alive and active, talk about them. If we talk about what we are to say and do, we become a church without a Head. On the other hand, if we hear and respond to the One to whom the Bible points us, we bring His life to be heard like the heartbeat that sustains us. Then the transforming work of Jesus will flow through our veins, and the Spirit will nurture our lives in action. If pastoral leadership has one life-sustaining task, it is to come to perform CPR weekly so that the people know and are known by the Jesus of the Bible as the kiss of life. A sermon cannot be mere amusement for applause; it must be more like mouth-to-mouth resuscitation to revitalize the breath that gifts life to the human.

INSIGHT FOR THEOLOGIANS: Any scientific community builds on disciplined research into the body of inquiry that precedes it and becomes its focus. In the Bible, we have the historical record, but that record reveals the One who speaks and desires to be known today. This availability makes possible the ongoing presence of the voice of Jesus. On this basis, Jesus becomes the corrective of what is wrongly claimed and the cohesion of all proper claims made of God, and His communication is what truly connects us as persons to the personal God. As a scientific community, we routinely discover and question the validity of what is said by any who make truth-claims regarding the triune God in the Bible.

The faithful examination of the biblical text is the means to hear what the authors, divine and human, have said. That leads to hearing what Jesus is still saying. God's intent is fulfilled when there is faithful provision for the academic and church communities to be an embodied expression of God's communication. This personified way of being exists as a vitalized relationship indwelling the concrete mystery of God.

CLARIFYING QUESTIONS: Does your theology of the Bible rest on the quality of the Bible's translation and exposition for doctrine or on how it has been developed and sustained for its authority? *Or* does your view of the Bible rest on the Bible's capacity to point to God in a dynamic and living way that trusts He is still at work in and through His Word?

## CHAPTER 27

FOLLOWING TRUSTWORTHY, TRAINED GUIDES IN A COMMUNITY OF EXPLORERS

§ 20. Authority in the Church

FOCUS STATEMENT: In journeying to explore the mountain, it is best to follow those who know the way. Their experience can help us explore with focused curiosity. Their voices invite us into an attentive journey of surprise, learning from others who have learned from other explorers before them. If we could get inside their thinking, we would find they still hear the voices of wise guides from the past. They too needed training to experience insight for the hike. Their wisdom opens the way to wonder so we can see more of what was unknown.

In this chapter, we find wise guides who function within the "Authority in the Church." Humans function under the Word of God: the living Jesus and the voices of the Bible. In this chapter, we recognize the value of the Church as having authority only as it exists under the authority of the living God. The Church is a community entrusted with the written Word. As a living community, the Church provides entry into a shared life with God. Ultimately, our confidence is in God, who leads us in Jesus' ministry, in which we participate by the Spirit. The Church lives as the present, confessing body of persons pointing the way to know the living God, who embraces and guides us.

INTRODUCTION: This paragraph is the second of three on "Holy Scripture." Having affirmed that God Himself establishes the authority of Scripture and that it must refer to Him, we now shift our focus to the function of the Bible in the Church. We must be prepared to see that the Church lives under the authority of the Bible. Additionally, it makes its witness available for humans in its confessions. The persons who constitute the Church have discovered God in Christ. They come to know God and find their belovedness through the Bible. They affirm their belonging by acceptance of its confessions. This leads to a life of joyful obedience. This is the fruit of discovering who has loved us.

The point of this chapter is to summarize § 20 in the *CD*, exploring the place of the Church in facilitating a hearing and responding to the Word of God.

IIII CONTEXT: *CD* 1.2
Pages in Paragraph: 123 pages (pp. 538–660)

Subsections
1. The Authority of the Word
2. Authority under the Word

TEXT: § 20. Authority in the Church

OPENING SUMMARY: The Church does not claim direct and absolute and material authority for itself but for Holy Scripture as the Word of God. But actual obedience to the authoritative Word of God in Holy Scripture is objectively determined by the fact that those who in the Church mutually confess an acceptance of the witness of Holy Scripture will be ready and willing to listen to one another in expounding and applying it. By the authority of Holy Scripture on which it is founded, authority in the Church is restricted to an indirect and relative and formal authority.[1]

SUMMARY:
1. The Authority of the Word (pp. 538–85)

The Bible makes known the revelation of Jesus as the Word of God to the Church and, consequently, to the world.

The Holy Spirit impacts the Church by bringing the power of God through witnessing to Jesus.

Those who wish to hear the living Word of God must hear Him through the written Word.

The effective communication and transformation of God's address approaches us through the Bible. It comes to us in a concrete form, namely

---

1. *CD* 1.2, § 20, p. 538.

by the incarnation of Jesus. It comes reflectively by the outpouring of the Holy Spirit at work in us. In every way, God is effectually at work with us and for us.

The truth and force of the Bible is present and active because it is an act of the triune God, who comes to us.

We need to distinguish between that which externally enlightens us (Jesus, who comes to us) and being internally enlightened (by the Spirit). The first is what God has made possible for humans. The second is what is possible in human reception for responsive hearing.

God's authority establishes His external coming as Lord. Paired with that, human freedom is what God has determined to make possible for humanity as the internal fulfillment of God's intention.

The Bible roots the life of the Church in the life of God. The Bible limits its authority, calling for a freeing obedience to God's call for the Church to respond. In this way, the Bible constitutes the Church as the place where God is at work and where humans attune to God's life.

The Bible has a unique and singular authority in the Church. It records the origin and basis of the existence of the Church.

The authority of the Bible in the Church is mediate, relative, and formal:

Mediate means that it is human, grounded in history and human time. It has human authority.

Relative means that it can only represent God's authority and be authoritative. It appeals to the living Word of God.

Formal means that the Bible is on the level with all other witnesses in the form of a promise. It is not the promise itself, but it points to the One who makes the promise.

Authority in the life of the Church is not obedience to the Bible but to the One revealed within it.

The Church must declare what and where revelation is, where it comes from, and to whom obedience is due.

In a life of loving response, two partners are necessary.

> The Bible was not given a godlike status in itself. It profoundly serves only to make Jesus Christ known and accepted as Lord of the Church.

A distinction exists within the unity of the relation between God and humanity. There is a revealer, and there are recipients of the revelation.

The Bible is the authentic copy of the revelation of Jesus Christ for the Church. Therefore, we have to deal personally with our Lord through it.

The Church cannot go past or around the Bible to the Father, Son, or Spirit.

The authority of the person of Christ is not limited to the time of the Old and New Testaments.

In the sphere of the Church, Jesus is present at all times, and subsequently, His authority is active through His Word.

> The Church confesses unity as a fellowship in space and time based on the Word of God as a gift.
>
> The Church confesses that it is made up of persons past and present who together speak because they have heard.
>
> The Church confesses a continuity of witnesses over time that brings the vitality and presence of the Lord again and again.
>
> The Church confesses a respect for those who have gone before and built a tradition as a human form which is a proper witness to the Lord.
>
> The Church confesses that it has been entrusted with the task of being a witness to the presence of Christ. Its authority rests in being that witness.

When we say that there is an authority *in* the Church, we also acknowledge that same Word having authority *over* the Church.

The scripture principle for the Church is that it lives as an act of obedience to a higher authority under whom it exercises its authority.

The Church renounces its authority when it gives authority to itself, any institution (as with neo-Protestantism), or human person (as with Catholicism).

If the Church knows no higher authority than its own, it invests in its own authority and resists all transcendent authority to protect its own.

When the Church chooses to protect its self-affirmed authority instead of choosing listening obedience, it forgets that it is confronted by its Lord, who will have no other lord.

"Its Lord is Jesus Christ. He has called it into life and He maintains it in life. In Him it believes. Him it proclaims. To Him it prays. It is related to Him as the human nature which He assumed is related to His divinity. It looks up to Him, as He is present to it, and it partakes of His Holy Spirit, as the earthly body looks up to its heavenly Head. He and He alone, with the Father and the Holy Spirit, can have divine glory and authority in the Church."[2]

---

2. *CD* 1.2, § 20, p. 576.

The faithful Church will have a humility that recognizes and is grateful for its fellowship with its Head. He is the unity between heaven and earth, and the Church lives from His blessings.

The faithful Church divides from the Catholic and neo-Protestant churches to be true to the One authority who gives life to the Church as its Word and authority known through the Bible.

The Reformation, the rediscovery and restoration of the Church, was not an innovation but was a return to the One who gives life to the Church.

The Reformers only affirmed the authority of Scripture where Jesus Himself has established it—in Himself.

The Bible was not given a godlike status. It serves only to make Jesus Christ known and accepted as Lord of the Church.

Still, we must confidently affirm that the Bible is the gate one cannot bypass to engage the life of God.

In the voice of Jesus and the voice of those called to witness to His voice, the Bible meets the Church in a living way with His authority.

> In the voice of Jesus and the voice of those called to witness to His voice, the Bible meets the Church in a living way with His authority.

The Church is filled with a multitude of parties vying for attention and authority (liberal and conservative, mystics and pragmatics, biblical and social, etc.)—all become forms of resisting the Lord of the Church with their own agendas.

The Church ceases to be the Church when it wants to be alone with itself.

The Church is not alone. It stands clothed with a divine dignity by the One who is present and gracious in concrete authority. The Bible is Jesus' authority active in the Church.

2. Authority Under the Word (pp. 585–660)

Under the living Word and therefore under His voice in the Bible, the Church exercises a genuine authority.

All claims for the Bible's interpretation must be submitted to the critical control of Jesus and the Spirit in order to confirm that the interpretation maintains a true intent.

Jesus' authority has a unique nature from which all other forms of authority derive their humble power.

No one will be a suitable teacher in the Church who has not first been a student of the Son of God under His authority.

The Church's authority stands under the authority of Christ.

The Church is the Church as a people constituted through hearing and accepting the Word of God.

The unity of this hearing Church occurs with a present listening. It also extends to the past and into the future as those who are His body. "Not listening" is cutting oneself off from the body.

The Word is not spoken to individuals but to a community of hearing who are a community by virtue of receiving it together.

We hear the Word of God in concert with those who have gone before and those currently in our community. In concert, we are confessing a faith that existed prior to ours and is larger than our belief. Only when listening in this polyphonic, harmonious context do we hear ourselves directly addressed.

How is authority worked out in the Church?

The Church's authority is relative to its shared confession, held under Christ Jesus.

The authority of the Church allows it to guide, inform, and govern while submitting to the presence of Christ. This happens through reading the Bible.

When the Church reads together, it becomes a chorus of voices, not a group of individuals. When they speak together as a community with a common witness, they affirm those who have heard as a community. As they mutually agree in hearing, they submit to the gift of the Word, graciously understood in the Church.

The Church is not a poor theological seminar or a religious debating club. It stands as a community of faith, together looking to Christ and participating by the Spirit in His love.

The confession of the Church cannot be merely an agreement between humans; the confession must humbly agree with Jesus.

There must always be an openness in the listeners to be corrected and redirected by the Word of God.

The Church cannot speak new revelation. It must always be open to realigning to revelation in fresh ways.

The Church's authority is narrow—a human, preliminary, and partial agreement of the community. The Church continually will be questioned and renewed by the Lord, who has final authority.

What is the concrete form of the Church in which it has authority?

The authority of the Church is heard in its common confession of the living God.

Church history is a discussion that may lead to common confessions. But it is not authoritative until it reaches a decision both within its own conversation and in alignment with Jesus.

The common confession of the Church arises when it answers God. It must agree regarding the hearing of what has been said and decide what can be confessed as it faces the witness of the Bible.

For unbiased observers, Church history appears as a whole, a mixture of opinions and voices. What is missing, however, is an overarching authority to bring unity. This can only happen when there is a humble submitting to the living Word through the written Word.

The authority of the Church arises as a result of the common decision, of those who spoke long ago and those who hear today, to listen to their Head.

Both those who speak with authority and those who hear its witness stand in the light of Holy Scripture, which is its validation. This authority is then expressed and realized in the acts of human speaking and hearing.

The Church is a spiritual authority. Wherever it exists, it has authority to speak in a specific form and historical context, under the Word.

1. The Church of the past and the present, existing everywhere, holds a common confession following the compass of the Holy Scriptures, the canon of the Bible. This confession is tied up with revelation; the Bible is God's concrete, earthly witness. The Church is a counterwitness—not in opposition but as spoken by awakened respondents.

2. The Church of the past and the present, existing everywhere, holds a common confession that respects certain teachers, expositors, and preachers of the Word. These "Church fathers" have taken part actively in the life of the Church to nurture its life together.

   Holy Scripture speaks to each generation in the Church. This speaking comes in a defined canon, that which is measured and approved. It speaks with human authority, respecting the preceding voices in the history of the Church. It is not limited by speaking to a generation or individual; it speaks to all who belong to the fellowship of the Church who have a place in history.

A Biblicist, one who wants only the Bible, becomes independent and then noticeably builds their own authority with an unwillingness to listen to others.

Neither in principle nor in practice can we deny the value of the great teachers of the Church.

The Reformers are genuine teachers of the Church. Until we have more trustworthy teachers, we would do well to be faithful students in their school in learning the authority of the Bible.

If we are going to introduce new teachers, they must meet certain qualifications:

a. Does the proposed person faithfully serve the Word of God in helping the Church's understanding?

b. Does the person listen attentively to the early fathers of the Church as well as the Reformation teachers?

c. Does this person consider the whole Church before them, to speak intelligibly and responsibly in addressing all its needs or just a selected part for a specific place?

d. Does this teacher bring Scripture home to us today as well as present timeless truth that will stand in the future?

3. The Church of the past and the present, existing everywhere, holds a common confession with specific declarations: a proclamation of insights with decisive elements.

a. It stands as a Church confession reflecting on and compliant with Scripture. It exclusively confesses Jesus Christ. It explains and applies the Bible in an understandable language.

b. It is a confession given to the Church as a source of knowledge for the universal Church in a manner consistent with Scripture.

c. It is a confession given to the Church, faithfully bound to what is discovered in Holy Scripture and as a gift of the Spirit. It is pronounced in such a way as to be believed or rejected. It challenges all persons to take a position with regard to the Word of God.

d. The confession of the Church has definite limits with regard to its source (originating in God) and object (focused on Jesus). It is a "Yes" and therefore a "No." It is a "Yes" to "we believe, we confess, and we teach." There follows a "we condemn," which limits what contradicts faithful confession.

The confessions stand to stop confusion. It is too late when an uncovered well has resulted in a drowned child.

Every confession is limited by its humanity. This limitation frees us to listen clearly with human ears.

A historical confession speaks for a particular place and time. The critical question then is whether it defers to its cultural context or to the Word of God.

e. The Church's confession is a common declaration achieved by deliberation and a final unified decision. The confession has to speak on behalf of the Church and to the Church.

   a. Confessing means entering into conflict and accepting its challenges and promise.

   b. Confession is the "Yes" of the Church in agreement with the Word of God.

   c. Confessors are those who stake their lives on the "Yes" of God.

Confession may come as a challenge, a question mark, or an insult to the world that surrounds us.

We relinquish our place as confessors when we try to spare our environment the confrontation and unpleasantness of our confession.

Confession as theory does not exert any pressure.

Publicity brings a confession to create a decision. Where the fear of God overrules the fear of humans, confessors become public in their confession.

No church lacks fellowship with those who stand behind them in the past and beside them in the present.

Firstly, the Church is the Church by virtue of the Church's confession. This word has been passed on from those before and is a human word that is given priority over other human words. Its recognition gives meaning to what follows.

Secondly, the confession is to be read as a commentary on Scripture, which gives it authority. It cannot replace Scripture or our exposition of it.

Having affirmed the confessions, we are responsible to go back to Scripture in understanding and living in light of the God we find there.

The Church has a confession to serve Scripture's reading. Confessions are not dogmas to stand over the Bible, laws to constrain the Bible's content, nor authority given by the Church through which these confessions hold power of their own.

The necessary affirmation of the Church's confession is its directing us toward a particular horizon. We stand before Scripture as it opens us to the revelation of the living God.

The authority of the Church's confession is relative, not absolute. The Lord, who is the Head of the Church, is infallible. Human dogmas are not final or unalterable. They must stand in relation to their proper horizon in Jesus for correction by the Spirit.

> Confession may come as a challenge, a question mark, or an insult to the world that surrounds us.

We must venture a new confession only as a faithful witness to the living God, to the brethren who went before us, and for the world that needs the confrontation of grace. The new confession must comply with the old yet bring a freshness that complies with the work of the Spirit. It must not tear down what the current fad opposes but must listen and proclaim anew within the horizons that are its proper limitation and freedom.

CONCLUSION FOR THE CHURCH: The Church was never intended to be an authoritative institution based on its own accomplishment or earned position. Rather, the Church's guiding role is entirely to be empowered by its relation to Scripture that is its sustaining authority. The Church must look through the window of the Bible to see the One who is always its source and who is supremely and clearly seen through this uniquely enabled text. The Church lives as an expression of Jesus' voice.

COMMENTARY:

- The question of authority is one related to power. Barth rejects granting autonomous power to any human organization or text. Authority belongs to Jesus alone.
- The only reason the Bible has authority is because its source and purpose for being are in making present the life and person of Jesus.
- The Church has a derived authority. It functions only under an authority. It has a responsibility to exercise its authority with a mindfulness that Jesus is the Lord. The Church is only an unworthy servant.
- Struggles in the Church, as to who has the upper hand in the world today, are missing the point. The quest for power in this world takes on many forms; all exhibit varying shades of denial with respect to belonging to the Church of Jesus Christ.
- To say the Church lives under the authority of the Word of God is to affirm that it is loved. It is granted a space to love and speak in return.

But it may not speak falsely of God or act in a manner that destroys what God's love is creating in the world by the Spirit.

- The great teachers of Church history are to be listened to and seen as our guides insofar as they point us to Jesus and the Bible.
- The confessions of the Church are lenses to help us read the Bible so that we may be shaped regarding what takes priority in our thinking and living in the light of God's presence.

INSIGHT FOR PASTORS: Pastors must be clear that they are not running a popularity contest or a successful church measured by profound theories or sheer numbers. A faithful pastor will clarify by teaching the "Yes" of God so that the "No" of God may have a corrective effect. A living church will know the confrontation of the Bible. It cannot conform to popular culture. Good preaching will always pull us out of our self-focus and return us to fix our eyes on Jesus through the Bible and the confessions of the Church that are signposts on the way. Confession ought never to be rote repetition; it should be more like the daily renewal of vows to love and cherish.

INSIGHT FOR THEOLOGIANS: Doing the work of an academic theologian without knowing the Bible and its revelation of Jesus is like being a doctor who does not prepare before seeing patients. What comes out of the doctor's mouth can only be foolishly spoken. The uninformed academic draws on wisdom from experience, which arrogantly would take over the diagnosis. The person needing help would be left ignorant. Proper theological method requires knowing Jesus in the most faithful way possible, through the Bible. Having come to know Him, we have wisdom in how to bring theology to serve those needing help. The investigations and conclusions that we come up with must be tested and tried against past teaching and understandability in the world today. Theology serves the Church by listening and clarifying what Jesus has said and wants to be said in the Church and to routinely reengage the life of the Church in the living God when it drifts away.

? CLARIFYING QUESTIONS: Does your theology acknowledge the authority of Scripture as residing in the book itself, in the Church that affirms it, *or* find its final authority in the person of Jesus?

## CHAPTER 28

FREEDOM FOUND ON THE TRAIL WITH COMPETENT OTHERS

§ 21. Freedom in the Church

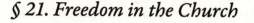

FOCUS STATEMENT: A freedom comes in the wilderness. This may happen when you are roped up on a glacier. It may occur to you when you are glad you are not alone when submerged in deep forests. This form of freedom comes when you appreciate that you are with others. You are under the care—yes, the authority—of persons who protect, guide, nourish, and connect with you—if you submit to their oversight.

This mode of existence is the case in the section called "Freedom in the Church." Human freedom is possible as it corresponds to the authority of the Church as the vessel of Jesus' presence and power to be graciously present, with us and for us. When we acknowledge and joyfully respond to His lordship of love, we are free to abandon the chaos and fear existing in our self-determination and disconnected self-seeking. Freedom comes in the companionship of love in the form of Jesus.

INTRODUCTION: In this section, we unfold § 21, which seeks to transform our sense of the experience of human freedom in the community of the Church. This inquiry is necessary because we have so many wrong ideas about freedom. In exploration, we find that freedom comes when Jesus is acknowledged as Lord over all things, even over those intrusions that bring chaos into our lives. Freedom comes when we read the Bible, learning to listen to God. Positioned to hear, we experience being included fully in a life of knowing with the God who sustains us. This is possible as a gift and made actual through His address that confronts everything that constrains us and as He then offers us life in Himself.

📖 **CONTEXT:** *CD* 1.2
Pages in Paragraph: 80 pages (pp. 661–740)

Subsections
1. The Freedom of the Word
2. Freedom Under the Word

📖 **TEXT:** § 21. Freedom in the Church

OPENING SUMMARY: A member of the Church claims direct, absolute and material freedom not for himself, but only for Scripture as the Word of God. But obedience to the free Word of God in Holy Scripture is subjectively conditioned by the fact that each individual who confesses his acceptance of the testimony of Scripture must be willing and prepared to undertake the responsibility for its interpretation and application. Freedom in the Church is limited as an indirect, relative and formal freedom by the freedom of Holy Scripture in which it is grounded.[1]

✠ **SUMMARY:**

1. The Freedom of the Word (pp. 661–695)

Jesus hovers over the Church with ultimate loving care as the authority who can ensure a life of active love. In this embrace, we also find our freedom in Him. We discover that human freedom is not a turning away to our own self-serving—freedom as liberation from others. Freedom is found precisely in focused listening to Him, placing ourselves within His care as a community who pays attention.

Having heard His voice, we may now act in a manner compelled by His love. We are newly awakened within His freeing hold to a distinctive life yet intended to be shared in community.

The Word who is Jesus does not overwhelm our ability to respond to Him in a forced manner. That would be a relational tragedy. Rather, He creates a new heart by His kindness. He invites, lovingly compels, and blesses us within the embrace He brings.

In freedom, our response comes from the heart. This is the reaction of one who receives and spontaneously generates an unconditional reply. Responsive acts flourish within the sphere of freedom created by His lordly grace.

---

1. *CD* 1.2, § 21, p. 661.

When we are humbled by His voice, we are raised up and comforted. We are stirred to a wholehearted assent to His faithful love.

Humans may feel an urge to grasp for power, thinking we may lose control to a tyrant God who wants to dominate us. This defensive response is a symptom of seeing the Word as overwhelming and forcing a constraining obedience. But this is not what we see in Jesus.

The command of Jesus sets us on our feet. He empowers us for a responsibility that is born of love.

Respecting the authority of the living God is to love God in return—this is a genuine, cooperative responsibility.

The fully Christian person is made to stand erect. They are lifted up because they have humbled themselves. This enablement is an act that receives a love not earned or forced. It is a resurrection made possible by the crucifixion of the old. It is a joyful response to the command of Jesus to return home—only because He has made the way.

"In the Word, by the Spirit" means we cannot pit the command of Jesus against us in an antithesis. To make that clearer, in the Word we see the One who is freely for us. By the Spirit we live in response to find our freedom lavishly fulfilled. The Word speaks and commands *that we be free*, and consequently, the Spirit brings us to participate in this love completed. Nothing is against us and all is actively for us.

Freedom comes through free obedience.

The Catholic Church fights for authority of the Church but usurps the authority of Jesus. The neo-Protestant fights for the authority of the individual human, who also usurps the authority of Jesus. Both exercise a kind of tyranny.

When we think of freedom in the Church, we must not begin with the free will of an individual. We must begin with the freedom that comes to us as a gift in the Word of God who frees us.

> The command of Jesus sets us on our feet. He empowers us for a responsibility that is born of love.

The freedom that concretely and personally comes to us is immediate, absolute, and meaningful. God is free for us, and His authority to free us makes us free indeed. Our freedom is under this living Word who comes to us.

Freedom is not an abstract concept in eternity or human thinking. It is human participation in the present and gracious person of Jesus.

Obedience is freedom. It is a choice to live in light of the actual freedom of Jesus and not to neglect this gift.

The Bible has to be heard as the principle and voice of both authority and freedom, igniting the Church to mutual love actively instilled and set in motion.

The true freedom of humans in the Church is found in following the living God, who precedes us through Holy Scripture.

1. The freedom of the Word of God consists in its faithful witness to the revelation of Jesus Christ, who stands with a permanent distinctiveness and uniqueness to free us.

2. The freedom of the Word of God is its ability, possibility, and power over against all other powers. The Word made flesh confronts and opposes other powers that operate in the sphere of humanity as the light that brings freedom.

    Scripture is victorious over the world even as it is hidden from the world. Jesus, who died and rose again, is its freedom, He who brings the Church into its reality in the kingdom of God.

    The rule of God in this world is not in the power of the Church. Rather, it is in the hands of Him who had to be nailed to the cross.

    a. The Word of God demonstrates its freedom and superiority by its ability to stand against the attacks made on it.

    b. The Word of God demonstrates its freedom and superiority as it distinguishes itself from the elements of the world that impose upon it for their own purposes.

    c. The Word of God demonstrates its freedom and superiority as it exercises the power to transform all alien elements it encounters into serviceable actions for the fulfillment of the kingdom of God.

    d. The Word of God demonstrates its freedom and superiority as the dynamic means of God's rule, the organ of His speaking. By the Holy Spirit, who is dynamically present, God says, "Lo, I am with you always" (Matthew 28:20 KJV).

3. The freedom of the Word of God is heard as a subject speaking within its sphere of influence in the Church.

    The Word of God chooses, defines, and rules the Church as the place of His working—not for the sake of the Church but for the work of God and His witness to the world.

    God speaks to the Church, in the Church, and through the Church so that He might speak to the world and thereby grow His Church.

The freedom of God's Word is actualized in that it unites to itself all people. This extends to all times and all places for people to hear the grace that overcomes all that threatens. His Word is His authority to overcome. It is also our freedom in our obedience as we hear and are restored.

The possibility of faith is our submission to His lordship and the reception of the freedom that follows.

The Church is not left alone like a widow when the Word of God is handed to the Church. The Church does not merely carry on a legacy.

The Word of God establishes the Church and is able to continually preserve and nourish it.

The resurrection of Jesus accomplishes a specific exercise as the Word of God, maintaining the Church in the world as it is drawn to Him who is its Lord.

From the life of the Word flows the life of the Church.

The Church is alive because it participates in the movements of His life with a "Yes." Consequently, its movements follow His movements, including worship, fellowship, preaching, and confession.

The Church is preserved as it lives under the care and authority of this sustaining Word of God.

The Church constantly tinkers with the gospel, trying to adjust it to meet human needs. When this happens, the power to maintain the Church is lost.

The continuation of the life of the Church depends on whether Scripture remains open to it, and not lost or twisted. Scripture's conceptions must remain clear, not muddied with other agendas. Finally, the Church must allow the Word to be free to speak authentically.

The atoning work of God has become for many a dim memory of an ancient past. The return of Christ for redemption is a vague, future goal. Neither the past nor the future seems to deeply impact those who live today in the interval between. The "faith" that is left is merely a human capacity for self-management and not dependence on the Lord of all times and places. That form is a false, autonomous faith.

Together, Jesus Christ and Holy Scripture explain one another. In harmony, they rule the Church. Each can be understood only through the other.

Holy Scripture is the bearer of the concrete governing of the Church. This is accomplished by virtue of its ability to establish the authority of Jesus Christ as its Head.

The Bible constitutes the immediacy of the relation between Jesus and His Church. This becomes a guarantee of His freedom as we abide in the relationship. Consequently, His freedom is experienced as ours.

Prayer precedes exegesis in the tasks of the Church. Prayer is the act of orienting the Church to hear. Only then can the Church be attuned to interpret what is said.

Real humans are gathered in the Church. They are called, not assembled, to experience freedom under the Word as gift. They are called by a human Word, who is Jesus.

> Freedom is not an abstract concept in eternity or human thinking. It is human participation in the present and gracious person of Jesus.

There is a human power and freedom that corresponds to the power and freedom of the Word of God.

God's freedom happens among those who are met, addressed, communicated with, and respond with a readiness to hear.

2. Freedom Under the Word (pp. 695–740)

To be ready and willing to listen and seek understanding of the Word of God is to experience freedom under the Word.

To have a conscience, as a theological affirmation, needs to be understood as knowing with God what God knows. Therefore, we submit to thinking with Him what is right and true and wise. This is freedom of the conscience over against a mere permission to do what we think is right for ourselves.

As we position ourselves under the authority of the Word, we are then enabled to live with freedom and become free toward one another. Human freedom is contingent on the freedom of the Word.

In prayer, we become open to the freedom of the gift of God's grace, enabled to be responsible in submission to His grace.

The Bible has its foundation in being God's Word, dynamically coming as a human word to humans.

We are aroused to believe and testify, which is not natural to us. The gift comes as Jesus intercedes before the Father and as we are illumined by the Spirit. In this process, we are claimed and compelled to tell what has happened to us as participants in God's gift.

Although we may experience doubt and despair, we are those who remember. Therefore, we give thanks and pray. We remember we are children, not strangers. We actively cooperate rather than passively look on. We are not ignorant; we have conscience—coknowing with God.

Human beings exist in decision. The Word of God questions us not in judgment but regarding our response to what the Word has spoken to us.

We can either persist in the alienation portrayed in the fall, or we can identify with what the Word of God has spoken to us. The latter is the truth that we are beloved of God, children of the Father, reconciled by Jesus, and redeemed by the Spirit's work.

"I am merely recounting a myth if I speak of the coming of the Word of God to man as of something other than the coming of the Word to me. Only as the Word which comes to me can I hear it as the Word which comes to the Church and therefore to others too."[2]

We hear the Word as particular humans who are called to communion with the Word. This Word calls us to Himself. We are never human individuals alone; we are always those who stand before the Word, whether in acceptance or rejection.

> Genuine freedom is realized under the Word as we become coknowers with God. We ought never to get lost in the illusion of freedom as self-determination without God.

In life, we become who we are with clarity specifically through the decision to find our identity in responding to the Word of God. We do not come into existence in our act; we become clear as to who we are in Him.

When were we saved? In the event of the birth, life, death, resurrection, and ascension of Jesus. Our faith is a sharing in the saving acts of God. Having heard the witness of Scripture, we are compelled to participate by the Spirit, as happened at Pentecost.

> We must be aware that we approach every text with lenses, logic, expectations, and ideals that filter our image of the relation of God and humanity and thus ourselves.

Divine freedom precedes human freedom. Thus, human freedom is grounded in the divine freedom, and divine freedom will not destroy or suspend it.

Genuine freedom is realized under the Word as we become coknowers with God. We ought never to get lost in the illusion of freedom as self-determination without God.

---

2. *CD* 1.2, § 21, p. 703.

Just as Church authority is not a human-created power but is under the authority of the Word, so too human freedom is not a human-created power but is lived under the freedom of the Word.

What are the real possibilities for human freedom under the Word of God?

1. Being free under the Word is more than hearing. It is to take seriously one's responsibility in the effective operation of the Word being expressed and heard in the Church and the world. In this response, we become the Church in person.

   Scripture needs interpretation that comes through exegesis and exposition.

   As members of the church, preachers intervene in the interpretation of Scripture, between its Speaker and the hearers.

   In the region of words, the clear sense of language is not always available in its intended meaning or its appropriate use.

   The Church exists for this mediatorial work between the original authors and the world—all to the glory of God and for the upbuilding of the Church.

   The form of exegesis that persons must employ is to practice the free subordination of all human concepts, ideas, and convictions to the revelation given us in the Bible. Subordination here means spontaneous activity in response to the Word of God spoken to us.

   The Word of God needs interpretation to correct the ideas, thoughts, and convictions that obscure its meaning when brought by humans from their own resources.

   When the Word of God comes to us, we are laden with images, ideas, and certainties that we have formed—this becomes a fog. Subordination to the Word is what happens when the fog clears.

   The clarity of the Word of God is intrinsic to the interpretation that He gives to it. His interpretation is the true interpretation.

   "The content of the Bible, and the object of its witness, is Jesus Christ as the name of the God who deals graciously with man the sinner. To heed and understand its witness is to realise the fact that the relation between God and man is such that God is gracious to man: to man who needs Him, who as a sinner is thrown wholly upon God's grace, who cannot earn God's grace, and for whom it is indissolubly connected with God's gracious action towards him, for whom therefore it is decisively one with the name of Jesus Christ as the name of the God who acts graciously towards him. To hear this is to hear the Bible—both as a whole and in each one of its separate parts."[3]

2. Scripture takes precedence in the interpretation of all interpretation, as Scripture interprets Scripture.

  Scripture unfolds what is hidden from us. If our interpretation is adjusted to our human world of thought as through a prism, it becomes darkened.

  We need to see the original texts as written by authors and understand them in their context.

  We must engage the historical aspect of the text, to know what it meant to the original writers and hearers. From this engagement, we form a picture of what was going on, a representation of what is now being spoken of to us. This field of engagement is not only within what is known but also opens to what is unknown.

  Our clarity in understanding the text depends on our forming an accurate picture of the object mirrored in the words of the writers.

  The meaning of a text needs to be controlled by its author and not by a human reading onto the text derived from our experience and bent to serve our purposes.

  The object, or speaker of the biblical text, is Jesus Christ. The texts of the Bible can be properly understood only when understood in the light of His intentions.

3. A distinguishable component of reading the biblical text is experienced in the act of reflection as listening: What is this text saying to us?

  Having heard the author's intention, we now listen for the explanation or clarification as to what the text means for us.

  We must be aware that we approach every text with lenses, logic, expectations, and ideals that filter our image of the relation of God and humanity and thus ourselves.

  No one is void of lenses. Everyone has a unique view on the nature and relationship of things that vacillate day in and day out, shaped within our changing encounters.

  We all read the Bible with fitted spectacles unlike those of others. Those who criticize others while assuming their own innocence are blind to their own lens as their particular point of view.

---

3. *CD* 1.2, § 21, p. 720.

We must not reject the fact that it is we who observe and seek to understand. We seek selfishly; we receive beyond our nearsighted perceptions.

We are like the self-seeking prodigal son. He still remembered where to get help when he was in his poverty. He received help beyond his expectations not only in getting food but, more importantly, his father.

Everyone uses some form of philosophy in interpreting. We must have some considerations.

a. An interpreter must be aware and honest about what he or she brings to the task. The meaning of the words belongs first to Jesus. The Spirit illuminates us.

Our thought does not originally default to biblical thought. We can participate in biblical thought only by submitting to the guidance of the Spirit in a venture of obedience.

b. When reflecting on the Bible, we need to use our tools unassumingly. We can do little more than create a hypothesis in the form of essays intended to give humble insight.

We are invited, as members of the Church, to explore the Bible in an experimental and provisional manner.

c. The philosophies and lenses we bring to the task of interpreting the Bible cannot have an independent end in mind. When used appropriately, they only serve the Word in being heard.

Imported modes of thought become dangerous when we are unaware how they may be different from the biblical intention. Subtly, Scripture becomes distorted. Our interpretations grasp for its power but do not seek the Speaker's intent.

The written Word can be separated from the living Word and become a deception.

The scriptural mode of thought must take precedence over our human modes of thought. In this way, following its lead will be good and equalizing. If we are dominating the text, its interpretation will always be bad.

d. Recognizing that we use some lens in our interpretation, there is no reason to prefer one lens over another. They must all be unveiled with honesty.

Then, we need to find what modes of thought can be particularly helpful for the current exegesis in hearing and advancing the scriptural intent.

e. Using a new mode of thought in scriptural exegesis is fruitful when controlled by the text and following its focus and intent.

    The truth of our reflections is determined by the critical control of the object which is mirrored in the text. That means the Speaker gets to determine what is meant.

    The object of biblical criticism is not Scripture but our thoughts about it. It is a testing of our thoughts to see if they are faithful. The criticism is a critique to distinguish what is originally meant from what we are reshaping in the interpretation.

    Scripture is the only truly free school for human thinking. It is freed from the tyranny of systems that favor human agendas. It frees us when we hear its freeing power to speak God's freeing Word.

4. Having observed and heard the Bible, we set ourselves to the task of reflecting and understanding its meaning. This leaves the final task to answer the question: "How does this freedom under the Word assimilate into our lives?"

    One cannot act in accordance with the Word if one has not read and contemplated the Bible.

    One cannot have read engagingly if its meaning does not find fruitful outcomes in one's life.

    Real transformation comes with a genuine openness to the One who meets us. The outcome is that our study becomes a real knowing-with the living God.

    Knowing that we are known becomes a fundamental reorientation of our lives. The outcome is that we act like it.

    The assimilation of the Word into our lives is an authentication that the intimacy offered us in the Word spoken to us has found its home in us.

    The Word wills not to be without us. The Word intends to be in communion with us and to permeate our whole existence.

    Reading and applying the Bible cannot be a question of theory and practice. No theory of falling in love, or learned practices that look like falling in love, can replicate the transformation of actually falling in love and thinking and acting from that new encounter.

    The Word itself shifts us from focusing on ourselves to beholding the One who meets us as faithful love and the fulfilling center of our existence.

By faith, we assimilate the grace that is enacted toward us by Jesus Christ, taking Him at His Word. In this is freedom indwelt as we live in Him.

🏠 **CONCLUSION FOR THE CHURCH:** The Church can never be in control of the Word of God as a resource for the Church's own ends or as a tool for attempting to be relevant. The freedom of the Church comes as we submit to the lavish love and authority of the One who loves us. We are free to come as hungry learners who did not know we were hungry. In our listening, we come to be filled as we discover the source of loving freedom that satisfies and empowers us to share what we have found.

🔬 **COMMENTARY:**

- Modern concepts of free will miss the point Barth is making in this section. Freedom can never be an act that claims autonomous power for ourselves. It always begins with God's freeing initiation.
- Freedom can never be an abstract concept; it can only come when we give ourselves to the One who sees our bondage and acts to free us.
- The Word of God is the sphere in which we are awakened to hear what was unknown. Our self-confidence, which feels like self-care, will deceive us regarding our self-capacity for freedom.
- Only in giving ourselves with freeing abandon to the One who loves us will we shed the urge to be worthy or capable of achieving our freedom.
- We need to become students of the Bible to know the fruit of freedom. We begin with a careful reading that is ready and open to hearing. In our reading, we come to ponder what is meant in the words as an opening to hearing from God's speaking. It is clear that we have heard when we love anew and act in a manner consistent with that love.
- The Bible is not a means for us to reach God; it is God's means of speaking to us.

📖 **INSIGHT FOR PASTORS:** The focus on the Bible in the Church cannot be an inspiring sermon. It must be an event that teaches all those present how to hear and that overwhelms us by who Jesus is as He meets us in the preaching of His Word. If those present congratulate us for a great sermon, we have missed the mark. If they walk out and confirm the wonder of hearing Jesus afresh and the challenge and joy of walking with Him out the door, then we know they are walking in the freedom of the Spirit. In that flood of unveiling that comes from God's Word, freedom is offered as a gift. All hear, but at the same time each hears a particular word for ourselves, some form of the address, "For you I have come and given Myself and speak to you today." The fruit of a Bible-based church is a love for Jesus, each other, and a loving self-giving that is evidenced in that order in the whole community.

INSIGHT FOR THEOLOGIANS: Theology must be a freeing discipline. If we build arguments and definitions from the Bible to construct a theology that does anything other than open the way to understand Jesus and the gift of freedom He brings, we are burying the point in abstractions. The Word liberates humans by helping them look at Jesus and perceive His intent as the One who is for us. The Bible ought not to be read to bring shame, guilt, or blame, looking first at our inadequacies and issues of bondage in our doctrine of sin. Using the Bible in this manner for self-achieved freedom is a clear example of sin at work. Freedom can only come in the form Jesus offers, and that is to give us Himself. In Him, we find that freedom is the life of Jesus overcoming whatever imprisons us. Seeking to build doctrines to clarify the outcomes for human life and connection with who God actually is might provide proper guidance for pursuing the clarifying work of academic theology.

CLARIFYING QUESTIONS: Does your theology build on a vision of the Bible as our tool for discovery in a life of searching for God? *Or* do you see the Word of God full of personal, mysterious openings to hear God? Does your study of the Bible keep bringing you and your thinking back to Jesus, thus helping you feel newly set free? Do you easily shed the tentacles of expectation that have constrained you and held you a hostage in reading the Bible? Is your life of study an accomplishment rather than a garden of meeting with your Beloved that will never leave you the same?

CHURCH DOGMATICS, CHAPTER 4

"The Proclamation of the Church"

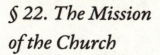 CHAPTER 29

LISTENING IN THE MOMENT, TELLING THE STORY, ENTICING OTHERS

§ 22. The Mission of the Church

FOCUS STATEMENT: When encountering wonder, it is hard to remain silent if we really let it impact us. We want to breathe in every moment. We yearn to hear and share all the joy we are experiencing. We are inspired to send pictures or texts that invite others. We want them to participate in the astonishment that makes us love this moment. What we have encountered moves us to care for others more than we previously thought possible. That is the heart of proclamation.

In this section, we explore the life of a community who is in the same moment both listening to and expressing what the Word of God has conveyed. Thus, "The Mission of the Church" is always a participation in the dynamic of God's self-giving. It is never a self-focused activity but is an expression blossoming from living in Christ, as witnessed to in the Bible, now propelling His Church. His body gathers in particular contexts to speak and live His Word. Together, they move with the pulse of this Word that calls them to love in action.

INTRODUCTION: This section begins chapter 4, "The Proclamation of the Church," as we continue through the seventeen chapters of the *CD*.

Remember the chapters in the *CD* so far: (1) "The Word of God as the Criterion of Dogmatics," (2) "The Revelation of God" ["The Triune God," "The Incarnation of the Word," "The Outpouring of the Holy Spirit"], and (3) "Holy Scripture." God is revealed in Jesus, who is revealed in the Bible and is revealed thereby in the ministry of the Church.

The rest of *CD* 1.2 will deal with the place of the Church in relation to the proclamation of the Word of God. The Church is a community who listens and then speaks as a witness to what the Word is saying. Thus, Barth affirms that Jesus continues to speak through the Bible as read, interpreted, and lived in the body of Christ, His Church.

The point of this chapter is to summarize § 22 in the *CD*, to make clear the place of the Church in discerning the sense of the Bible in revealing God, explaining it to the Church and world, and then assimilating this hearing into the life of listeners.

▐▌▌ CONTEXT: *CD* 1.2
Pages in Paragraph: 54 pages (pp. 743–96)

Subsections
1. The Word of God and the Word of Man in Christian Preaching
2. Pure Doctrine as the Problem of Dogmatics
3. Dogmatics as Ethics

📖 TEXT: § 22. The Mission of the Church

OPENING SUMMARY: The Word of God is God Himself in the proclamation of the Church of Jesus Christ. In so far as God gives the Church the commission to speak about Him, and the Church discharges this commission, it is God Himself who declares His revelation in His witnesses. The proclamation of the Church is pure doctrine when the human word spoken in it in confirmation of the biblical witness to revelation offers and creates obedience to the Word of God. Because this is its essential character, function and duty, the word of the Church preacher is the special and immediate object of dogmatic activity.[1]

✠ SUMMARY:
1. The Word of God and the Word of Man in Christian Preaching (pp. 743–58)

Having listened to the living Word of God (Jesus) and become attuned to hearing Him in the written Word of God (the Bible), we are now ready to engage the Word of God (preaching) within the Church. We must attend with a unified listening within these informing contexts.

Key question: To what extent is the preaching of the Church also the Word of God?

The Word of God, living and divinely personal, has been spoken once for all in Jesus Christ.

---

1. *CD* 1.2, § 22, p. 743.

The Word of God, written and scriptural, is near the Church, given in the prophets and apostles in the form of Holy Scripture.

The Word of God, humanly spoken and enacted, lives in the Church. It is given to bearers and speakers commissioned to preach as servants with freedom under the authority of the living and written Word.

The living, written, and preached Word of God are each and together truly God's Word. But they are each Word in a different sense. The third form depends on the second, which depends on the first and primary revelation.

The Church is the body of Jesus Christ built on the foundation of the prophets and apostles. By the Spirit, the Church is now calling humble servants to witness to the One who holds all together in unity.

The Church must be reminded that the Word is given to it only by the revelation of Jesus and the witness of the biblical writers. Built on this knowledge, the Church speaks. This recognition acknowledges that the Word of God is alive and active in the Church.

By the grace of revelation, God commits Himself to the preaching of His Word in the Church so that it is His own proclamation.

The Word of God is entrusted to those who are members of Jesus' body. Proclamation belongs to the Church.

The Church's commission to preach corresponds to the resurrection. Its testimony is a gift that transcends human possibility. It surpasses in its own power every human accomplishment or failure. The living God is here at work.

The Word of God must be believed as it stands, fulfilled in Jesus Christ.

> The living, written, and preached Word of God are each and together truly God's Word. But they are each Word in a different sense. The third form depends on the second, which depends on the first and primary revelation.

What needs to happen for the Word of God preached in the Church to be believed has already happened. It is also true that all that is necessary for the Church to live has already happened.

Our business is to accept that something has happened that pertains to us. What is accomplished has been performed and fulfilled in Jesus Christ. It is in this acceptance that the Church lives its life rooted in Him. The same is true of the Bible. This is also true of proclamation. Each refers to what has happened before.

When the Church holds faithfully to Jesus' commission to preach, the Church has Him in its midst as the Lord. In and through its speaking, He bears witness to Himself.

Our greatest concern to beware of ought to be our inclination to turn to ourselves and not to the Lord who addresses us.

There is a genuine authority and freedom in the Word of God who speaks, the Word that witnesses, and the Word in the Church. At each level, this authority must be apprehended, accepted, and reckoned with. This is not deciding on the truth of a theory but is answering God, who speaks to us here and now.

Where the Word of God succeeds in being heard, it is a divine victory. God makes possible what we do poorly.

The Word of God may seem to be drowned in the history of the Church's sea of proclamation. Therefore, we can affirm that hearing the Word is a miracle that is achieved by God's Word to accomplish its own proper task.

When we are overconfident in our ability to preach, we become weak in our faith in God. When we are humble and feel inadequate, we are confessing that it is only by God's miracle that the Word is heard, and this is a confident faith in God.

Unless God sustains and transforms us, the greatest preaching and theology are empty and meaningless.

Human powerlessness in understanding God is not absolute. Only God is able to overcome this inadequacy. It will not be because of our human capacities.

In ourselves and by ourselves, we are left empty before God. By being aware of that, we are able to receive and be filled. In the end, all merely human attempts to grasp God become futile.

God alone can speak about God. This is what God has done.

The power of preaching is established on the fact that the Son of God has come in the flesh. His Spirit has been poured out in the Church. Now the duty of speaking about God has been laid on the Church.

The recognition of God's speaking must deeply inform the service of preaching. Only then will we distinguish human words that disclose the grace that comes from God alone.

Faith in the human is realized through a faithful participation in what God has done, will do, and is doing in this place and time. This is not our work, but an acceptance of His work transforming in us and through us.

As the Church speaks about God in human words, it proclaims God's own Word. This Word stands against all that imprisons humans. This freedom is fulfilled as God speaks the word of grace that is His freeing love for all humans.

Christian preaching is speaking about God, not generally but specifically, as known in Jesus' self-revelation.

Preaching is a human activity. This declarative activity may take place because God has spoken and still speaks for those who are willing to hear.

Through preaching we receive the gift of grace and miracle. We also hear and heed the call to be responsible by living in the light of this grace and miracle.

The service of preaching is incomparably greater than any other service. It makes available the living God who has come to us. But it is God and not the preacher who makes available the personal connection.

The recognition of God's speaking must deeply inform the service of preaching. Only then will we distinguish human words that disclose the grace that comes from God alone.

2. Pure Doctrine as the Problem of Dogmatics (pp. 758–83)

Pure doctrine is a term used to describe the content of the activity of preaching. It is born of God's grace. Then, it is spoken and lived in the Church attuned to God's grace and love.

The Word of God is not only a word but also an action of God.

Pure doctrine can never be limited to an abstract intellectual business. Doctrine does not mean theory.

A theory builds on chosen acts of observation and interpretation. Building one is a human task created to develop a human expression of something to be known.

Doctrine acknowledges the impartation of something other than ourselves. That which is other is to be understood in such a way, through right communication and reception, as to responsibly provide a sense of clarifying for a community. The intended meaning needs to be conveyed to make possible a faithful hearing by the listener.

A theory has a value in itself. It is intended to clarify and enrich other theories or express the delight of its creator.

Doctrine is always directed toward others. It is not to be an expression of opinions but ought to bring insights in stating the truth and aligning the community with it.

Doctrine serves to clarify and point to the Word of God, but it is not equal to the Word of God.

Doctrine has the task of building up the Church into its Head. The goal is for humans to hear this living Word.

When humans preach, the speaker's desire is not that the hearers focus on the human voice but that they hear Him whose Word it truly is.

As the Church speaks about God in human words, it proclaims God's own Word. This Word stands against all that imprisons humans. This is fulfilled as God speaks the word of grace that is His freeing love for all humans.

All preaching is an attempt to incite and inspire the hearers to hear the Word of God for themselves. The listener is focused where God has spoken and has been heard.

In its preaching, the Church must be a transparent word, like a window, or a reflecting word, like a mirror. Originality must arise from a fresh breath of the Spirit, who brings us back to the origin of the Word. Freshness must not merely introduce new, contemporary concepts in the attempt to be relevant. Those endeavors merely distract.

Orthodoxy points to correct opinion. We need a faithful teaching that brings a ministerial character of mediating the life of God to the life of humans.

Pure doctrine brings the presence and activity of God to the speaking of the Church. This is a unique activity, not to be replaced by other human activities.

In pure doctrine, human words yield to the living Word of God.

The task of dogmatics lives within the whole of Christian theology.

In biblical theology, we ask questions regarding the foundation for preaching.

In practical theology, we ask questions regarding the form of human response to the Word.

In dogmatic theology, we ask questions regarding the content of Christian preaching.

The dogmatic task is about clarification. It is utilized to ensure that preaching is in agreement with the revelation of God attested to in His written Word.

Each of the three tasks implicitly implies the other tasks; they cannot be done properly if in isolation from the others.

Biblical/exegetical theology aids in observation.

Dogmatic theology provides for explanation.

Practical theology helps with assimilation into our lives.

The question of the Church's ministry is determined in dogmatics. Good or bad dogmatics will create good or bad theology. It aims to provide criteria to distinguish good from bad preaching. These criteria are based on how faithful we are to the One whose Word it is.

Pure doctrine is a deed. It is not in words or thoughts. It is not a formula, a theological system, a creed, or even a text of the Bible.

Pure doctrine is not limited to a text. It is an event, like the incarnation and the outpouring of the Holy Spirit. Doctrine lives in the dynamic of engagement.

When the Church turned the Bible into a human text, it changed the biblical texts into tools for its own authority.

The Church transferred the authority and freedom of the Word of God to its own control. Its own authority and freedom have steadily intensified in this pursuit.

Purity of doctrine is an event that happens when the Word of God is heard and accepted with freedom. It is a loving response in the form of joyful obedience.

To teach dogmatics means to have a preliminary acquaintance with what has gone before. Only then can one participate in the dogmatic task. Understanding what God is saying here and now follows listening. This requires an attitude of learning.

Preaching becomes real when it is situated between the witness of biblical revelation and the Church in the present-day world. In this space the hearing Church becomes the teaching Church.

In shaping and evaluating its fidelity to speaking of God, the Church must take seriously the inseparable unity of reflection and action. The whole of God speaks to the whole of the Church.

Theology lives in a midway position between the Bible and the Church.

Dogmatics lives by first listening to the Word of God and then hearing it proclaimed in the Church. Both forms must be attentively attuned to the voice of the Word of God.

The contribution of dogmatics both confirms and guides the Church in preaching. Dogmatics serves the Church by clarifying its preaching so as to be both God's Word and a human word.

One who engages in dogmatics must prepare for the listening work by hearing the problems of the day. This begins with listening to God in prayer—the most significant concern in hearing. This happens only as we avail ourselves to the Holy Spirit.

All dogmatics has one function: to question whether the words, phrases, sequence of thought, and the logic of the preaching have the capacity to make clear the Word of God who speaks in self-giving.

The question of dogmatics is not whether all is included that could be included but whether what is done is done well. This involves keeping the meaning faithful and true to the Word of God as pure doctrine.

We must go beyond what is said to discern what is meant. With this approach, we clarify our task in aiming at pure doctrine with listening discernment attuned to the source.

The Church has an unrest of knowing in that it cannot merely speak about God. This is true because the Church must ever live afresh, transformed by God to speak again with transparency what God is saying.

God Himself wishes to speak to His Church and to the world.

Every person or claim that speaks of God or the Church or God's creature must be interrogated for the sake of the real thing and be evaluated in light of the real thing.

The task of dogmatics is to carefully and critically examine all claims that humans make about God. This acknowledges that everything falls under His lordship.

Dogmatics should prove itself competent for the task of examining. Therefore, it must be able to confirm or contest human speech about God by comparing human claims against God's self-revelation.

Dogmatics must prove that its method is competent to assess the truth of words about God.

What are the criterion and standards by which we judge pure dogmatics? What is the dogmatic norm? These questions address the objective possibility of finding answers in the task of assessing.

How does one rightly use the criteria and standards of examination? What is dogmatic thinking? These questions address the subjective possibilities within the task of assessing.

By reality, we mean the Word of God in the form of Scripture, standing under the triune God.

The objective possibility of the Church is the authority of the Church to stand as a servant under the living Word, the incarnation of God in self-revelation.

The subjective possibility of the Church is living in freedom under the Word through the outpouring of the Holy Spirit.

3. Dogmatics as Ethics (pp. 782–96)

When discussing the Christian life, is our behavior a living out of dogmatics or is it a discipline separated from our dogmatic clarification?

In determining some Christian ethics, it has been a practice of some to set up an ideal of the good and to have Christian ethics serve this ideal. Rather than ethics being derived from Christ, they appeal to a foundation in the human sense of goodness, independent of Jesus.

When ethics takes the priority over biblical studies and dogmatics, it forces the Bible to be subsumed with lesser influence. This marginalization is done in order to serve in creating dictates and dogmatics, in order to develop theories of goodness in action that are based in human sensibilities. In the end, Jesus gets retired.

The history of Christian ethics is replete with attempts at determining behaviors that have a foundation other than Jesus for developing a Christian vision of ethics. Rules, models, imitations, and systems based in philosophy flourish everywhere.

Christian ethics cannot be based on a universal mode of human feeling founded on philosophical foundations. These modes of thinking separate our ways of knowing from our ways of acting. A moralizing movement easily develops in such a way that it moves the focus to self-feelings as the source of knowledge, without referring to Christ.

People easily attach to questions of "how should I behave?" and lose interest in knowing about the God they cannot see.

We cannot separate emotional contemplation of the eternal from moral teaching about life in our finite relationships.

Dogmatics cannot refer to a state of mind separate from ethics as a state of will.

God's being, expressed in doctrine, is realized in life together.

If human goodness and conduct become the focus of theology, we will have abandoned our dogmatic task, surrendered to the preferred interests of human inquiry.

The worst thing we can do is to write a sequel book on the *Holy Human* as a second volume after *Holy God*. In this separated state, we fool ourselves into thinking we have a detached subject to discuss. But we must continue to engage the one book in which God is always the context of human being and acting.

The Word of God turns toward humanity and restores, and this ordering cannot be reversed. Proper theology cannot be informed by beginning with human concepts of failure or potential.

The problems of ethics are theological, not human. Perhaps they are *the* great theological problems.

Studying Christians, Christianity, Church history, and all religions is to engage phenomena of this world.

Our first reference as humans is not with reference to the created world but is with the Living God. Therefore, in response to other misguided studies, ethics needs to refocus on being a theological question, not a human dilemma.

The Word of God turns toward humanity and restores, and this ordering cannot be reversed. Proper theology cannot be informed by beginning with human concepts of failure or potential.

Christian ethics can never be about what we hope to become. It cannot concentrate on the effects of Christianity on us. That turns our back to revelation, the very place from which our transformation comes.

The Word of God is our point of departure; through it we hear the Word of God addressed to humanity, heard by humans, and claiming and gripping our attention.

Humans are gripped by the actuality of their existence. This focuses us on a life of thinking, acting, and suffering.

When humans become hearers of the Word, it becomes possible to become doers of the Word.

Once a hearer, a human is reoriented to being determined by the Word.

All theological topics have a bearing on the human as determined by God's Word.

Humans exist in that they act. How far humans act rightly is determined by how far they exist rightly.

The theme of dogmatics is always exclusively the Word of God. The theme of the Word is human life, volition, and action.

Dogmatics has to be ethics as well as listening. Because it refers to the Word of God, it must refer to human existence as well.

Ethics must be included within dogmatics.

We cannot affirm any separated treatment of ethics.

The inclusion of ethics within dogmatics is that it provides greater clarity and consistency.

We must consider the material and problems of ethics but only within the general plan of dogmatics.

CONCLUSION FOR THE CHURCH: The Church is a place where those who want to know God are able to hear God. This can happen when the Bible is preached to make God known. The Church is not a place for human improvement. It is a place to know who God is and what He is doing as He addresses humanity. The Church's task is to engage in careful study, insightful understanding, and transformed behavior. This is the result of meeting with God in His Word. Meeting with God is a nourishing event for the Church as a listening, speaking, and acting community.

🔬 COMMENTARY:

- The Church is to be understood with regard to its manner of relating to the living God. The Church is not a set of programs or services. It is a people bound up with the life of God. The gathered community acts as though this is the case.
- The Word of God as preached in the Church has a duality in character. It will be affirmed as making known *God's Word*. It uses *human words* for this task. God has taken our humanity into His service through the tools of language.
- God affirms humanity by speaking our language. This creates accessibility but is also the cause of some people thinking God's words are merely human words.
- The Church has a task in learning to develop quality exposition. This skill informs the disciplines of biblical theology. This develops our theological understanding, knowing that the Bible is like a mountain that is both delightful and dangerous. We must learn to listen to those who have climbed it and lived to tell the story.
- Reflection on the Bible is a second task of the Church. Skills of reflection allow the Church to deeply clarify and distinguish what is and is not meant in following the Bible's lead. This guiding task is similar to dogmatics. It keeps us on a faithful path to our destination and prepares for us an acceptable route.
- The Church has not fulfilled its task without application. Practical theology utilizes the teaching of the Bible so that it functionally transforms the life of a community. The people not only think differently but act as newly awakened persons who live the grace they receive. In this way, the Church works out its operations in order to scale the heights, not merely to talk about what it would be like if the quest was actually attempted.

📖 INSIGHT FOR PASTORS:
This section is a clarion call to become true servants. To minister is to serve. The preacher's tasks are to assist in the announcing and ongoing conversing that facilitate God's present life in the Church. All other demands and marketing schemes are simply missing the point. And those words that are spoken as the Word of God must come

from the heart of God. Additionally, they must speak clearly in the language of the people present. The question "What does my Lord have to say to His people through this text?" is a proper orientation in preparation.

INSIGHT FOR THEOLOGIANS: Theology was never intended to merely be a seminar for the academy. Theology functions best when it provides a dynamic contribution. This moves us beyond trying to find the best definitions and descriptions or create vast libraries and successful conferences. Theology, as an academic endeavor, is for equipping the Church. Leaders need to learn the skills of knowing and responding to God. This includes starting with the God revealed in Jesus, witnessed to in the Bible, and finally made available by trained servants. Theologically equipped servants make God so well heard that people come prepared to hear God. They leave knowing that they are known, beloved, and able to act accordingly. Functional academic theology trains students in all the subsets of theology under their proper Head, the living God, including how we are to behave as humans.

? CLARIFYING QUESTIONS: Does your theology of preaching begin with "What do these humans want?" *or* "How can I help people understand the free unveiling of Jesus?" From whom is it most important to hear "Well done" at the end of your preaching or ministry?

CHAPTER 30

LISTENING TO THE GUIDE FOR SAFE AND SENSATIONAL EXCURSIONS

§ 23. Dogmatics as a Function of the Hearing Church

FOCUS STATEMENT: A guide can be both a person and a book. In this case, both are active in leading, protecting, and maximizing our experience. The value of these authoritative voices for our journey may be as simple as staying alive. But they also facilitate learning to appreciate and be sensitive to our place in our environment. But first, we must learn to listen. Then we need to learn to act on what we hear. Thus, the point of "Dogmatics as a Function of the Hearing Church" is to orient our exploration by beginning to listen. Being properly attuned, we are positioned to proceed in engaging reality, especially in relation to the persons who lead us.

INTRODUCTION: This section continues discussion on the place of the Church in making the Word of God known in the world. The concern for faithful listening is paramount. Listening can become divisive. This often happens within the Church. Proper hearing of the Word also gets hijacked by other ideologies that lead the Church and its leaders away from Jesus.

This chapter summarizes § 23 in the *CD* on learning to listen to the revealed God. Careful listening is not natural to humans, especially regarding hearing God. By learning to be attentive, we avoid getting off track. Initial listening to religious, political, or philosophical schemes leads us off the trail, and then we can get lost. We need to be guided to listen to Jesus before engaging the task of teaching and proclaiming.

CONTEXT: *CD* 1.2
Pages in Paragraph: 47 pages (pp. 797–843)

Subsections
1. The Formal Task of Dogmatics
2. The Dogmatic Norm

📖 **TEXT: § 23. Dogmatics as a Function of the Hearing Church**

OPENING SUMMARY: Dogmatics invites the teaching Church to listen again to the Word of God in the revelation to which Scripture testifies. It can do this only if for its own part it adopts the attitude of the hearing Church and therefore itself listens to the Word of God as the norm to which the hearing Church knows itself to be subject.[1]

SUMMARY:

1. The Formal Task of Dogmatics (pp. 797–812)

The hearing Church has no spectators. All persons are oriented to listen and learn. This means the whole Church together, at all levels of skill in leadership and service, must learn to tune in to what is said.

We are all intended to be wise stewards of the Word, sharing a common responsibility to participate in the life of the Word.

There is a proper ordering between hearing and teaching. One receives in order to serve. Having become listeners, we are made teachers.

Dogmatics evaluates the human words of Church proclamation to make sure they are trustworthy as the Word of God.

Human errors may creep into preaching. Dogmatics brings a clarifying conversation for edification and truthfulness with respect to the God who speaks.

Dogmatics fulfills a role of critiquing. The questions for consideration relate to how well the preacher is speaking of God.

All human reflections and actions that are put out in varied forms of proclamation are confronted by another reflection and action—God's.

God has spoken, will speak again, and speaks now. Because of this, the Church can hear as God speaks in its proclamation.

What is to be preached? The answer is found in recognizing and adjusting to what has already been said by the Word of God, newly realized in the present context.

The content of Church preaching is not to be determined by the human hearer but by the divine speaker whose Word it is.

---

1. *CD* 1.2, § 23, p. 797.

The task of dogmatics is to remind the Church that the Word it preaches belongs first to its Lord. Whatever is said must always draw from Him, lead to Him, and bring His free, loving lordship to bear in its preaching.

The redemptive nature of the Church's proclamation consists in its listening, its being spoken, and its regularly being heard afresh.

> Before heresy exists in the Church there is a forgetting that makes Jesus an honorary member.

How likely will the Church enjoy being told that it has gotten off track? How can it hear that it may need to stop teaching and begin anew, to really listen from the beginning?

The main concern of the Church in its proclamation is that Jesus be heard in His Church as the Lord of the Church.

When the Church stops being obedient to the voice of Jesus, it begins to slip into a form of self-righteousness and idolatry.

Before heresy exists in the Church there is a forgetting that makes Jesus an honorary member.

In preaching, at the other end of the spectrum from idolatry is a false moralistic earnestness.

The real possibility for the Church is inherent in listening to the voice of Jesus Christ.

2. The Dogmatic Norm (pp. 812–43)

The dogmatic theologian cannot look down on the preacher but comes alongside as a member of the listening Church. The dogmatic task in partnership with the preacher is to conform the clarity and validity of the message in relation to the Word of God.

> The task of dogmatics is to remind the Church that the Word it preaches belongs first to its Lord. Whatever is said must always draw from Him, lead to Him, and bring His free, loving lordship to bear in its preaching.

The church that becomes a teaching church and does not listen will miss out on the voice of God. The great error in that void is that the word that is preached is not guided and corrected by God.

The church that teaches without listening will end up in a dialog with itself if it misses the one true starting point. With this neglect, the preacher will lull people to sleep and not awaken them to joyful proclamation.

Dogmatics must determine a concrete understanding under the Word of God.

1. Its investigations, formulations, and demonstrations must have a *biblical character.*

    Its thinking must correspond to the obedience of faith. Its listening must recede its acting. Believing what is true from God leads to adequate speaking. We must not merely respond to the questions we put to ourselves.

    A biblical attitude is not merely explaining the text of the Bible.

    Dogmatics must always focus on "God said." Subsequent thinking must live in the light of God's speaking and not depend on human explanations of the text through appeals to human experience.

2. Its investigations, formulations, and demonstrations must have a *confessional attitude.*

    This is a criticism, examination, and correction that is lived for the benefit of the life of the Church. It is an exercise in being faithful to the Word of God. The confessional attitude is a call to serve the whole Church as God's servants.

    This attitude is required for the whole ecumenical Church. There is only one Church under the Word.

    There can only be a dogmatics of the one, holy, universal, apostolic Church.

    Roman Catholic and neoorthodox are opposed to Reformed dogmatics. Lutherans and Anglicans simply have a debate within the Evangelical Church.

    The Church must look beyond its different positions. Together, all must inquire with faithfulness to the intention of God to have wholehearted fidelity in the one confession of the Church.

    Under the recognized authority of Holy Scripture, different schools and movements must listen to one another.

    In applying oneself to dogmatics that are biblical and confessional, the principle at work requires focusing on the form of thought, not the content. We are not trying to correct teachers or confessions; we are only focused on hearing the Word most concisely and clearly by learning from them.

3. It must determine to listen to the teaching Church of today, the requirement of a *Church attitude.*

    In testing the Church's proclamation, there must be an orientation and awareness of the actual situation in which the message is expressed.

The Word of God must be proclaimed by the Church in the present.

While listening attentively to the Word of God, it must address the problems, concerns, difficulties, and hopes of current situations with meaningful connection.

Dogmatic theologians must work with the teaching Church in an attitude of prayer. This means being attentive to the past and present and speaking to the future.

Servants of God must have an attitude of thanksgiving and praise. This arises because God has made Himself known in Jesus. Humility is needed to acknowledge the failings of the Church in appreciating God's benefits. But finally, there is a coming together to pray for the Holy Spirit to open a more vital and impactful hearing of the Word of God.

The essence of the Church attitude is to listen to the voice heard in its prayer. This includes and corresponds to speaking on behalf of humans before God. This is a priestly role in preparation for its prophetic role in speaking to humans for God.

The Church's whole life of speaking and teaching must be informed out of its attentiveness before the Word of God as the teaching Church.

- The Church attitude has several restrictions.
- A Church attitude cannot think and speak as though it were timeless. It cannot be a detached inquiry.
- The Word of God founded the Church, not an academy.
- Dogmatics gives counsel to the Church. Its task is to answer questions regarding the relations of God, humanity, and the world so that the Church may do so responsibly.
- The Church must be prepared for its own times, with all its hopes and needs.
- The Church attitude precludes speaking in such a way as to make preaching into an idol. The implicit beauty of the Word is self-revealing; any added agenda will distract from what is there.
- The quest for a form of beauty may include conformity to logical, historical, linguistic, or juristic ideals. Any of these can distract and overshadow the primary task of revealing the Word.
- The business of dogmatics is to edify the Church. It does this by means of clearly hearing the Word of God.

- When the Church is aligned in its action with the Word of God, it will display its proper beauty. Its worship will call forth true, thankful reflection born of the Word's speaking.
- A Church attitude excludes a romantic dogmatics. That means it must resist the temptation to uncritically speak from any idealized, romanticized period in Church history.
- The Church attitude must stand against becoming secular dogmatics. It must not serve the spirit of each time, the spirit of the age. It cannot become the mouthpiece of the cares and concerns of contemporary culture.
- Dogmatics must orient itself in the prayer of the Church, which speaks before God and to God—it listens to the voice of God, not the voice of the day.
- The real work of dogmatics is to summon and guide the Church. Dogmatics must teach the Church to think and proceed in light of its basis in Jesus and learn its proper nature as His body.

CONCLUSION FOR THE CHURCH: The Church needs the practice of dogmatics like chefs and doctors need to wash their hands. What these stewards have in common is that they are servants, committed to bringing and sustaining health. They are required to practice care by preparing well. There are real but unrecognized threats that could destroy what is to be a caring skill. In the case of the caretakers of the Church, heresy and idolatry resemble germs that could infect the Church. In its noble yet humble task, dogmatics serves the Church in maintaining health by staying true to Jesus.

COMMENTARY:

- The Church needs to be informed and nourished by Jesus. Therefore, it must first be a listening Church, resisting what might threaten its existence.
- When the Church tries to exercise any authority or logic other than reasoning out of Jesus, the Church creates an idol that decentralizes its being and consequently serves some other end. Orienting toward any focus other than Jesus ends up leading the Church down a path of estrangement.
- Establishing the authentic basis of life together is a necessary precursor to critiquing both preaching and planning. This is provided in Jesus. The great temptation is to turn to the simple distraction of appealing

to the wants and desires of the surrounding culture and consequently abandoning Jesus.

- There is only one Church, even though there are many traditions and denominations. The one Church has one Head, who is Jesus.
- There needs to be an openness between those communities who operate in the several branches of the Church in the world. Only then can there be a conversation to explore what it will mean to be true together to live in unity in the person of Jesus Christ.
- Doing dogmatic work in the church requires that one have a character attuned to the Bible, a faithful attitude to the intent of the confessions, and a genuine concern for the Church as the body of Christ. Any other definition of success, following agendas of popularity and relevance or defaulting to engagement with current issues and ideals of the day will lead to the church's demise when it misses living within the threefold Word.

INSIGHT FOR PASTORS: The first job of a pastor is to know, love, converse with, and speak for the living Word of God. This comes as a result of being immersed in prayerful listening. The task of preaching is not merely to give tools for Christian living, especially if in any way that is conceived in a manner separate from Jesus. Rather, with a bold determination to know Jesus, we find ourselves responding and attuning our lives to Him who loved us first. Faith is attuning our thinking and acting to that love. This happens because we come to know His voice as attentive listeners. If we hope to practice good leadership, we will lead people to know His voice and to resist imposters. Knowing the real is the best way to spot imposters.

INSIGHT FOR THEOLOGIANS: Theologians are not permitted to study from an orientation based on the interests of a particular moment in time. Rather, true theologians listen to the living Word. They listen to serve the Church in hearing what rings true to Jesus' revelation, as well as being attentive to what has taken the Church on divergent paths. Rather than just making sure people think and behave well, theologians must serve the integrity of relationships with God and neighbor. They must ensure the Church lives in faithfulness. They must safeguard relationships so that the Church is not seduced by the worldly voices that bombard it. The Church and human persons can be easy prey for the ideals of happiness, success, and sustainability other than what is nurtured by Jesus. In this sense, the theologian is like a seasoned marriage counselor. She will make sure that the involved parties' listening cultivates the relationship not by rules and principles but by each falling in love with the other so that appropriate actions follow. This requires guiding in such a way as to avoid the possibility that each person might pursue their separate desires. They each must do one thing: know the other as a faithful companion.

?　CLARIFYING QUESTIONS: Does your theology begin with listening and attending to Jesus in the Bible? *Or* are you pulled by the Jesus who has been shaped by a tradition, denomination, congregation, or your favorite author? Do you come to the Bible looking for what will benefit you, or do you come intent on hearing what Jesus is saying to reveal His heart?

## CHAPTER 31

THE INVITATION TO SHARED REALITY

§ 24. Dogmatics as a Function of the Teaching Church

FOCUS STATEMENT: Good news is intended to be shared. We are called to invite others into the vastness of what we are discovering. This call proposes meaningful engagement with the reality of the world with others. We are to avoid being stuck in our heads or houses, thinking God wants to "improve" us alone.

The grand revisioning aims at recovering the immense value of persons and personal relationships. As we are outward bound with God, we find this companionship transforms our experience of life in this world. We are in a recovery process. Walking with God fills us to overflowing, which compels us to unveil the wonder of who and what is right before us but is often missed. That is to engage the freely loving God, and see how God makes all things to operate according to His loving intent. Thus, "Dogmatics as a Function of the Teaching Church" is a community awakening to be a neighbor who will not remain distant. Together, we answer the call to speak to those who do not know God and to help others discover life experienced in the light of God's grace.

INTRODUCTION: This section is the final paragraph of the two-volume set of *CD* 1.1 and *CD* 1.2. We have come to see the personal God revealed in Jesus, witnessed to in the Bible as the text that makes Him known, and have seen the church as a community that participates in making this God known. Now, we are given a brief glimpse of the lay of the land of the dogmatics that is coming in all its massive expanse.

This chapter summarizes § 24 in the *CD* on the revealed God. Here God is revealed as Creator, Mediator, and Redeemer. God is not a map for the good life. God does not leave us with principles for right living. God's life cannot be reduced to a system. We enter only to be met and known as we meet the Lord of the universe, who is already embracing humanity. He is known as the living God, beginning of everything. Knowing Him, we are now properly oriented to go on and to get to know this triunity in the following volumes. With listening ears, we come to hear the meaning of life found in discovering our context of meaning. We are His people blessed to respond to His love and to avoid what detaches us from this loving life.

▌▌▌ CONTEXT: *CD* 1.2
Pages in Paragraph: 41 pages (pp. 844–84)

Subsections
1. The Material Task of Dogmatics
2. The Dogmatic Method

📖 TEXT: § 24. Dogmatics as a Function of the Teaching Church

OPENING SUMMARY: Dogmatics summons the listening Church to address itself anew to the task of teaching the Word of God in the revelation attested to in Scripture. It can do this only as it accepts itself the position of the teaching Church and is therefore claimed by the Word of God as the object to which the teaching Church as such has devoted itself.[1]

✠ SUMMARY:
1. The Material Task of Dogmatics (pp. 844–53)

To hear the Word of God is not enough. The Church hears so that it may go on to teach.

The Church lives with a simultaneity of hearing and teaching.

The Word of God is the object and norm of the Church's proclamation. Thus, we must hear His voice, which calls us to listen. Then we share what we hear.

When we hear the Word of God, we are called to service, employing our human tongues, speech, words, and actions.

Life is found in the presence and address of the One who sustains and makes us whole again.

The presence of Jesus Christ is made known in the biblical recollection that brings His speaking to a contemporary realization in the Church.

Because Jesus speaks, the Church should act.

---

1. CD 1.2, § 24, p. 844.

The Word of God is our Creator, by whom we exist. We may deny His existence and consequently lose ourselves.

The Word of God is our Reconciler, whose existence deals with our sin and guilt. He preserves us, if we will be preserved.

The Word of God is Redeemer, who is able to restore the existence of humanity to its former splendor.

The Church must make the Word of God clear to listeners not merely as a task but as a gift.

The presenting of the Word of God must awaken, strengthen, and invigorate the Church.

In serving the Word of God, the Church brings the gospel with incomparable freedom.

To disconnect from the freedom offered by the Word of God is to self-destruct.

Life is found in the presence and address of the One who sustains and makes us whole again.

2. The Dogmatic Method (pp. 853–84)

The method of Christian dogmatics unfolds and presents the contents of the Word of God.

In dogmatics, we are called to dare to say what we have heard. We proceed with the intention of summoning the listening Church to become a teaching Church.

When the Church forgets that it is a teaching and speaking Church, it becomes bewildered, joyless, inactive, and dead.

The power of the Word of God becomes visible when the light of divine being and doing is reflected onto human being and doing.

Dogmatic thinking is committed to comply with the Word of the Father, Son, and Holy Spirit that is given in the revelation to which Scripture points us.

Dogmatic thinking is a wall that reminds us that God is unique, but it is also a gate that affirms God makes Himself available. We must proceed while affirming both.

The ordering of dogmatics must correspond to God's work and action.

Dogmatics describes what is first true from the point of view of God but told from the human point of view.

We may allow ourselves to be drawn into the sphere of the effective operation of the Word of God. Consequently, our obedience may be free in our thinking and speaking as those embraced by grace.

God freely acts for humans. This occurs so that humans may have a free act of encounter that is truly freeing in the meeting of persons.

Freedom cannot be based on the arbitrary will of the human. Freedom is a gift received only in encounter with the activity and work of God.

Obedience is not a human willing: our choice for God. It can only be a response to the free offer of God that meets us as we reply with a free acceptance.

If obedience cannot be rendered freely, then it is not the obedience required. Loving obedience must also leave others free.

Dogmatics cannot be a system that sets in place laws and structures that are self-contained and complete in themselves. That course brings the end of freedom. What will follow is a life conformed to human limitation.

Church dogmatics cannot submit to a system of theology but only to the Word of God.

The object of study for theology is not a concept; it is a person.

The personal center of Scripture is not under our control but exercises control over us.

We must know no other starting point for theology than the living Word witnessed to in the Bible.

Jesus must be the center of dogmatics in a manner similar to the center of a wheel that sustains its spokes.

Dogmatics is a crucible in which methods are refined and purified by the person of Jesus so that the Word of God is respected and loved above all things.

Dogmatics is a method that creates a path, an ordering to get at the heart of things. It ought not to become a boat without a rudder that is filled with chattering voices and going nowhere.

We cannot build dogmatics on an analytic system in order to lay a foundation of fundamental principles. We need a center from which to explore and expand.

The task of dogmatics must proceed with obedience and daring. Obedience behaves in response to the source. It develops a daring character of freedom that is at play in exploring human responsibility.

By beginning with God's self-revelation, we have the starting point for engaging God in His work and activity in His Word.

God's work and activity with us is Jesus Christ. He has accomplished the once for all positive relation between God and humanity.

God's revelation becomes synonymous with atonement. Jesus overturns the human plight in their darkness and contradiction to life.

Jesus gives His reconciling self to restore humanity back to light and life in relation.

We cannot reduce dogmatics to the single, important issue of atonement, or it becomes a principle that replaces the Word of God.

Also, we cannot reduce dogmatics to the theme of God as Creator. This precedes atonement—humans must exist before they need reconciliation.

Beginning with the doctrine of creation, we make the mistake of trading God in for things that relate to human existence. As a result, God fades to the backdrop.

Human language and laws easily take over the dogmatic pursuit. This happens when we try to make sense by determining what we think will meet the needs and desires of the human.

In God's redemption, we see created humanity placed on the far side of the conflict with God as a result of God's act of reconciliation.

God is the Redeemer. He meets us as the God who has everlasting faithfulness and allows us to find Him. The Holy Spirit is the pledge of His faithfulness and coming.

At four points God provides the basis of our knowledge. They all arise from the Word of God:

1. Regarding God
2. Regarding Creation
3. Regarding Reconciliation, Atonement, and Mediation
4. Regarding Redemption

The content of the doctrine of God is known in the Trinity. God's triune being precedes God's relations as Creator, Reconciler, and Redeemer.

We have to do with God Himself in the revealing of Father, Son, and Spirit in their differentiated life of free and freeing love.

God is the Giver, the Gift, and the Giving all in one.

> God is the Giver, the Gift, and the Giving all in one.

Barth begins his dogmatics with the classical position. This means we begin with God, not any acts or elements of God's life.

Barth's brief survey:

1. We must begin with the *being and attributes of God* as subject. Four complexes of questions will engage our attention:
   a. What is the reality, possibility, and actual realization of our knowledge of God, based on revelation?

    b. How can we make statements that can both contain and truly express the reality of God?

    c. How do we engage the unfolding of God's freedom toward humanity in the actuality of God's choice to extend grace to us?

    d. How does God's freedom for humanity imply a claim and a command over humanity that creates a theological ethic of command and free response?

This shapes the chapters of *CD* 2.

2. We continue with the *doctrine of creation* and therefore turn to Jesus. He serves as the one who concerns our very existence, through whom our existence came into being, who sustains all existence, and who sustains and controls all that has been, will be, and is existing. Three circles must be described:

    a. The relation of God to His creatures and to His creation.

    b. Humanity in a relation as God's creature and the focal point of creation and the current state of the relation.

    c. The claim and command of God over our lives as His creatures, whose behavior is shaped by God's being toward us.

This shapes the chapters of *CD* 3.

3. The *doctrine of atonement* is the center of God's revelation. God is present to us to mediate His being so that we become hearers. The atonement confirms God's covenant to us despite our unfaithfulness. Humans are fallen but sustained as beloved children upheld by the Spirit. We have four circles of concern:

    a. God has established a covenant between Himself and humanity, known within the light of grace, in response to which we must discuss the shadow of sin.

    b. The objectivity of the atonement is fulfilled by the Mediator, Jesus Christ.

    c. The subjective reception of atonement is accomplished by the Holy Spirit making present Jesus' finished work, nurtured in the Church through Word and sacrament.

    d. Humans accept the acceptance of God and so respond to the grace of God in submission to the command of God to love, having dealt with our sin and now being restored to become friends and neighbors.

This shapes the chapters of *CD* 4.

4. In acknowledging *God's redemption*, we see that the One who speaks to us is not only our origin but also our destination. In His

kingdom, discord is destroyed, and a new day dawns. Humanity is seen from the perspective of the completed outworking of love that comes under the lordship of Jesus. The promise of the resurrection life is an advance acknowledgment of the future God has for humanity. There are three circles to explore:

   a. the life of hope born of the presence of Jesus,
   b. the promise to be realized as the culmination of Jesus' kingdom coming, and
   c. the ethical goal of a better future, where the command of God is realized in living response to His Word.

This would have shaped the chapters of *CD* 5.

Dogmatics addresses the content of the Word and therefore the work and activity of God.

Dogmatics must remain secured to God's Word. It must unfold what God reveals in the past, present, and future.

God is revealed in event, in what occurs in space and time in Jesus Christ.

Dogmatics is threatened by systemization. Systemization is human self-will that produces error.

We begin in exegesis because exegesis reveals God's address. We move to explanation and interaction to understand what the Word has said. Finally, we move to assimilation, an actualization of the human response to God's presence that compels and transforms us.

In the dogmatic task, we are summoned, authorized, and empowered in our thinking and speaking by the grace of God.

God is the One who has thought His thoughts and spoken His words, and He now gives Himself through humans to bring light to the darkness.

CONCLUSION FOR THE CHURCH: The Church cannot be silent, self-serving, or managers of God's Word. This is especially true when the mortal manner usurps the living voice of the eternal God for the Church and the world. The Church must begin with the dynamic of listening and speaking from what is heard. Having started in attentive silence, it then may speak. This process accommodates God's speech within human speech. This ordering allows human understanding to be aligned in meaning with the One who has spoken. He preeminently is the One who brings the address that gives life. He brings restoration again in those whom He gathers as His people. He ought not be reduced to an agenda for the Church to promote.

The Church is not a fan club. He must be its breath and life. Jesus must show up as our brother, not as one who has sent a memo. Absent from attending to the Father through the Son, participating by the Spirit, a church dies as a person dies from lack of air.

COMMENTARY:

- When we speak of dogmatics, we are not creating statements to be held with fervor. We are confirming that what is said in the Church has a true connection to the One whom we serve.
- Entering the field of dogmatics cannot be achieved by trying to reduce theology to principles or themes. Teaching that replaces the living Head with a skeleton or developed portrait of Him is merely an idol constructed by human insight.
- The work of *CD* 1 has been to open human ears to hear the God revealed in Jesus. He shows us the triunity of God, whose address to humanity is not a historical record but is a present means of connection to facilitate a current and active relationship.
- Having prepared the way to talk about God, this section scans the horizon to apprehend God, who is the subject of our study.
- We now may proceed to *CD* 2 in a manner that reveals who God is, and we may come to understand how God has related to His creature in a free choice to love.
- In *CD* 3, theology will go on to unfold the One who creates all that is as the initiation of the existing relationship of God and creation.
- This God-human relation has a tension in which God has been covenantally faithful to bring restoration.
- In the end, humanity needs God's ongoing restoring work to open God's intended future fulfillment.

INSIGHT FOR PASTORS: This paragraph is a challenging look that bypasses all attempts at "relevance for our day" by leaders. It is so tempting to try to attract people to attend church and neglect the powerful presence of Jesus. But people need one thing, to be focused on the One who is the source and future hope for humanity. With that, the Church does have a clear focus. This also means resisting all attempts to tame any vision of God. We must resist programming that is constructed by or fits the needs of a church for "its success." With humility, we must go where we are instructed in a challenging but reality-engaging adventure. This reorientation for the life of the Church is like getting on to a hang glider and learning to respect the challenge, as well as embrace the opportunity, of seeing the big picture. Thus prepared, we now discover how to go where the Spirit takes us and then be filled with wonder.

INSIGHT FOR THEOLOGIANS: Dogmatics is a scientific discipline that develops a quality-control sensibility. In order for this discernment skill to be developed, we must have significant exposure to and comprehension of the original focus of study—the living God revealed in Jesus. Then, as we progress, we must learn to listen ever more attentively. We will come to recognize all the ways people in the Church or academy speak of God and learn to call into question any approach that goes amiss. This section warns, as well as welcomes, the dogmatician to stay on course. Dogmatic theology prepares for the important task of serving the Church and God. The goal is to clarify who we are dealing with, what He has done to establish a true and faithful relationship, and how we live in the light of God's present and active reality.

? CLARIFYING QUESTIONS: Does your theology attempt to fit Jesus into a thematic structure designed to make sense of God in logical progression? *Or* does your theology look like a humble offering brought repeatedly to the author of life to gain clarity? Are you positioned to sort out honest authenticity in your truth claims? Are you willing to discuss the application of your insights? Are you ready to fulfill the task of inviting people to know the One whom you serve in a manner that brings delight and freedom?

PART 4

VOICES VALUING
CD VOLUME 1

The Doctrine of the Word of God

THE VALUE OF *CD* 1 FOR BIBLICAL STUDIES

Douglas Campbell

Douglas Campbell is professor of New Testament, Duke
Divinity School, Durham, North Carolina, USA, and
author of numerous books on Pauline theology, including
Pauline Dogmatics: The Triumph of God's Love.

Barth's account in *CD* 1.1 of how to read the Bible is both insightful and
inspiring. Many scholars either claim too much or too little for their readings
of the Bible. *Either* its exegesis reveals the very word(s) of God, inspired and
inerrant, creating an exegetical papacy that has been notoriously vulnerable
to cultural capture, not to mention notoriously insensitive to the recognition
of unacceptable archaisms and mistakes in the text. *Or* its analysis reveals
only a dissolution into underlying fragmentary texts that preserve the words
of ancient people who were very unlike ourselves culturally and as detached
from genuine divine realities as we are assumed to be. Faced with this divided
and destructive situation, Barth pronounces "a plague on both your houses."
In its place he provided a brilliant and essentially orthodox—albeit rather
Protestant—account of how biblical interpretation is to be coordinated
with "the truth question" concerning God and
thereby to find its true place and correct method
within the Church. Barth breaks through the
impasse by recovering something that the Bible
itself knows well.

> This truth is known because God
> has made it known, actively,
> through revelation. And that
> revelation is centered in terms
> of content on Jesus Christ.

The truth about God must be grasped, both
in modality and content, prior to the interpre-
tation of the Bible. This truth is known because God has made it known,
actively, through revelation. And that revelation is centered in terms of content on Jesus Christ. He is the place where God is fully known among us.
Furthermore, this definitive truth, that God is fully disclosed through Jesus
Christ, is revealed by the Holy Spirit. God is therefore revealed through
a triune act of revelation that discloses God's triunity within that revelatory process.

It follows that the Bible does not and cannot establish this truth. We cannot grasp this truth for ourselves. We are always in the position of gratefully receiving and obeying it after the fact. Hence, we cannot go on to specify too strongly just where God will make this truth known, which would be to try foolishly to control it. However, God has used the Bible to witness to this truth and continues to do so.

The first witnesses, namely, the apostles, have their testimony recorded there, that is, their attestation of this revelation. And the Bible should continue to be read in the light of the rule of faith they confess—namely, Jesus—with this rule ultimately taking shape in the creeds. Moreover, the Word, Jesus, was actively at work in the proclamation of the first apostolic witnesses and is and will be at work as their apostolic words are taken up and proclaimed again by preachers in our day. As first witnesses did, the proclaimer or preacher must still seek the guidance of the Holy Spirit, who can and will inspire the preacher and the listener. Inspiration is only coherent in this broad sense. The Word of God, Jesus, is then known as the biblical word, itself centered in the proclamation of the first witnesses, and is proclaimed through the preacher's words again, likewise under the impress of the Word and his Spirit and received by listeners who also are under the impress of the Word and his Spirit.

In view of this, the modern preacher has nothing to fear from modern biblical scholarship. The most rigorous techniques and questions can all serve the true function of biblical proclamation within the Church— provided they are not captured in advance by a false overarching ideology ultimately of human derivation. Rudolf Bultmann is a prime example of this with his *a priori* commitment to existentialism, not to mention to an essentially Newtonian worldview within which God's action in the world is inconceivable. All valid biblical exposition remains grounded in and by Jesus Christ and flows from this place—from this person! Barth provides numerous powerful examples of just what this looks like, expounding texts, often in lengthy excurses, from both the Old Testament and the New. Volume one of the *Church Dogmatics* thereby instantiates the approach that it argues for: the God revealed definitively through Jesus Christ, known by the Spirit of Christ, continues to speak through the proclamation of the Bible as that task is undertaken faithfully by the witnesses it has summoned to do this.

THE VALUE OF *CD* 1 FOR SYSTEMATIC THEOLOGY

Myk Habets

Myk Habets is senior lecturer in theology, Laidlaw College, Auckland, NZ, senior research fellow, Australian College of Theology, author of numerous books on Trinitarian theology, and coeditor of *Trinitarian Theology after Barth*.

Barth's *CD* is 8,000 pages, 13 volumes, 16 chapters, 73 paragraphs, and 6,000,000 words, and I have less than 500 words to speak about the two-part volume 1: that is some ask!

CD 1.1 is concerned to lay out for the reader Barth's prolegomenon to theology wherein, first, he makes a radical distinction between theology that is done in response to revelation and for the Church from theology that is predicated upon some *a priori* or prior system of thought (philosophical ideas, for instance), and second, he attempts to reclaim the faith of the ancient Church on the doctrine of the Trinity and reframe it for a contemporary audience. Two central theological ideas occupy Barth's mind in 1.1: the task, sources, and parameters of theology, focused as they must be upon the Word of God as the criterion of dogmatics; and the doctrine of the Trinity. In 1.1 the main theme is that God reveals himself as the Lord: Father, Son, and Holy Spirit. No less a thinker than Thomas F. Torrance, the lead editor of the *CD* in English, states in the preface to 1.1 that this is "the greatest treatise of the kind since the *De Trinitate* of St. Augustine" (ix). Now I don't think this is the case myself, given the fact that in *CD* 1.1 Barth all but merely restates Augustine's particular doctrine of the Trinity, but the fact that after so many years of neglecting the Trinity Barth makes it front and center is perhaps what Torrance was referring to, and at that point we can all agree.

CD 1.2 develops themes introduced in 1.1 and especially teases out the idea of the threefold Word of God, namely: revelation, Scripture, and preaching. *CD* 1.2 starts where *CD* 1.1 left off, with part 2 of the chapter on the revelation of God, this time focusing on the incarnation of the Word and the outpouring of the Holy Spirit, before chapters 3 and 4 are given on Church and proclamation. Throughout 1.2 Barth makes the trenchant claim that theology is done by the Church and for the Church and that Christology must be the foundation for all of it (see § 24.2 for the summary). By the end of 1.2 the reader is not in two minds about what theology is, how it is to be done, and who it is done for: it is critical reflection upon the revelation of God (primarily in Christ), it is done as an aspect of faith seeking understanding (*fides quarens intellectum*), and it is by and for the Church for the sake of the world.

> Theologians are not to stand over the Word of God and seek to control or manipulate it; rather, the Word of God encounters us, moving us to faithful service to him.

With Barth's prolegomenon, I am struck by the very poor style, the long-winded prose, and the viscous circularity of it all, *as well as* by its brilliance, mastery of the topic, and relentless pursuit of the goal. It is breathtaking in more than one sense. Theology must be done on the basis of revelation, must be confident in its call to speak faithfully of who God is and what he has done, and must not fall into the trap of looking for validation, or worse still, foundational principles, in anything but the dynamic Word of God. Barth reminds us that revelation is another word for reconciliation (§ 11.1) and herein lies the method for theology, to move from faith to understanding. Theologians are not to stand over the Word of God and seek to control or manipulate it; rather, the Word of God encounters us, moving us to faithful service to him. When theology keeps this truth close to heart, it stays on the right path.

THE VALUE OF *CD* 1 FOR PASTORS

Richard Keith

Richard Keith is minister at Corowa Presbyterian
Church, New South Wales, AU, former stated moderator,
Presbyterian Church of Australia, New South Wales,
AU, and administrator of the website Karl Barth for
Dummies, as well as the Karl Barth Discussion Group
and Karl Barth Translation Group Facebook pages.

In a perfect world, this would be the easiest chapter for me to write and for
you to read. For one thing, Karl Barth considered himself a pastor rather
than an academic theologian. As a lecturer, his students warmed to his pastoral heart. In his later years, Barth regularly visited the prison, led worship,
and preached for the inmates. Additionally, Barth wrote his great work,
the *Church Dogmatics*, to help pastors with their theological thinking and
preaching. Six million words written by a pastor for pastors! What could
possibly go wrong?

Sadly, we do not live in a perfect world. Barth's dense writing style, long
sentences, and dialectical way of thinking complicate what could be simple.
Critics like Cornelius Van Til and Francis Schaeffer have caused many to
treat Barth with suspicion. Finally, Barth's relationship with his assistant
Charlotte von Kirschbaum has become more widely known. Pastors, more
than anyone, have to be on their guard against moral failure. It breaks our
hearts to hear of it in our teachers.

Over the years I have tried to translate what Barth wrote into simpler
English in order to understand him better. I have put this into practice in my
Facebook page and website Karl Barth for Dummies. I am therefore grate-
ful for the opportunity to share the insights from volume 1 of the *Church
Dogmatics* for pastors, from one dummy to others.

1. REVELATION

For Barth, the foundation for his theological work is the Word of God in
which God himself reveals himself. We do not have to wonder what God

is like. We do not have to climb up to heaven to see God for ourselves. God has spoken. This is crucial, for without this Word of God from God, pastors have nothing to say to their congregation except their own opinions and best guesses. Without this Word of God from God, pastors would be better off writing self-help books instead.

> Preaching is simply drawing a curtain so that God can take the stage and recount what he has done.

This concept of revelation reminds us that pastors have a prophetic ministry. God uses us to speak in such a way that God's people hear him and know that they have encountered the true and living God. In his Word, God fulfils the promise of Emmanuel. He becomes God with us and for us. It reminds us that we don't have to dare to speak for God. God speaks for himself and calls pastors to put his Word in modern day words. Preaching is simply drawing a curtain so that God can take the stage and recount what he has done.

2. JESUS CHRIST

This revelation is not a book gathering dust on a shelf. It is not a set of doctrines that can be codified and analyzed. It is not a system that fits neatly into a theological box. God's Word is Jesus Christ, God himself in human flesh. Jesus Christ, in his whole life, reveals the true God and our true humanity in perfect unity. It is not just that he shows us what God is and what we could be. But in the unity of his divinity and humanity, we see the promise of God's presence among us and of our fellowship with God. He is God with us, the gospel written in our flesh. He is the first and last word in our faith, theological thinking, and ministry for others.

God is Christ shaped, and as pastors our ministry and preaching must be Christ shaped too. In our words and deeds we are simply retelling what God has already done for us in Christ and revealing the glory that will be ours in and with Christ.

3. HOLY SCRIPTURE

God's revelation in Jesus Christ does not undermine God's Word in the Bible. Instead, the Bible is the Word of God because of Jesus Christ. The Old Testament witnesses to the coming of Christ. The New Testament testifies to what God has done and will do for us in Christ. Together they are Holy Scripture, God's authoritative document through which he rules his Church.

Theological thinking, therefore, as well as the preaching it informs, must be based on the words of the prophets and apostles from Genesis to

Revelation. Our specific task is to make those words live again for the men and women of our time. We have not been left as orphans to muddle through life on our own resources. The Father of Jesus Christ longs to speak again to his people and to make them hear him.

Barth's detractors make much of the errors that Barth found in the Bible. Barth believed that if the Bible is, like Christ, both truly divine and truly human then it comes with all our human frailties. In his use of the Bible throughout the small print sections of the *Church Dogmatics*, Barth never undermines the authority of the Bible or goes out of his way to point out its mistakes. It is Holy Scripture, God's written Word, and the only Jesus we can know and trust and obey is found in its pages.

I personally want to affirm the inerrancy of Scripture. The Bible exposes my faults, not its own. However, Barth's reflections are a good reminder that the Scripture does not exist to support our agendas but to recruit us for God's agenda. The Bible is not a truth-mine from which we can extract all sorts of principles to build the perfect nation state or to reconstruct a worldview from heaven's viewpoint. Its greatest value is in how it unerringly witnesses to Jesus Christ on every page. For this reason, the gospel of Jesus Christ must be the interpretive key that unlocks God's message in every chapter and verse for us pastors and for our congregations through our preaching.

4. RELIGION

The section of *Church Dogmatics* on the relationship between revelation and human religion is a master class on dialectical theology. For me, dialectical theology is theology in conversation. It does not undermine the truth of God's Word but examines that truth from every angle. Dialectical theology has the courage and humility to say, "but on the other hand."

For example, Barth cannot fail to observe that God's Word in Jesus Christ finds a human response through the work of the Holy Spirit. And that response has all the characteristics of what we call religion. What we call the Christian religion also exists as a member of a class along with other religions. The existence of both religion and other religions raises the question of the validity of revelation. How can we dare to confess Jesus Christ is Lord when other gods and demigods make the same claim?

Barth argues that human religion at its core is unbelief. Religion is the original sin, grasping after divine power by rejecting God's grace and trying to justify itself. Instead of worshiping the true God in whose image we have been created, religion creates gods in our own image out of silver and gold, or philosophical principles and worldviews. Even Christianity did not escape

Barth's blowtorch. In many ways, it can be just another excuse to reject God's grace and build our own kingdom.

"But on the other hand," Barth ultimately acknowledges the existence of true religion. However, what makes the religion true does not lie within the noun *religion*. It lies in the adjective *true*, which depends on Jesus Christ, God's truth. Jesus Christ is God's Word made flesh, his revelation.

In this way, the truth of Christianity does not lie in its impressive institutions or buildings, in its theology or ethics, or even in any benefit it provides to humanity. The truth of Christianity is Jesus Christ, who makes himself heard within its sphere of service. The presence of Jesus Christ himself, working through his Spirit, makes Christianity not just a religion but also the Church, his own body. It makes its members not just Christians but also children of God. Religion is unbelief trying to justify itself. Jesus Christ justifies us and our unbelief by his grace and not by our works.

Pastors are in the business of facilitating human religion, and the same problem of religion confronts us every day and twice on Sundays. How can we justify our calling, our priorities, our service, our liturgy? How can we become the matchmakers between God and his people and not just the peddlers of human sin and unbelief? What makes anything we do valid or good or lasting or true?

The simple answer is that God and God alone can and may make our ministry valid and true. God alone by his free grace given freely can justify us and our work and works. That is his promise in Jesus Christ: to meet his people again and speak to them so that they hear his voice and believe and obey. And in Jesus' name he calls us to this service: to proclaim the gospel of Jesus, to assert his exclusive claim to lordship, and to live that day by day. God is with us and calls us to complete his mission to the world to redeem it in Christ and to make all things new.

CONCLUSION

The word *Barthian* is a terrible noun and a wonderful adjective. As a noun, it means a disciple of Barth, which Barth himself never wanted. But as an adjective it is a summons to theological thinking and preaching like Barth's that is humbly daring and bravely humble. To me, Barth tried to be a herald, an evangelist, a proclaimer of the gospel of Jesus Christ, and a pastor for pastors. His success or alleged failure does not discredit the attempt, because Christ is not justified by our service, but our service is justified by Christ. And the great influence of Barth on my life is that although I don't want to be him when I grow up, I do want to be what he wanted to be.

THE VALUE OF *CD* 1 FOR ORDINARY PEOPLE

Julie Canlis

Julie Canlis is lecturer at Whitworth University, Spokane, WA, USA, and Regent College, Vancouver, BC, Canada, and author of *Calvin's Ladder* and *A Theology of the Ordinary*.

For the ordinary Christian (that is, the nonprofessionalized Christian) who can hardly get through their nightstand books in a year, Karl Barth's 10,000-page *Church Dogmatics* might feel like an exercise in either extreme luxury or extreme masochism. But Barth didn't see it that way. He described his project as "for pastors"[1] and even as Christian "youth instruction on a higher grade."[2] Barth believed that every practical issue we face in our lives is at root a theological one, and that even this kind of deep theology must never exist for its own sake but only to serve the Church and the ordinary people who fill its pews. So what could be gained for an "ordinary Christian" by reading Barth's *CD* 1?

> Barth believed that every practical issue we face in our lives is at root a theological one, and that even this kind of deep theology must never exist for its own sake but only to serve the Church and the ordinary people who fill its pews.

As I read through *CD* 1, I feel as if I am on a beach watching three enormous waves come in and break thunderously upon the shore. I can run forward as each wave is sucked back in succession and see what has been deposited—ancient crustaceans, startling shells, infinitesimally small pebbles—but the most important thing is to get out of the way of the next crashing breaker. These are the breakers from *CD* 1 for the ordinary Christian:

1. GRATITUDE (ALSO CALLED "REVELATION")

Barth's theology begins on a note that doesn't seem to hold much promise: We can know nothing unless God tells us. We can never know God unless God reveals himself to us. The words of our local pastor are empty unless

---

1. In Eberhard Busch, ed., *Final Testimonies* (Eugene, OR: Wipf & Stock, 2003), 23.
2. *CD* 1.1, p. 48 (I'm using the T&T Clark edition, 2010)

God decides to fill them with himself. Even the Scriptures do not hold life unless they point to and are animated freely by the God who chooses to reveal himself.

Is there nothing I can do, as a stay-at-home mother, to know God? Can I not even rely on my local church to guide me? How do I know whether my personal Bible reading is full of God or my own self-justifying fantasies about God?

But Barth actually uses this "negative" point in service of a much larger observation: the reality that we *are* actually hearing from God; we *are* able to know God; and we *are* able to speak of God. This is the mystery—that we know God at all. All theology is done from this mystery: that God, who cannot be known without God's help, has already reached out to us, has already given us words to speak about Him, and has already brought us into the Church. And this is good news indeed for ordinary Christians. It is good news for the world.

In this way, Barth is like the older fish of David Foster Wallace's parable: "There are these two young fish swimming along, and they happen to meet an older fish swimming the other way, who nods at them and says, 'Morning, boys. How's the water?' And the two young fish swim on for a bit, and then eventually one of them looks over at the other and goes, 'What the hell is water?'"[3]

For Christians, the most obvious and important reality is the one we most take for granted: God. And not just God, but God's constant outward motion toward us in love. Barth highlights the innate "hurdle" in human (dis)ability to receive and understand God ("What is water?") in order to highlight grace. Even though revelation is something that God (not us) brings about, God has already overcome this problem and is pouring out his revelation on a daily basis. This is God's free choice, again and again. We don't have to conjure God in our daily lives—he is already there. No vocations of "super revelation" or spiritual disciplines can bring God more clearly into our lives. God is always revealing.

And yet because revelation is mystery and also commonplace, Barth also gives a word of caution: "God may speak to us through Russian Communism, a flute concerto, a blossoming shrub, or a dead dog. We do well to listen to Him if He really does. But unless we regard ourselves as prophets and

---

3. David Foster Wallace, "This Is Water," speech. This was his 2005 commencement speech which has since been ranked by *Time* as one of the best commencement speeches ever delivered: https://fs.blog/2012/04/david-foster-wallace-this-is-water/.

founders of a new Church, we cannot say that we are commissioned to pass on what we have heard as independent proclamation."[4]

Here Barth celebrates both how the ordinary, and even unpredictable, things in life mediate God to us (communism . . . dead dogs) and yet also the frailty of human receptivity: Will we discern him? Will we turn this into a book and market it and twist it for our own ends? Will we respond with gratitude or with indolence?

God never ceases revealing himself in our ordinary lives. Will we respond? Will we be awake?

2. WHAT DOES GOD REVEAL? THE TRINITY

If the first wave that crashes upon the beach is Barth's thunderous summons to gratitude for the miracle of revelation, the second wave that rushes in its wake clarifies what has been revealed. Or to use the metaphor of the older and younger fishes: since we have woken up and discovered that we are indeed swimming in water, our next discovery is that it has a Trinitarian shape. It is not just that we get to know "something" (some facts about the salinity of water) but that the actual revelation itself is wet. Barth is not trying to prove (apologetics) that water exists; rather, he is engaged in describing the effects of water—and how in the very knowing of water, we cannot help but become wet.

Barth always moves from the particular to the general, not the other way around. He carefully reveals how our knowledge of the Trinity arises from the New Testament and not prevailing Greek philosophical trends. But more than this, Barth outlines how the miracle of revelation already immerses us in the Trinity, because revelation has a Trinitarian shape. And so, whether or not the ordinary Christian understands the Trinity, she can rest in the assurance that even her day-to-day life with God is already happening in a Trinitarian manner. It is this mysterious reality that is happening, with or without our awareness. And this is something every ordinary Christian is already engaged in. We don't need to do anything! The very structure of Barth's *Dogmatics* was culturally radical in that he presented the Trinity as foundational to the whole not only of his *Dogmatics* but as the inner cohesiveness of life itself.

And so, the next step is to realize that God's personal nature, his inner life as Father, Son, and Spirit (or "Revealer, Revelation, Revealedness"[5]), has

---

4. *CD* 1.1, p. 57.
5. *CD* 1.1, p. 296.

already organized our lives in a personal manner. By placing all of life in the sphere of the Trinity, Barth has thrown open his dogmatics for ordinary people. Our life is inescapably relational because its very structure is Trinitarian, and we get to figure out how to respond to this with the rest of our lives.

3. HOW HAS THIS BEEN REVEALED? THE INCARNATION

As would be expected by now, Barth doesn't spend time defending the incarnation—proving it could happen, or had to happen. This doesn't interest him. He already is wet. He already is swimming in the water. Barth wants us to *understand the water.*

Earlier in this volume, Barth indicated that there was a pattern to discern how God is speaking to us, how God is proclaiming himself to us (in Scripture, in preaching, and in our everyday lives). We can know the God who has chosen to reveal Himself in our everydayness, but Barth wants to alert us to a pattern that he calls "the Christological doctrine of the two natures."[6] What this means is that the "riddle"—that we cannot know God, and yet here we are, in our everyday lives, knowing God and teaching our children about him and praying for guidance and following him—is answered in the person of Christ. This riddle, which we never asked, and its answer, which we often gloss over, provide the principle for understanding our ordinary lives and relationships in the world.

Just as God gave himself to us in the human body and nature of Jesus, so too God's self-giving always occurs through everyday, created realities. The incarnation is the rule, not the exception, for God's way of being with us. So even if we hunger for direct (and ravishing) communication with God, we must look at the christological principle and see the gracious pattern by which God gives himself to us "veiled" under our ordinary lives. This is not to downplay the desire but to give eyes and ears to the hunger. Our "ordinary" suddenly ceases to be ordinary because communion is geocached in the ordinary. This is the God who is revealing his Son under the cover of an ordinary man from Nazareth. Those who sought a thrilling spirituality missed the one of whom they said, "Can anything good come from Nazareth?" We too, amid mortgages and kitchen squabbles, might miss the "Can anything good happen in my ordinary life?" Yes, says Barth. Because God, in His freedom, is constantly pulling us into the life of His Son.

---

6. *CD* 1.1, p. 58.

For the ordinary Christian, what could be better news? Barth summons us to wake up to the water in which we live and move and have our being, and this summoning causes gratitude at what we have been taking for granted for years. This not only gives dignity to our ordinary lives but also tells us something about God. If the incarnation is God's permanent blessing on the created order (where we spend all of our time and energy), it is not just our residence *but His*. His humanity established life with us forever. In this way, our division of sacred and secular has to be rethought according to the revelation of the incarnation.[7] Revelation is not a spectator sport—either for us or for God.

---

7. Our thinking about God's "transcendence" and "sovereignty" must bow to this revelation. This is "The majesty of God in his condescension to the creature" (*CD* 1.2, p. 31).

THE VALUE OF *CD* 1 FOR MENTAL HEALTH

James Chaousis

James Chaousis is a retired principal social worker and
clinical discipline lead with the Mental Health Divisions of
Northern Adelaide Local Health Network-Dept. of Health
and Wellbeing, Adelaide, AU. He received postgraduate
training in behavioral-cognitive psychotherapy with the
Department of Psychiatry, School of Medicine, Flinders
University, with a special interest in the spectrum of anxiety
disorders, psychological trauma, and affective disorders.

Grace must find expression in life, otherwise it is not grace.
—*Karl Barth*[1]

There has been a long-standing tradition in the mental health field in employ-ing negative metaphors, such as abnormal psychology, mental disability, and mental illness, to the detriment of investigating positive ones that delineate the contours of mental *health* and *wellbeing*. It is not an either-or proposition. Both metaphors are needed. We need to understand what stifles a person's life and compromises their mental health and what revitalizes their wellbe-ing. In view of the majestic theological panorama laid out in Barth's *Church Dogmatics* 1, what might its ramifications be for mental health and wellbeing?

For me, the preeminent standout theme here in *CD* 1 (1.1 and 1.2) is the stunning revelation that this God does not want to be God *without us*. To that end, our attention is directed to God's initiative of stepping inside of human flesh, reaching out in awesome humility and grace to seize hold of us in the mystery of the incarnation as the man Jesus, and taking us into the home life and hospitality of His Father, with the Spirit. In other words, reading the *CD* 1 is like listening to someone gossiping about the very secret to our human existence on earth.

---

1. Helmut Gollwitzer, *An Introduction to Protestant Theology*, trans. David Cairns (Philadelphia: Westminster, 1982), 174.

Mental health and wellbeing are a huge and complex topics. In the interest of making my contribution meaningful and manageable, I will point to one very influential development in the field of mental health and wellbeing—namely, the Positive Psychology (PP)[2] movement spearheaded by Professor Martin Seligman and colleagues over two decades ago to supplement the lopsided preoccupation with mental illness research. It is continuing to develop and refine its study of a well-lived life, which is often summed up as a life of human flourishing. PP advocates focus on five factors to harness human flourishing and wellbeing: positive emotions, engaging with others and one's environment, relationships that foster intimacy and authentic connections, meaning that answers the question, "why are we on earth?" and accomplishments based upon goals and informed by one's core values.

This constellation of human flourishing factors highlight the importance of strong emotions, participatory and relational themes, and imperatives that give rise to a purposeful existence and achievements directed by one's goals and values. In all, these are invigorating themes because they pull together the importance of actions, intentions, emotions, and cognition in a way that does indeed generate vitality, prospectively enabling one to achieve a richness in life and living. And in the case of discovering the God of *CD* 1, we locate the source of such human flourishing to be grounded in the person of Jesus Christ.

> The opening offering in *CD* 1 is an immersion in the ground and grammar of the living God, encapsulated in the person and work of Jesus Christ and expressed as the beginning place for unravelling the hope for humanity.

But what emotions can be stronger than those that arise from the knowledge that we are the beloved of God in Christ, and which in turn give rise to inexpressible joy and gratitude for such a gift? What propels us to engage with others, vulnerabilities aside—is it also not the love of God constraining us to actions of joyful service, while the triune God subdues the fears and anxieties we may harbor? What settles our hearts and minds, energizes us in worship, services and directs our purpose? Is it not in our encounter with Christ that we finally understand that the purpose of our existence lies with sharing in the glorious community of love in the household of Father, Son, and Spirit? To flourish then is surely to know God

---

2. Martin Seligman, *The Hope Circuit: A Psychologist's Journey from Helplessness to Optimism* (Sydney: Penguin Australia, 2018); and Corey L. M. Keyes and Jonathan Haidt, eds., *Flourishing: Positive Psychology and the Life Well-Lived* (Washington, DC: American Psychological Association, 2003).

in Christ—His lavish Fatherly blessings and goodness and purposes for life and living.

Does the gospel of Christ as narrated in *CD* 1 guarantee optimal mental health and well-being? No, it does not! We should therefore caution against any stratagems that seek to market the gospel of Christ as a panacea for achieving good mental hygiene. Our sheer honesty and integrity require us to avoid making such inflated and unsustainable claims. When we consider such fine Christian exemplars as William Cowper, Charles Spurgeon, and Peter Taylor Forsyth, we know that they suffered from mentally and physically challenging conditions that incapacitated them for lengthy periods of time. And yet we need to recognize equally that they were incredibly productive saints—of great service to the Lord and His Church. So, while sainthood, mental health, and wellbeing are not necessarily commensurable, and the gospel of Christ is not a prescription for positive mental hygiene, we must nevertheless acknowledge that one's encounter with Christ has significant transformative value, stability, and dynamism for persons, communities, and cultures.

The opening offering in *CD* 1 is an immersion in the ground and grammar of the living God, encapsulated in the person and work of Jesus Christ and expressed as the beginning place for unravelling the hope for humanity—for "In him was life; and the life was the light of men" (John 1:4 KJV).

THE VALUE OF *CD* 1 FOR SPIRITUAL FORMATION

John Vissers

John Vissers is principal and professor of historical theology, Knox College, University of Toronto, ON, Canada, and author or editor of numerous books and articles on theology and Christian formation, including *Calvin@500: Theology, History, and Practice*.

It would be a grave injustice to the theological achievement of Karl Barth in volume 1 of the *Church Dogmatics* to describe its value for spiritual formation if we use this term as it is commonly understood in contemporary spirituality: a spiritual process or a set of spiritual practices for cultivating a religious life based on human experience. In fact, the 1,400 pages of this volume can be read as an indictment against this kind of thinking about the Christian life. And yet we commit an equally egregious error if we assume that Barth's theology in *CD* 1 has no significance whatsoever for the formation of a life in Christ. It does, and what Barth offers here is a grand vision of the triune God of grace as the One who creates relationship with us in Jesus Christ.

The value of *CD* 1 for spiritual formation is found primarily in Barth's doctrine of the threefold form of the Word of God and in Barth's Trinitarian doctrine of revelation. For Barth, human beings can know God and speak about God because God has first spoken and revealed Godself in Jesus Christ. The Scriptures of the Hebrew Bible and the New Testament, as the written Word of God, testify to Christ the living Word. Through the preaching of this Word, and the outpouring of the Holy Spirit, we are formed in faith.

The spiritual life, then, is a response to the God who meets us in revelation as Father, Son, and Holy Spirit. The God who exists and acts in Jesus Christ makes a judging-saving claim upon our lives. For Barth, the Christian life is not the fulfilment of some general spiritual longing. It is joyful assurance that in life and death we belong to Christ. Spiritual formation is not the process of becoming virtuous. It is learning to live with God and with one another in right relationship, which has been created through the life, death, resurrection, and ascension of Jesus Christ.

For Barth, then, the *possibility* of spiritual formation is grounded in the *reality* of divine revelation, and we grow in the grace and knowledge of Jesus Christ as we tell ourselves what God has already told us. In revelation, God shares God's self-knowledge with us so that our knowledge of God is a participation in God's knowing of Godself as Father, Son, and Holy Spirit. When by faith we know ourselves as those redeemed by Jesus Christ, we understand that our lives are lived in relationship with God as a response to God. The living God remains free in our experience of God. Jesus Christ is always Lord in this relationship.

With this understanding, it should not surprise us that, as a Reformed theologian, Barth privileges the Word of God in the spiritual life. Through the hearing and reading of Holy Scripture our lives are conformed to Jesus Christ. Reformed spiritual practices have traditionally focused on the ordinary means of grace: Word, sacraments, and prayer. Barth resists such language because he believes it creates the impression that we can constitute our own spiritual lives or institutionalize grace. Jesus Christ is the only means of grace, and in the freedom of grace God elects to speak to us through the testimony of the written Word.

For Barth, spiritual formation is being formed by the living Word of God in a relationship that has been created by the Word of God in its threefold form. This is the primary context; the rest is microclimate. Spiritual formation is not a process through which I make God relevant for my life in the so-called real world. Spiritual formation is the grace of God at work in my life making me fully alive in Jesus Christ to flourish in God's world.

> For Barth, spiritual formation is being formed by the living Word of God in a relationship that has been created by the Word of God in its threefold form. This is the primary context; the rest is microclimate.

In later volumes of the *Church Dogmatics*, Barth began to work out what this emphasis on God's freedom and grace might mean practically for the formation of the Christian life as a life of genuine human freedom. But the value of *CD* 1 for spiritual formation is Barth's relentless insistence that in Jesus Christ we have to do with God and that God comes first. What most people foreground when they speak of spiritual formation, human experience, Barth backgrounds. And what Barth foregrounds, God, is often backgrounded in contemporary discussions of spirituality.

So, simply put, spiritual formation is the reality of God's grace at work in our lives, shaping us into the likeness of Jesus Christ, through the work of the Holy Spirit, with one another in the life of the Church, for the sake of the world. In *CD* 1 Barth calls out every preoccupation we might have with ourselves and our own experience as the basis of a spiritual life, and he points us to the only ground and goal of a genuine Christian existence, Jesus Christ. It is a radical reorientation of our thinking about spiritual matters, and this is precisely its value for spiritual formation.

THE VALUE OF *CD* 1 FOR THE SCIENCES

Andrew Torrance

Andrew Torrance is senior lecturer in theology, School
of Divinity, St Mary's College, University of St Andrews,
Fife, Scotland; program leader, Scientists in Congregations,
Scotland; and author of *What Can the Christian Theologian
Learn from the Scientist?* and many other books and
articles on Christian theology and the sciences.

In *CD* 1.1, Karl Barth presents theology as a science among the sciences. As
a science, theology does not give free rein to the imaginative and speculative
activity of its investigators. Rather, it commits to the relentless yet humble
endeavor to attend to, learn from, and be directed by a given object. As he
writes in *Evangelical Theology*, theology "seek[s] to understand [its object]
on its own terms and to speak of it along with all the implications of its *existence*."[1] At the same time, however, he is also clear that the object of theology
is not an object among natural phenomena but is the one who creates, orders,
maintains, and defines natural things. This makes the object of theology
more relevant for understanding the object of the natural sciences than the
other way around. Whereas God defines what the natural order essentially
is, the natural order does not define who God essentially is—even if there
are (veiled) ways in which the natural order witnesses to God's creative activity. Consequently, there is an asymmetry in the relationship between God
and the natural order. The methods of theology are therefore unique from
those of the natural sciences. The task of theology is guided by the Word of
God, as it is mediated to theologians through Scripture, within the sphere of
the Church.

This does not rule out the possibility of the natural sciences serving the
task of theology. Barth is clear that theology "is itself no more than human
'talk about God.'"[2] "Theology does not in fact possess special keys to special

---

1. Karl Barth, *Evangelical Theology* (London: Weidenfeld and Nicolson, 1963), 4.
2. *CD* 1.1, p. 4.

doors."[3] So other human disciplines, such as the nontheological sciences (particularly human sciences), can inform our interpretation of Scripture by helping us to understand better the sociocultural world in which it was written.

Despite the limitations that humans face when undertaking the theological task, Barth does believe that theology can be a positive science. With a confidence in its given content, theology can venture to be a positive witness to God's Word. As it does so, theology understands that it is not open to critique from sciences that see themselves as secular or naturalistic, sciences that rule out *a priori* the existence of that reality who shapes the science of theology. If it is challenged by such sciences, theology must be aware that it is being met by "alien principles rather than its own principle"—principles that would "[increase] rather than [decrease] the mischief which makes critical science necessary for the Church."[4] Moreover, the theologian can know that there is something unscientific about secularistic or naturalistic commitments insofar as such commitments are discordant with the very nature of reality.

> By drawing on God's revelation, theology has a deeper insight into the nature of creation—insight that we are unable to discern from observing the visible surface of the cosmos.

At the table of the sciences, theology "makes a necessary protest against a general concept of science which is admittedly pagan."[5] Cognizant of the bigger picture of reality, theology can keep the other sciences in check by preventing them from veering into metaphysical error. It can do this because, as a science, it recognizes that it has been given to know the truth of metaphysical reality—that the triune God is the first principle who defines and is the source of all else that exists. So if a natural scientist puts forward a theory that is somehow incompatible with the mind of the Church, then the theologian can be ready to challenge such a theory because it is metaphysically overdetermined. The theologian can show that such a theory goes beyond the means of the natural sciences in ways that distort the conclusions. Because the theologian speaks to the ultimate source of the natural order and therefore knows creation beyond its immediate appearance, theology has a much wider scope than the other sciences.

By drawing on God's revelation, theology has a deeper insight into the nature of creation—insight that we are unable to discern from observing the visible surface of the cosmos. This means that there is a sense in which

---

3. *CD* 1.1, p. 5.
4. *CD* 1.1, p. 6.
5. *CD* 1.1, p. 11.

the natural sciences are subordinate to theology. On this point, Barth quotes Francis Turretin: "Theology . . . is thus the judge and lord of all things, so that it judges concerning them and is itself judged by no other science; for all other disciplines must be examined according to its criteria, so that whatever they have that is not consonant with theology is to be rejected."[6]

By understanding theology as a science among the sciences, theology can help us to understand the second-order place of the natural sciences. This can give us a better appreciation of both their scope and potential as well as their limitations. On the one hand, theology holds the natural sciences back from closing themselves off from theological reality in favor of a "heathen pantheon," by drawing "too clear-cut a distinction between theology and the sciences."[7] On the other hand, while theology may not have practical impact on the day to day work of the natural sciences, it can help scientists to appreciate the deeper context that surrounds the object of their study. By so doing, the natural sciences can be a discipline and vocation that is most at home within the life of the Church: the community whose activity seeks to track the fundamental reality of things.

---

6. *CD* 1.1, p. 6
7. *CD* 1.1, p. 11.

THE VALUE OF *CD* 1 FOR THE ARTS

Steve Guthrie

Steve Guthrie is professor of theology and religion and
the arts, Belmont University, Nashville, TN, USA, and
author of several books, including *Creator Spirit: The
Holy Spirit and the Art of Becoming Human*; *Resonant
Witness: Conversations between Music and Theology*;
Faithful Performances: Enacting Christian Tradition.

As Kingfishers Catch Fire

As kingfishers catch fire, dragonflies draw flame;
As tumbled over rim in roundy wells
Stones ring; like each tucked string tells, each hung bell's
Bow swung finds tongue to fling out broad its name;
Each mortal thing does one thing and the same:
Deals out that being indoors each one dwells;
Selves—goes itself; *myself* it speaks and spells,
Crying *Whát I dó is me: for that I came.*

I say móre: the just man justices;
Keeps grace: thát keeps all his goings graces;
Acts in God's eye what in God's eye he is—
Chríst—for Christ plays in ten thousand places,
Lovely in limbs, and lovely in eyes not his
To the Father through the features of men's faces.
—*Gerard Manley Hopkins*

JOURNEYING OUT TO MEET US

"What I do is me."

It is a striking line from one of Gerard Manley Hopkins's best-known
poems. Kingfishers are small, brightly colored birds with shocks of brilliant
golden plumage across their breast. And they do indeed seem to "catch fire"

as rays of sun are drawn to and then flash out from their iridescent feathers. Moreover—and this is Hopkins's theme throughout—just by virtue of being a kingfisher, just by virtue of having the plumage it has, does heavenly light burst from it. In the same way, Hopkins says, stones ring out as they tumble into wells, and the sound that rises up to us is an expression of this stone's particular shape and weight and texture and composition. (Sounding in melodious counterpoint, we might add, with the particular shape and depth and contents and composition of the well into which it has tumbled.) "Each mortal thing," Hopkins says, "deals out that being indoors each one dwells." In its very being, the stone, the kingfisher, the dragonfly, the bell "flings out broad its name." Each created thing, Hopkins suggests, is created to reveal itself: "Selves—goes itself; *myself* it speaks and spells, Crying *What I do is me: for that I came.*"

The kingfisher (we might say) is a revelation, and it is meant to reveal itself. This revelatory act is not an addendum to its being, but rather its act *is* its being: *What I do is me.*

Hopkins's poem is about "each mortal thing," and so I worry (just a bit) that I may be accused of violating a fundamental principle of Barth's theology and reasoning from the creature to the Creator rather than the other way around. I will run the risk, however, simply because there is such a clear resonance between Hopkins's poem and much of what Barth has to say in the first volume of the *Church Dogmatics*.

Even stones and kingfishers, Hopkins says, "deal out that being dwells indoors." The world is not just there. The world gives itself; makes itself known. But we can say more than this. The very God who made these is, according to Barth, an "outgoing" God. "*God* is the one who reveals himself,"[1] Barth writes. Indeed, "God Himself is not just Himself. He is also His self-revealing."[2] This is true to such an extent that Barth can speak of God the Father, Son, and Holy Spirit, as Revealer, the Revelation, and the Revealedness. The God of the *Church Dogmatics* then is a God who speaks. The starting place in this account of God is the affirmation that God ventures out of himself to meet us.

This is good news for all of us, of course. It also is good news in a particular way for the artist. "In order correctly to define art," Tolstoy writes, "it is necessary, first of all to cease to consider it as a means to pleasure, and to consider it as one of the conditions of human life. Viewing it in this way

---

1. *CD* 1.1, § 8, p. 380.
2. *CD* 1.1, § 8, p. 298.

we cannot fail to observe that art is one of the means of intercourse between man and man."[3] It is an imperfect definition of art, but Tolstoy is certainly right to suggest that art, like speech, is rooted in a deeper feature of our humanity, namely, our desire to journey beyond ourselves toward others, to "deal out that being indoors each one dwells." We see this impulse expressed, and expressed artistically, everywhere:

> We are accustomed to understand art to be only what we hear and see in theaters, concerts, and exhibitions, together with buildings, statues, poems, novels. . . . But all this is but the smallest part of the art by which we communicate with each other in life. All human life is filled with works of art of every kind—from cradlesong, jest, mimicry, the ornamentations of houses, dress, and utensils, up to Church services, buildings, monuments, and triumphal processions. It is all artistic activity.[4]

We embark on this outward journey not simply to share information or accomplish tasks but "to communicate with each other in life" in order that we would know and be known. We might say then that we are not only *made by* a God who reveals himself, but we are likewise *made to* reveal ourselves. The God who has a voice has brought about a world of voiced creatures.

This is one place where this volume of *Church Dogmatics* speaks to the artist and to human artistic experience particularly. In these pages Barth describes a God and a reality in which the experience of the artist and the human attachment to art are entirely comprehensible. It is not that our experience of art explains God. But the character of God does make sense of our experience of art.

A FREE WORD

As human beings, we not only desire to reach beyond ourselves; we must. We reach out to others, as a matter of both psychological and practical necessity. We must learn to make ourselves known, and learn what others mean as they attempt to make themselves known. At this point, God's self-revelation is markedly different than our own. God, as Barth famously says, is the One who loves in freedom, and this love and this freedom characterize God's revelation as well. God does not make himself

---

3. Leo Tolstoy, *What Is Art?*, trans. Aylmer Maude (Indianapolis: Hackett, 1960), 49.
4. Tolstoy, *What Is Art?*, 52–53.

known out of necessity or because God "just can't help himself." God's self-communication is grace.

This too is a good word for the artist. The artist likewise engages in an act of self-communication marked by freedom, excess, and gratuity. We must not exaggerate here. It would be wrong to say (with Oscar Wilde) that "all art is quite useless."[5] As Tolstoy observes in the preceding quotation, we use art in all sorts of ways: to get our children to sleep, to pass along the stories of a community, to support and animate the ordinary work of a given day, and so on. And yet works of art (whether they are cradle songs or symphonies) are distinguished as such and commend themselves to us precisely by the ways in which they *exceed* necessity. I had a conversation once with my father-in-law—before he was my father-in-law, and when I was trying to make a living as a professional musician. He is an extraordinarily good man, but one who spent his entire professional life as an engineer and, as such, struggled to understand my work in music. We were in fact discussing the possibility of my future with his daughter when he looked at me with genuine perplexity. "The thing is—if I design a strut for the landing gear on an airplane," he said, "I know what that does. It *accomplishes* something. So—what I'm trying to understand. . . . When you write a song and play it for someone. . . ." He faltered. "Please help me to understand what that *does*."

The freedom of God's self-revealing underwrites a world in which communion exceeds function and necessity. A free word, a gratuitous word, pushes back against a culture that asks of each thing: What does that *do*? This is true first of all of God's free word. It is true likewise of the excess that characterizes the word of the artist.

A NATURAL AND PHYSICAL WORD

God's word to us is not only free; precisely because this word is God journeying out to *meet* us, it is an enacted word. God's revelation is not a disembodied abstraction or the simple delivery of a concept. "There is no Word of God without a physical event," Barth insists. "The Word of God is also natural and physical because without this it would not be the Word of God that is directed to us men as spiritual-natural beings, really to us as we really are."[6] Many of us grew up in churches where the arts often served an instrumental and illustrative function. They were treated as attractive but ultimately disposable containers, carrying some more essential conceptual content.

---

5. Oscar Wilde, *The Picture of Dorian Gray and Other Writings* (New York: Pocket, 2005), 4.
6. *CD* 1.1, § 5, p. 133–34.

But Barth's treatment of God's revelatory act pulls hard against this distinction between inner truth and outer vessel. Indeed, Barth writes that "the distinction between form and content cannot be applied to the biblical concept of revelation."[7] God is not just the agent of revelation; God is the content of revelation. What we want is not some other idea behind God but to encounter God himself. In the instance of God's self-revelation, this revelation "is not referred to anything other, higher, or earlier. . . . Revelation in fact does not differ from the person of Jesus Christ nor from the reconciliation accomplished in Him. To say revelation is to say 'The Word became flesh.'"[8]

Certainly, human beings make themselves known to one another by all sorts of means. Barth's discussion, however, underwrites the validity of the particular means by which the artist engages in this human connection. This artistic engagement is not the delivery of a bare concept but one in which the meeting is inseparable from these sounds, these colors, these movements and syllables and textures and rhythms that encounter our senses at this particular time and place. The meaning of the work is inseparable from its material form because the work of art is more than an attempt to "say something." It is not less than this either. But as Tolstoy suggests, in and through our art we hope also to meet, to encounter, and to be with one another. And being with another—as Zoom calls and FaceTime meetings regularly remind us by their shortcomings—involves an enacted, embodied presence. What Barth says about the Word of God can be said of the artwork: apart from this "natural and physical" element, it "would not be directed to us as spiritual-natural beings, really to us as we really are."[9]

The point here is not to suggest that God's self-revelation is a specific instance of a more general principle. Instead, the point, as before, is that God's way of speaking and acting may help us better make sense of the artist's own way of speaking and acting. What we value about the artist's word particularly is that it is an embodied, enacted word.

A VOICE OTHER THAN OUR OWN

Is the first volume of *Church Dogmatics* really a resource for the artist? It's worth acknowledging that for many, it does not have this reputation. When thinking of this volume, students of Barth might recall a well-known passage where Barth seems to dismiss any sort of special claims attaching to art or beauty. "God may speak to us through Russian Communism, a flute

---

7. *CD* 1.1, § 8, p. 306.
8. *CD* 1.1, § 4, p. 119.
9. *CD* 1.1, § 5, p. 134.

concerto, a blossoming shrub, or a dead dog," Barth writes. "We do well to listen to Him if he really does," he concludes, drily.[10] This really doesn't sound very promising. What is Barth saying? Are we really just as likely to hear God's voice through a rotting corpse as we are through a beautiful piece of music or a stunning vista?

The passage is a response to Paul Tillich, who proposed that in a modern, secular age we might "think and speak about the Church equally well, if not better, from outside than from inside."[11] So, Tillich wonders, can we not hear God speaking through art and culture ("a flute concerto")? Through beauty ("a blossoming shrub")? Through historical and political developments ("Russian Communism")? And if we can, then does not Barth—with his insistent emphasis on preaching, Scripture, and Jesus—have a rather narrow and restrictive vision of revelation? Indeed, at first blush, Tillich's understanding of revelation seems to be far more expansive and welcoming to the artist than does Barth's Church-oriented, Word-centered theology.

In response, we might turn once again to Hopkins's poem:

> Each mortal thing does one thing and the same:
> Deals out that being indoors each one dwells;
> Selves—goes itself; *myself* it speaks and spells,
> Crying *Whát I dó is me: for that I came.*

The kingfisher points to God, yes, in the same way that "the heavens declare the glory of God." But the kingfisher is not a mere pointer or a bare cipher through which God is revealed. Rather, what the kingfisher reveals is itself. "*Whát I dó is me: for that I came.*" It is precisely as a creature that the creature declares God's glory. Because it is other than God, it can praise God, "in limbs and eyes not His."

Barth offers a vision that makes room for creaturely voices, precisely by differentiating between the voice of the creature and the voice of the Creator. Our art is not God speaking. Rather, here we speak, in the space opened up for us by God. God's revelation frees humanity to respond. Indeed, the language of revelation and encounter makes it clear that response is precisely what God wants. If God meets me as a voice from outside—rather than simply being the projection of my own voice, rather than simply the articulation of my own ultimate concern—then between me and God there

---

10. *CD* 1.1, § 3, p. 55.
11. *CD* 1.1, § 3, p. 55.

is created a space in which I may answer. This answer shines forth, like the kingfisher's plumage, and is "not as a second, repeated light of revelation, but as the light of *our human and earthly witness to revelation.*"[12]

What sort of answer should we give? The principal response Barth outlines is that of love and worship. "This love," Barth writes, "is our answer to His loving."[13] There are of course, many ways to respond in love and worship. But it is not an accident that the love song or the poem are a more typical demonstration of love than is the logical syllogism. It is not a coincidence that worship takes place in the domain of careful attention to architecture and decoration, with attention to the pacing and placement of words and sounds and gestures. Christian worship is clothed in poetry of melody and harmony because here we are in the domain of love.

> Barth offers a vision that makes room for creaturely voices, precisely by differentiating between the voice of the creature and the voice of the creator. Our art is not God speaking. Rather, here we speak, in the space opened up for us by God. God's revelation frees humanity to respond.

In this response of love and worship, we find ourselves once again in territory familiar to the artist. In love, we not only journey out beyond ourselves, but we do so adorned "like a bride beautifully dressed for her husband" (Rev. 21:2 NLT). In love, we not only speak a word, freely and naturally. We also make that word winsome and delightful for the Beloved; "lovely in limbs, and lovely in eyes not his / To the Father through the features of men's faces."

---

12. *CD* 1.2, § 18, p. 414. My emphasis.
13. *CD* 1.1, § 18, p. 414.

ACKNOWLEDGMENTS

This book has its roots in thirty years of studying and teaching people to appreciate Karl Barth. James B. Torrance introduced me to Barth as a pioneer to be followed. Alan Torrance and Douglas Campbell furthered my understanding of Barth as a theological genius. My students over the years have helped build a relationship with Barth as a faithful companion. That journey is what led to the creation of this book.

I would like to thank my daughter Abigail for her creative partnership, Wyatt Houtz for images and insights to light the way, and many friends who have read drafts and offered feedback. Many thanks to Matt Estel and Katya Covrett for their encouragement and thoughtful engagement. Special thanks to Anna Lyn Horky for many hours of fine-tuning and addressing editorial issues.

This is the start of a long journey in exploring a monumental text, *Church Dogmatics*. My greatest hope is that those who have been daunted and discouraged will find help in the vision and thinking of Barth. His work has the potential to do for theology what Einstein did for science.

Deep gratitude is in order for Cindy, my wife, who has made it possible to undertake this expedition. Without her, this series would never have been born.

To the essayists who added their voices from multiple disciplines, you are courageous community builders. Thank you! Each volume will add to this international community creative expressions from diverse perspectives. Each one will invite a network of learners to look with new eyes and see what is possible as theology meets the mosaic of disciplines that are joined in this conversation.

To you, the reader, be patient and persistent to discover your own break-throughs. This may begin with Barth, but it has the possibility of expanding and learning to attune to the triune God who loves in freedom. This God knows and desires a life of intimacy, a family in the life of the Church, and participation in sharing in the acts that translate love into creative expressions and activity born of God.

God is.
God speaks.
God loves in freedom.
May this book whisper to you God's voice anew.

Marty Folsom
Advent 2020

FURTHER READING

BACKGROUND AND INTRODUCTION

Busch, Eberhard. *Karl Barth: His Life from Letters and Autobiographical Texts*. Grand Rapids: Eerdmans, 1975.

Franke, John. *Barth for Armchair Theologians*. Louisville: Westminster John Knox, 2006.

Green, Clifford, ed. *Karl Barth: Theologian of Freedom*. Minneapolis: Fortress, 1991.

McKim, Donald, ed. *How Karl Barth Changed My Mind*. Grand Rapids: Eerdmans, 1986.

Morgan, D. Densil. *The SPCK Introduction to Karl Barth*. London: SPCK, 2010.

Torrance, Thomas. *Karl Barth: Biblical and Evangelical Theologian*. Edinburgh: T&T Clark, 1990.

SURVEY

Allen, R. Michael. *Karl Barth's Church Dogmatics: An Introduction and Reader*. London: T&T Clark, 2012.

Bender, Kimlyn. *Reading Karl Barth for the Church: A Guide and Companion*. Grand Rapids: Baker, 2019.

Bromiley, Geoffrey. *Introduction to the Theology of Karl Barth*. Grand Rapids: Eerdmans, 1979.

Guretzki, David. *An Explorer's Guide to Karl Barth*. Downers Grove: InterVarsity Press, 2016.

THEOLOGY

Hunsinger, George. *How to Read Karl Barth: The Shape of His Theology*. Oxford: Oxford University Press, 1991.

Jenson, Robert. *Alpha and Omega: A Study in the Theology of Karl Barth*. Eugene: Wipf & Stock, 1963.

SPECIFIC SECTIONS IN *CD* 1

Barth, Karl. *On Religion: The Revelation of God as the Sublimation of Religion*. Translated and introduced by Garrett Green. London: T&T Clark, 2006. Focuses on paragraph 17 in *CD* 1.2 for a helpful guide, including the title of the section.

HANDBOOKS

Burnett, Richard, ed. *The Westminster Handbook to Karl Barth*. Louisville: Westminster John Knox, 2013.

Hunsinger, George, and Keith L. Johnson. *Wiley Blackwell Companion to Karl Barth*. Hoboken, NJ: Wiley, 2020.

Jones, Paul Dafydd, and Paul T. Nimmo, eds. *The Oxford Handbook of Karl Barth*. Oxford: Oxford University Press, 2020.

Webster, John, ed. *The Cambridge Companion to Karl Barth*. Cambridge: Cambridge University Press, 2000.

ONLINE RESOURCES

Center For Barth Studies, Princeton, https://barth.ptsem.edu/

Karl Barth Archive, Basel, https://karlbarth.unibas.ch/de/

Barth Literature Search Project, http://barth.mediafiler.org/barth/index_Eng.htm

Theological Studies: Karl Barth, https://www.theologicalstudies.org.uk/theo_barth.php